Carl Peter Thunberg

Travels in Europe, Africa and Asia made between the years 1770 and 1779

Volume IV.

Carl Peter Thunberg

Travels in Europe, Africa and Asia made between the years 1770 and 1779
Volume IV.

ISBN/EAN: 9783742812650

Manufactured in Europe, USA, Canada, Australia, Japa

Cover: Foto ©Andreas Hilbeck / pixelio.de

Manufactured and distributed by brebook publishing software (www.brebook.com)

Carl Peter Thunberg

Travels in Europe, Africa and Asia made between the years 1770 and 1779

TRAVELS

IN

EUROPE, AFRICA, AND ASIA,

MADE

BETWEEN THE YEARS 1770 AND 1779.

IN FOUR VOLUMES.

VOL. IV.

CONTAINING

TRAVELS

IN THE EMPIRE OF

JAPAN,

AND IN THE ISLANDS OF

JAVA AND CEYLON,

TOGETHER WITH

THE VOYAGE HOME.

BY CHARLES PETER THUNBERG, M.D.

Knight of the Order of Vasa, Professor of Botany in the University of Upsal, and Member of various Academies and learned Societies both in Sweden and other Countries.

LONDON:

PRINTED FOR F. AND C. RIVINGTON, N° 62, ST. PAUL'S CHURCH YARD.

1795.

THE AUTHOR'S PREFACE.

AT length I have the happiness to send from the Press the *concluding Volume* of my Travels. It contains a farther Account of the Japanese nation, my departure for Batavia, and the description of the Island of Java; after that my Voyage to Ceylon, and my Travels on the coasts of this island; and finally my Voyage home by the Cape of Good Hope, through Holland, England, and Germany.

With a view to illustrate a part of what I have here treated of, I have added a few Plates, descriptive of the Japanese and Indian Utensils and Furniture.

In this volume I have mentioned several articles, which are either in general use at present, or at least may be rendered beneficial and serviceable, and applied to some useful purpose, *e. g.*

ARTICLES used as Food,—1. In *Japan.*—2. In *Java.*—And 3. In *Ceylon.*

1. The flesh of Whales, the Perca 6-lineata, the Clupea thrissa, Shrimps, and Crabs, Salmon, Oysters, and univalve Shell-fish; Rice, Buck-Wheat, Barley, and Wheat, the Holcus Sorghum (or Millet), the Cynosurus coracanus, Panicum corvi and verticillatum, Sium sisarum, Solanum melongena, and tuberosum, Brassica rapa, Arum esculentum, Sagittaria sagittata, Polygonum multiflorum, Dioscorea japonica, Daucus carota, Convolvulus edulis, Lactuca sativa, Pisum sativum, Vicia faba, the Phaseoli, and various species of Dolichos; China and Seville Oranges, Lemons, Shaddocks, Pears, Peaches, Plumbs, Cherries, Medlars, Kaki-figs, Grapes, Pomegranates, Chesnuts, and Walnuts.

2. Birds-nests.

3. The Musa paradisiaca and troglodytarum, the Radermachiæ, Bolange, Paningai, and Cocoa-nuts.

For *Preserves* and *Spices:*

1. The *Amomum mioga,* Bamboo, Raphanus sativus, or Radishes, Lycoperdon tuber, or Truffles, the Agarics, the Fagara piperita, and Capsicum, or Cayenne Pepper, the Cucumis melo, Pepo and Conomon.

2. The

2. The Cardamomum compactum, and Cubebs.

3. Alpinia, the different Peppers, the Cherimelle and Marmelle.

Oils for *dressing Meat*, for *Lamps* and *Candles*.

1. The Sisamum, Camellia japonica, Bignonia tomentosa, Dryandra, Rhus succedanea and vernix, Taxus baccata and Ginko, Brassica orientalis, Laurus camphora and glauca, Melia azedarach, Cocoa-nut.

For *Quickset-Hedges:* The Jatropha curcas, Ophioglossum scandens and Cocoa-tree.

For *Paper*, *Fans*, and *Umbrellas:* The Licuala and Borassus.

For *Bottles:* The Cucurbita lagenaria.

For *Lackering:* Gum Lac, from the Croton.

For *Materials for dying:* The Polygonum chinense, barbatum and aviculare.

For *Combs:* The wood of the Myrica nagi.

For *Furniture* and various sorts of *Cabinet* and *Joiners-Work:* The Pinus sylvestris, Cupressus japonica, Taxus macrophylla, and Calaminder-wood.

For *Cloaths:* Cotton, Silk, and the Urtica nivea.

For *Remedies:* Camphor, Moxa; the Dolichos pruriens, Aristolochia indica, Periploca indica, various sorts of Cinnamon, Lopes-root, the Moringa, Stink-tree, Serpent-stones, the Lignum Colubrinum, Ophiorhiza

orhiza mungos, Rhinoceros's-horn, and a variety of other articles, which are noted down separately and by themselves, for Java, from p. 145 to p. 150.

Japan is in many respects a singular country, when compared with the different states of Europe. In it we behold a Form of *Government*, which has existed without change or revolution for ages; strict and unviolated *Laws*; the most excellent *Institutions* and *Regulations* in the towns, the villages, and upon the roads; a *dress*, coiffure and customs, that, for several centuries, have undergone no alteration; innumerable inhabitants without *parties*, *strife*, or *discord*, without *discontent*, *distress*, or *emigrations*; *Agriculture* in a highly flourishing state, and a soil in an unparalleled state of cultivation; all the *Necessaries* of life abounding, even to superfluity, in the land, without any need of foreign commerce; besides a multiplicity of other advantages.

Among the Rulers of the Country are to be found neither *Throne*, *Sceptre*, *Crown*, nor any other species of Royal Foppery, which in most courts dazzles and blinds the wondering eyes of the simple multitude; no Establishment of a *Royal Household*, no *Lords in waiting*, nor *Maids of Honor*; no extensive and magnificent range of *Stables*, no profusion of *Horses* and *Elephants*,

nor

nor *Masters of Horse*; no *Equipages, Wheel-Carriages*, nor *Cavalry*; no *Wars* nor *Ambassadors*; no *Public Functionaries*, unused to or unqualified for their respective posts; no *Corporations, Imposts*, nor other *Monopolies*; no Play- nor Coffee-houses, no Taverns nor Ale-houses; and consequently no consumption of Coffee, Chocolate, Brandy, Wine, Bishop, or Punch; no privileged *Soil*, no waste *Lands*, and not a single *Meadow*; no National *Debt*, no *Paper Currency*, no *Course* of *Exchange*, and no *Bankers*.

Java and *Ceylon* are, in fact, two of the most fortunate islands on the whole face of the globe, with respect to their situation under a warm climate, their abundant supply of rain, and the fertility of their soil; but the Government of these islands is of various kinds, always despotic, and the Religion, for the most part, Mahometanism; whereas the happiness of the people must be in a restraint which renders them stupid and superstitious, cringing and rebellious, poor and slothful, constantly objects of commiseration; and this wretched state has been rendered the more oppressive to them, inasmuch as the Europeans, who trade with them, have, by their superior information, their Christianity and Humanity, in the last centuries, neither meliorated their condition, nor made their fetters sit lighter

lighter upon them; but rather, by their infatiable avarice, aggravated their yoke, and increafed both the degree and number of their unmerited fufferings. And, indeed, how is it poffible for the people of a country to be happy, where no law obtains but the caprice of individuals; where the life of man is not more regarded than that of the brute creation; where there is no fecurity, nor real property, and where there is fcarcely the leaft idea of liberty, or of great and noble actions?

During the fpace of nine years, which I fpent in foreign countries, I have had many defirable and happy opportunities of difcovering and collecting new and hitherto unknown treafures from the exhauftlefs mine of Nature. Thofe, which I have already been enabled to arrange and defcribe, amount to a confiderable number; the new animals to nearly 400, the new genera of plants to 75, and the fpecies of plants to upwards of 500; not to mention all thofe, which I ftill keep by me for farther examination.

On my arrival in Stockholm, in the month of April, 1779, I had the honor, at the Levee in Drotningholm, and ftill farther afterwards on the fame day, in a private audience, to render an account to a great and gracious King of the general termination of my foreign Travels abroad,

the

the most remarkable things and occurrences in them, especially with respect to the almost unknown country of Japan, of my own private adventures, and the discoveries, which might be considered as being in a greater or less degree useful.

During my absence I had, on the 31st of May, 1777, been appointed by the Privy-Counsellor RUDENSCHIOELD, Chancellor of the University of Upsal, Botanical Lecturer at that University, to which office I now received my patent from the hands of my Patron, the King's first Physician, the Chevalier BAECKS. March 5th, 1781, on occasion of Professor LINNÆUS's making a Tour into foreign parts, I was appointed Overseer of the Botanical Garden, and to preside over the public Lectures. November the 7th, 1781, I received his Majesty's Patent to be Professor Extraordinarius, together with an increase of salary. September 7th, 1784, I was appointed Ordinarius Medicinæ Professor, and Professor of Botany. In the same year, I had the honor to be elected President of the Academy of Sciences in Stockholm. In June, 1785, I was chosen Rector of the Academy in Upsal, and on the 21st of November of the same year, was created a Knight of the Royal Order of Vasa.

Divers foreign Philosophical Societies have at different times done me the honor to chuse me a Member of their Learned Associations.

The

PREFACE.

The IMPERIALIS Natur. Curiosor.
The NORWEGIAN Society, 1772, October 17.
The LUNDEN Physiogr. 1773, December 8.
The UPSAL Society, 1777.
The STOCKHOLM Society of Sciences, 1780.
The HAARLEM Society, 1781, May 21.
The AMSTERDAM Society, 1781.
The STOCKHOLM Oeconom. Patr. 1782, March 16.
The MONTPELIER, 1784, July 1.
The PARISIAN Society of Agriculture, 1785, July 7.
The ZEELAND Society in Flushing, 1785.
The BERLIN Soc. Nat. Scrut.
The EDINBURGH Nat. Stud. 1786, May 4.
The EDINBURGH Medical Society.
The FLORENTINE, 1787, Feb. 7.
The PARISIAN Academy of Sciences, 1787, September 5.
The HALLE Soc. Nat. Scrut. 1787, May 12.
The LONDON Royal Society, 1788.
The LONDON Linnæan Soc. 1788, March 8.
The LONDON Medical Soc. 1789.
The BATAVIAN Ind. Orient.
The PARISIAN Society of Nat. History, 1791, January 7.
The PHILADELPHIAN Society, 1791, April 15.
The COPENHAGEN Society of Nat. History, 1792, June 8.

The

PREFACE. xi

The Works I published after my return home, were as follows:

1ft, My TRAVELS, in four Volumes, printed at Upsal, between the years 1788 and 1793. Translated into German, at Berlin; into English, at London, and into French, at Paris.

2ndly, My INAUGURAL ORATION, on the Species of Coin, that have been struck in Japan, held before the Academy of Sciences at Stockholm, the 25th of August, 1779. Translated into Dutch, and printed at Amsterdam in 1780, and afterwards into German in 1784.

3dly, My SPEECH, on laying down the office of President in the Stockholm Academy of Sciences, on the Japanese nation, Nov. 3, 1784. Translated into German by Stridsberg, Francfort, 1785.

4thly, My ORATION in COMMEMORATION of the Assessor and Provincial Physician, Doctor MONTIN. Stockholm, 1791, 8vo.

5thly, FLORA JAPONICA, printed at Leipsic, 1784, 8vo. with 39 Plates.

6thly, My ACADEMICAL DISPUTATIONS have been as follows:

1. De venis reforbentibus. Præf. C. v. LINNÉ. 1767. 4.
2. De Ischiade. Præf. J. SIDRÉN. 1770.

3. De

3. De Gardenia. Resp. Djupedius. 1780. Tab. 2. Recenserad i Upf. Salsk. Tidn. 1781. No. 49.
4. De Protea. Resp. Gevalin. 1781. Tab. 5.
5. Oxalis. Resp. Hast. 1781. Tab. 2.
6. Nova Plantarum genera. P. 1. Resp. C. Hornstedt. 1781. Tab. 1.
7. Novæ Insectorum Species. p. 1. Resp. Casstrom. 1781. Tab. 1.
8. Nova Plantarum genera. p. 2. Resp. Sahlberg. 1782. Tab. 1.
9. Iris. Resp. Ekman. 1782. Tab. 2.
10. Novæ Insectorum Species. p. 2. Resp. Ekflund. 1783. Tab. 1.
11. Nova Plantarum genera. p. 3. Resp. Lodin. 1783. Tab. 1.
12. Ixia. Resp. Rung. 1783. Tab. 2.
13. Novæ Insectorum Species. p. 3. 1784. Tab. 1. Resp. Lundahl.
14. Novæ Insectorum Species. p. 4. 1784. Tab. 1. Resp. Engestrom.
15. Gladiolus. Resp. Ajmelæus. 1784. Tab. 2.
16. Nova genera Plantarum. p. 4. Resp. Berg.
17. Nova genera Plantarum. p. 5. Resp. Blumenberg. 1784. T. 1.
18. Insecta Svecica. p. 1. Resp. Borgstrom. 1784. Tab. 1.
19. Aloë. Resp. Hesselius. 1785.
20. Medicina Africanorum. Resp. Berg. 1785.

21. Erica.

21. Erica. Resp. STRUVE. Tab. 6. 1785.
22. Ficus. Resp. GEDNER. 1786. t. 1.
23. Museum Natural. Acad. Upf. p. 1. Resp. RADLOFF. 1787.
24. - - - - p. 2. Resp. HOLMER. 1787.
25. - - - - p. 3. Resp. EKEBERG. 1787.
26. Museum Natural. Acad. Upf. p. 4. Resp. BJERKÉN. 1787. Tab. 1.
27. - - - - p. 5. Resp. GALLÉN. 1787.
28. Moræa. Resp. ZACH. COLLIANDER. 1787. Tab. 2.
29. Museum Natural. Acad. Upf. p. 6. Resp. SCHALÉN. 1788. Tab. 1.
30. Restio. Resp. PETR. LUNDMARK. 1788. Tab. 1.
31. Arbor toxicaria Macassariensis. 2. Resp. AJMELÆUS. 1788.
32. Moxæ atque ignis in Medicina rationali Usus. Resp. HALLMAN. 1788.
33. Myristica. Resp. RADLOFF. 1788.
34. Caryophylli Aromatici. Resp. HAST. 1788.
35. Museum Natural. Acad. Upf. p. 7. Resp. BRANZELL. 1789.
36. Characteres generum Insectorum. Resp. TORNER. 1789.
37. Museum Natural. Acad. Upf. p. 8. Resp. RADEMINE. 1789.
38. Novæ Insectorum Species. p. 5. Resp. NORÆUS. 1789. Tab. 1.

39. Muræna

39. Muræna et Ophichtus. Resp. AHL. 1789. Tab. 2.
40. Remedia nonnulla indigena. Resp. HOLMER. 1790.
41. Museum Natural. Acad. Upf. Append. 1. Resp. LUNDELIUS. 1791.
42. Museum Natural. Acad. Upf. Append. 2. YMAN. 1791.
43. Museum Natural. Acad. Upf. p. 9. Resp. EKELUND. 1791.
44. Novæ Insectorum Species. p. 6. Resp. LAGUS. 1791.
45. Museum Natural. Acad. Upf. p. 10. Resp. KUGELBERG. 1791.
46. Flora Stregnesensis. Resp. CARLSON. 1791.
47. Insecta Svecica. p. 2. Resp. BECKLIN. 1791. Tab. 1.
48. - - - p. 3. Resp. AKERMAN, 1792.
49. - - - p. 4. Resp. SEBALDT. 1792. Tab. 1.
50. Genera nova Plantarum. p. 6. Resp. STROM. 1792.
51. - - - p. 7. Resp. TRAFVFNFLDT. 1792.
52. Museum Natur. Acad. Upf. p. 11. Resp. SJOBERG. 1792.
53. - - - p. 12. Resp. LINDBLADH. 1792.
54. - - - p. 13. Resp. FERELIUS. 1792.

7thly,

7thly, TREATISES on Miscellaneous Subjects, sent in to different learned Societies.

a. To the Academy of Sciences at STOCKHOLM.

1. An accident, that happened from White-lead being used in food, through mistake. 1773. 1st. qu. p. 29.
2. Description of a curious and unknown Mushroom, the HYDNORA AFRICANA. 1775. 1st. qu. p. 69. Plate.
3. Description of a new Genus of Insects, the PNEUMORA. 1775. 3d. qu. p. 254. Plate.
4. ROTHMANNIA, a new Genus of Plants. 1776. 1st. qu. p. 65. Plate.
5. Description of a new Genus of Plants, called RADERMACHIA. 1776. 3d. qu. p. 250.
6. Remarks on the HYDNORA AFRICANA. 1777. 2d. qu. p. 144. Plate.
7. Description of a BEZOAR EQUINUM. 1778. 1st. qu. p. 27.
8. A new and, with respect to its Genus, hitherto unknown Grass, called the EHRHARTA. 1779. 3d. qu. p. 216. Plate.
9. Observations upon CINNAMON, made at Ceylon. 1780. Translated and inserted into the Transactions of the Flushing Society. Tom. 12. Part 1. by Dr. HOUTUYN. p. 296.

10. Description

10. Defcription of the WEIGELIA JAPONICA, a fcarce Plant from Japan. 1780. 2d. qu. p. 137.
11. Defcription of fome WARM BATHS in Africa and Afia. 1781. 1ft. qu. p. 78.
12. Defcription of two new INSECTS. 1781. 2d. qu. p. 168.
13. NOCTUA *Serici*, a new Silk-Worm. 1781. 3d. qu. p. 240. Plate.
14. Defcription of two Species of genuine NUTMEG, from the ifland of Banda. 1782. 1ft. qu. p. 46. Plate.
15. Some Obfervations in ORNITHOLOGY. 1782. 2d. qu. p. 118.
16. Defcription of a new Genus of Plants, the FAGRÆA *Ceilanica*. 1782. 2d. qu. p. 132. Plate.
17. On the *Oil* of CAJOPUT, and its ufe in Medicine. 1782. 3d. qu. p. 223.
18. NIPA, a new Genus of Palm-tree. 1782. 3d. qu. p. 231.
19. On PALM-TREES in general, and particularly on the Licuala Palm. 1782. 4th. qu. p. 284.
20. Defcription of the HOUTUYNIA *cordata*, a Japanefe Genus of Plants. 1783. 2d. qu. p. 149. Plate.
21. Farther Obfervations on ASTERIAS. 1783. 3d. qu. p. 224.

22. De-

22. Description of the MINERALS and PRE-
CIOUS STONES of Ceylon. 1784. 1st. qu.
p. 70.
23. Observations on BIRDS of the *Loxia* kind,
at the Cape of Good Hope. 1784. 4th.
qu. p. 286.
24. Observations on and Description of the
Genus of Plants called ALBUCA. 1786.
1st. qu. p. 57.
25. Observations on the Plants called OR-
CHISES. 1786. 4th. qu. p. 254.
26. Description of some rare and unknown
Species of Lizards. 1787. 2d. qu. p. 123.
Plate.
27. Description of three species of TORTOISE.
1787. 3d. qu. p. 178.
28. Description of the WILDENOVIA, a rare
and new Species of Grass. 1790. 1st. qu.
p. 26. Plate.
29. Description of two FISHES from Japan.
1790. 2d. qu. p. 106. Plate.
30. Description of the WAHLBOMIA INDICA.
1790. 3d. qu. p. 215. Plate.
31. Two foreign Fishes, the GOBIUS *patella*,
and SILURUS *lineatus*. 1791. 3d. qu. p.
190. Plates 6.
32. Two Japanese Fishes, the CALLIONYMUS
Japonicus, and the SILURUS *lineatus*. 1792.
1st. qu. p. 29. Plate 1.

33. De-

33. Description of the unknown Fishes, the PERCA 6-*lineata* and *picta*. 1792. 2d. qu. p. 141. Plates 5.

β. *To the Literary Society in* UPSAL.

1. Cycas Caffra. 1775. cum figuris. Vol. 2.
2. KÆMPFERUS illustratus. p. 1. 1780. Vol. 3.
3. Cussoniæ Genus. 1780. c. f. Vol. 3.
4. Novæ Species Insectorum Sveciæ. 1783. c. f. Vol. 4.
5. KÆMPFERUS illustratus. p. 2. 1783. Vol. 4.
6. Curculio Cycadis. 1783. Vol. 4.
7. Descriptiones Insectorum Svecicorum. 1792. Vol. 5. p. 85.
8. Observationes in Linguam Japonicam. 1792. Vol. 5. p. 258.

γ. *To the Physiographical Society in* LUNDEN.

1. Retzia capensis. 1776. cum figuris.
2. Montinia et Papiria.
3. The Preparation of Gum Aloë in Africa.
4. Aitonia capensis.
5. Falkia repens.
6. Syngnathi nova Species.

δ. *To the Norwegian Society in* TRONDHEIM.

1. Hypoxis.
2. Cliffortiæ Genus.

1. *To the Society of Sciences at* HAARLEM.

  1. Obfervationes Thermometricæ in Japonia habitæ.
  2. Cryptogamarum fructificatio in Cycade et Zamia.

2. *To the Royal Society at* LONDON.

  1. Account of a Voyage to Japan.
  2. Citodium, or the Oeconomical Ufes and Preparation of the Bread-fruit.

3. *To the Imperial Society Naturæ Curioforum:*

  1. Craffulæ novæ Species 28.
  2. Mefembryanthemi Species novæ 21.

4. *To the Society Naturæ Scrutatorum at* BERLIN.

  1. Dilatris genus.

5. *To the Society of Natural Hiftory at* PARIS.

  1. A new Genus of Plants, called the BOSCIA *undulata.*
  2. Defcription of 13 Species of Japanefe and 341 Cape Plants, before unknown.

THE TRANSLATOR'S PREFACE.

AFTER the warm reception the preceding Volumes have met with from the public, it would be needless to say any thing in recommendation either of the Work or its Author. It may suffice to observe, that this Volume is much more interesting than any of the former; and that, if any thing be wanting to make it complete on the subjects of which it treats, the Reader will find the deficiency amply supplied, in a little Tract, lately published, entitled "The Life and Adventures of Christopher Wolf, with his Voyage to Ceylon;" particularly with respect to the Vegetable Productions of that island, the Rollewai, the Elephant, and the manner in which this latter animal is captured.

ERRATA IN VOL. IV.

Page 36, line 12, *read* By this means all the viands are extremely well dressed;
      l. 21, *for* are *read* have been
—— 40, l. penult. *read*, To Batavia Sacki is imported as an article of commerce; but it is also drank there out of
—— 57, l. 10 from bottom, *for* must *read* would
—— 62, l. penult. *for* has an opportunity of seeing r. sees
      l. 8 from bottom, *for* blacker *read* black or
—— 63, l. 10, *for* portable stools *read* Norimons
—— 77, l. 4 from bottom, *for* exterior *read* hindermost part of the
      l. 6, *for* Haki *read* Kaki
—— 84, l. 9, *for* Cabbages; *read* Coleworts;
      l. 10, *after* of which *read* last
      l. 21, *for* like Cabbage-seed, in beds. *read* and thick, as Cole-seed is in boxes.
      l. 24, *for* Cabbage-plants, *read* Colewort-plants,
      l. 25, *for* bundles, *read* tufts,
      l. 26, *for* bundle. *read* tuft.
—— 86, l. 10 from bottom, *read* leave an empty space between them.
—— 87, l. 13 from bottom, *for* Cabbage-seed *read* Cole-seed, *for* grows wild *read* is cultivated
      l. 4 from bot. *for* Cabbage-seed *read* Cole-seed
—— 88, l. 11, *read* as is likewise the whole bean
      l. 6 from bottom, *for* Turnips *read* Turneps
—— 89, l. 13 from bottom, *for* amonium *read* Amomum
      l. penult, *after* Lemons *read* Shadocks
—— 90, l. 1, *after* Japonica r. Figs of a very delicious taste.
—— 93, l. 2, *after* succedanea *read* indeed, *for* seed r. seeds
      l. 3, *for* yields, *read* yield,
      l. 14 and 15, *read* The finer oil of Sesamum they use in the kitchen,
      l. 4 from bottom, *for* is *read* be
——112, l. 15, *dele* roundish, and *read* oblong plate of gold, rounded off at the four corners,
      l. 17, *after* broken off *read* at intervals
——146, l. 16, *after* Vitex *add* (or Agnus Castus)
——218, l. 4 from bottom, *for* Purperagan *read* Pusperagan
——237, l. 7 from bottom, *after* Mature *read* back again
——272, l. 13 from bottom, *for* the defence of their country *read* their mutual defence.
——289, l. 5 from bot. *read* the *British, Leverian*, and other Museums.
      l. 4 from bot. *for* The former *read* The first

IN THE PRECEDING VOLUME.

Page 183, *for* Daikoku *read* Daikokv.

Explanation of the Plates

For the Fourth Volume.

Plate I.

Fig. 1. A *Japanese Slipper*. These are used every day in common, instead of Shoes.

2. *Another*, which is used on Journies, and is tied fast round the foot.

3. A *Horse-Shoe*, which is tied round the foot.

4. A *Razor-Case*. *a*. The *Case* itself, for two Razors, and *b*. the *Razor*.

5. A *Medicine-Box*, with several compartments in it. *a*. The *Box*, with its partitions. *b*. The *Cord*, by which it is supported. *c*. The *Ball*, by which it is made fast to the belt.

Plate II.

Fig. 1. A *Japanese Lady*, with *a*. her *Lute*, in her usual dress.

2. *Touche*, or *Japan-Ink*, with which the Japanese and Chinese usually write, and which they use instead of ink.

3. A *Box*, which contains *a*. a *Reckoning-board*, with moveable *Counters*, strung upon a steel-wire, denoting Units and Decimals; *b*. a *Steel-yard*, together with its *Scale*, and *c*. the *Weight* hanging to it; *d. e.* an excavated *Stone*, to rub the Touche upon; *f*. a *little Trough*, for holding water for that use, and *g*. a *Writing-pencil*.

Plate

Explanation of the Plates.

PLATE III.

Fig. 1. A *Steel-yard*, with its Cafe. *a.* The *Cafe*, which fhuts up with great eafe and convenience. *b.* The *Steel-yard* itfelf, formed of ivory. *c.* The *Scale* with its Strings. *d.* The *Strings*, by which the Steel-yard is held, when ufed. *e.* The *Weight*.

2. A *Tooth-brufh*, of foft wood, to clean the teeth with.

3. A common *Writing-pencil*, made of a reed and hare's hair.

4. A *Spring Steel-yard*, or *Weight* upon a Spring, which is very elaftic, for weighing fmaller articles.

PLATE IV.

Fig. 1. A *Tobacco-pouch*, with a Pipe and its Sheath. *a.* The *Pipe-fheath*, made of filk. *b.* The *Pipe* in its fheath. *c.* The *Pipe* made of a reed, with a mouth-piece and bowl of metal. *d.* The *Tobacco-pouch*, made of filk.

2. A *Cafe* for Inftruments for the Ears and Teeth. *a.* The *Cafe*, made of horn. *b.* The *String*, by which it is faftened to the belt. *c. Ornaments* of Silk. *d.* Divers fmall *Inftruments*, to clean the ears and teeth with.

TRAVELS

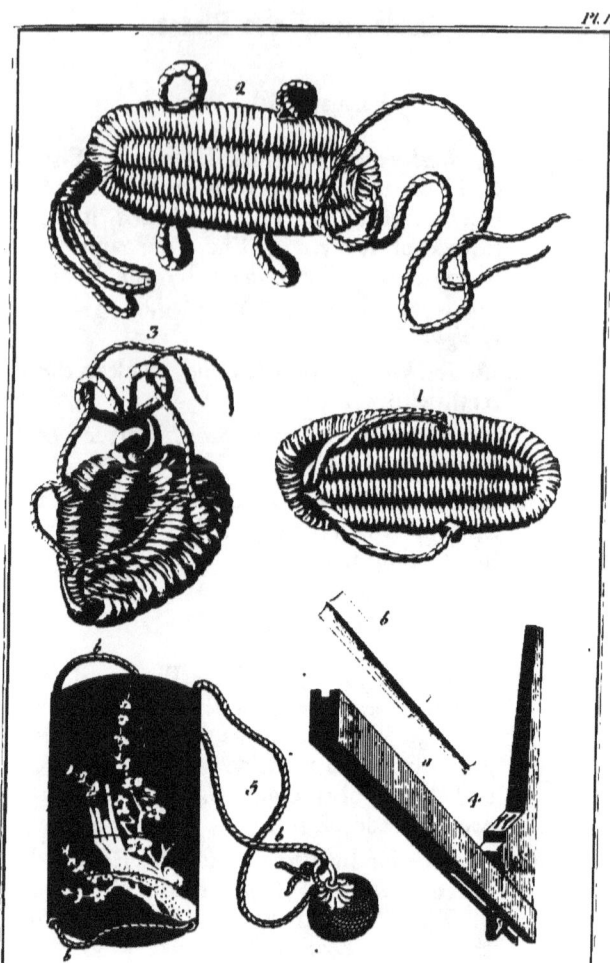

Pl. 1.

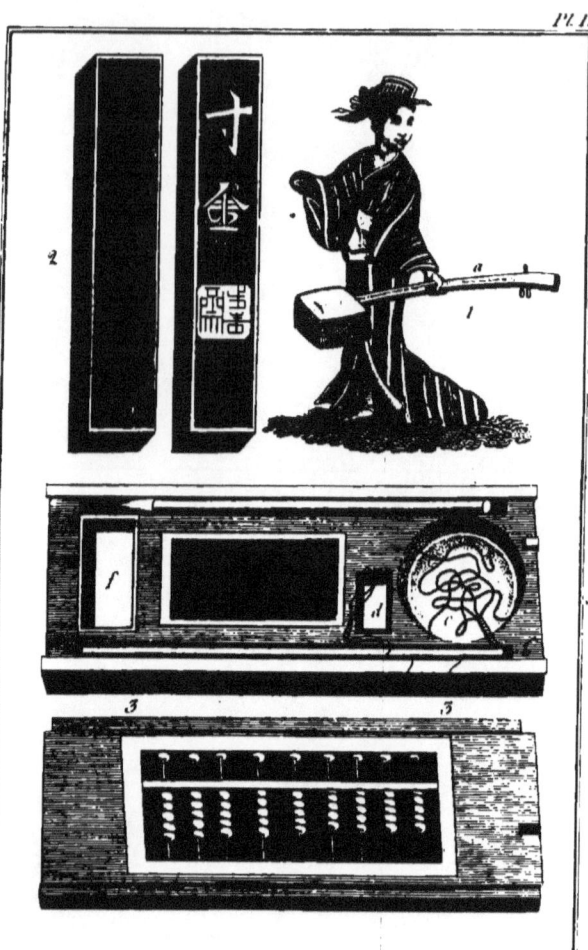

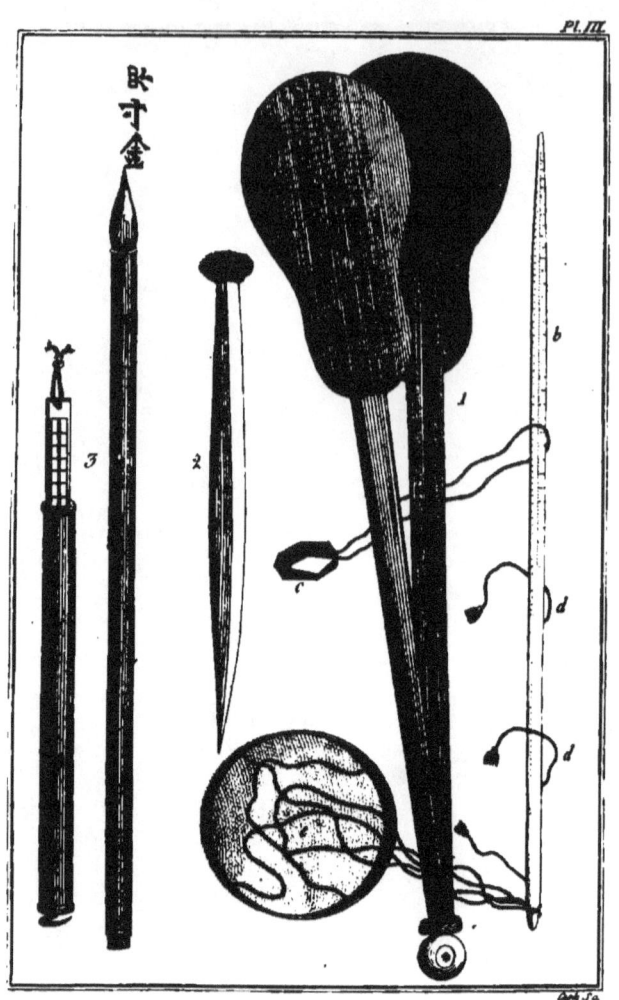

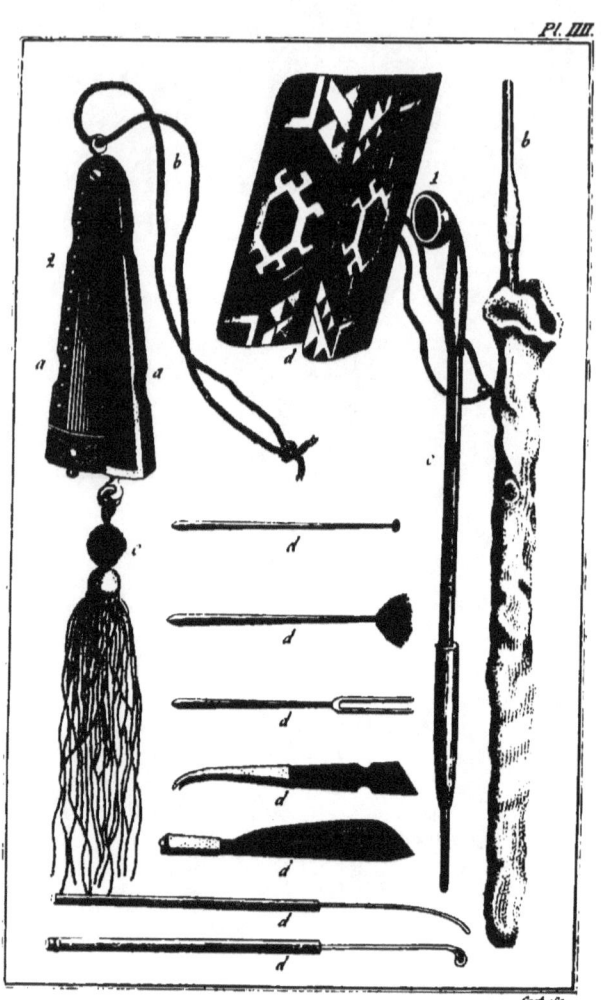

TRAVELS

IN

EUROPE, AFRICA, AND ASIA.

THE GOVERNMENT.

THE empire of Japan is encompassed on all sides with water, and consists of three large islands, together with a vast multitude of smaller ones. All these are divided into seven departments, which again are subdivided into sixty-eight provinces, and these into six hundred and four districts.

At present, *Kubo*, or the Secular Emperor, is Lord of the whole country, and under him rules a Prince or Governor in each province. The Princes that are first in dignity, are called *Daimio*; those of an inferior rank are denominated *Siomio*. If any of them is guilty of misdemeanors, he is amenable to the Emperor, who has a right to dismiss him; to banish him to some island; or even to inflict capital punishment

ment upon him. It is farther incumbent upon all these Princes to perform a journey once every year to the Imperial Court, to reside there six months, and to keep their whole family there constantly, as hostages for their allegiance.

But, besides this Monarch, there is a Spiritual or Ecclesiastical Emperor, whose power at present is totally confined to the concerns of religion and the church establishment; although this Spiritual Regent or Pope, derives his descent in a direct and uninterrupted line from the ancient Rulers of this country, for upwards of 2000 years back.

If we carry our researches back to the remotest ages of antiquity, which are enveloped in obscurity and uncertainty, it will appear probable, that Japan, like other countries, was governed by Patriarchs, or petty Chiefs, who afterwards united together under one head. The most authentic History of the Japanese Monarchs commences about 660 years before the birth of Christ, when the government was bestowed upon SYN MU, of a very conspicuous race, called TENSIO DAI SIN. This SYN MU is the founder of the monarchy; he introduced an accurate Chronology, called *Nin O*, and improved not only the laws of the country, but likewise the very form of the government. The Emperors of this tribe were most usually denominated

minated DAIRI, and sometimes, but not so frequently, *Mikaddo, Dai, Tai, Tenfin,* and *Oo*. One hundred and nineteen DAIRIS have ascended the throne in succession, from that period down to the time of my residence at Japan; although their power and authority have been very different and dissimilar at three different periods. These reigned alone with unlimited authority, till the year 1142. From that time the secular power was divided between the oldest and lawful Potentate of the country and the secular Rulers or Generalissimos of the army, till the year 1585, since which time his authority has only manifested itself in matters which concern the government of the church.

The veneration which is entertained for DAIRI, falls little short of the divine honours which are paid to the gods themselves. He seldom goes out of his palace, his person being considered as too sacred to be exposed to the air and the rays of the sun, and still less to the view of any human creature. If at any time he has absolute occasion to go abroad, he is generally carried upon men's shoulders, that he may not come into contact with the earth. He is brought into the world, lives, and dies within the precincts of his court, the boundaries of which he never once exceeds during his whole life. His hair, nails, and beard are accounted so sacred, that they are never

never suffered to be cleanfed or cut by day-light, but this, whenever it happens, muft be done by ftealth, during the night, whilft he is afleep. His holinefs never eats twice off the fame plate, nor ufes any veffel for his meals a fecond time; they being for the moft part broken to pieces immediately after they have been ufed, to prevent their falling into unhallowed hands. For this reafon, the furniture of his table confifts of a cheap and inferior fort of porcellain. The cafe is pretty much the fame with refpect to his cloaths, which are diftributed among thofe who refide at his court. Without the precincts of the court there is none, or at leaft hardly any one, that knows his name, till long after his death. His whole court, with very few exceptions, confifts of none but fuch as are of his own race; all of whom have their appointments at court, in like manner as others of them, who are not employed at court, are promoted to the richeft benefices, and the beft convents. He has twelve wives, only one of whom, however, is Emprefs. The pomp which reigns in his court, though not fo fplendid as formerly, is yet very great. Since the retrenchment of his power, he derives his revenues from the town and adjacent country of *Miaco*; and has likewife an allowance from Kubo's treafury, befides immenfe fums which he acquires by the conferring of titles;

and

and yet his revenue is frequently inadequate to his expences. The right of bestowing titles of honour remains to this day vested in the person of the ecclesiastical Emperor, and serves considerably to increase his income. Even Kubo himself and the hereditary Prince, receive titles at his hand; as do likewise, on Kubo's recommendation, the highest officers of state at his court. Those who have spiritual titles, are distinguished both at court and in the churches all over the country, by a particular dress, conformable to their rank and dignity. I had the honour to see one of these Prelates at a convent in Nagasaki; his dress consisted of a pair of trowsers, and a large cloak with a long flowing train. I found him very affable and courteous, and we had a long conversation together, through the medium of our interpreters, respecting various matters; which, however, afforded me far less pleasure than the shrubs I met with in the vicinity of his church.

DAIRI's court was formerly removed at pleasure from one part of the country to the other; but now his residence is fixed in the town of *Miaco*. This court is very extensive, and forms of itself no inconsiderable town, being provided with walls, fosses, ramparts, and gates: in the centre stands DAIRI's palace, adorned with lofty turrets, and round about it are the mansions of

both

both the superior and inferior officers of his household, and other attendants. A Governor is kept here for his service by Kubo, and a guard appointed for his safety, to defend the sacred person of Dairi, and by way of security to Kubo, that no disturbances or insurrection can be raised there. At this court literature is cultivated, and academic studies are pursued with vigour. It is the only university in the country; and here the students are maintained, brought up, and instructed. The principal objects of their application are poetry, the history of the country, mathematics, &c. Music is a very favourite study with them, especially with the ladies. Here it is that all their almanacks are compiled, which are afterwards printed in *Isie*.

Although Dairi has lost his authority in temporal concerns, yet he is still considered as so august and holy, that Kubo, either in person or by his ambassador, is bound to pay him a visit, and that either annually, or at the expiration of a certain stated time; bringing with him, according to the general custom of the country, presents of great value. Yoritomo and many more of the secular Emperors, have visited *Miaco* in person, to perform this homage, which latterly however, and by degrees, has been more and more neglected, and is at last entirely given up. Neither the Princes of the country, nor the Dutch, when

they

they go up to *Jedo*, pay their respects to the ecclesiastical Emperor in *Miaco*. Seventy-six Emperors of this race have reigned with unlimited power, till the year 1142, when civil commotions arose among the Princes of the land, and a calamitous war was waged between them. With a view to compose these disturbances, the command of the armies was given to YORITOMO, in the quality of Generalissimo. This valiant commander suppressed, indeed, the growing disturbances, but at the same time also arrogated to himself and his successors great part of the Emperor's authority; which continued to be divided between DAIRI and the Imperial Generals till the year 1585. About this time a peasant's son, named TAIKO *Samma*, had raised himself by his superior abilities to the rank of General, reduced all the Princes of the Land under his authority, and in the end deprived DAIRI of all the power he had hitherto possessed, with respect to secular affairs, and the government of the empire. From the reign of YORITOMO, the first of the secular Monarchs, to that of YE VARU, who swayed the sceptre of Japan, at the time of my residence in that country, one and forty KUBOS had sat upon the throne, and kept their court at *Jedo*. The secular Emperor does not, however, hold the reins of government entirely in his own hands, but reigns conjointly with six Privy Counsellors, who

who are moftly men in years and of found judgment. Befides the confiderable prefents which each ruling Prince fends to court of the produce of his province, KUBO derives his revenue from certain crown lands, as they are called, or five imperial provinces, and fome imperial towns, which are fubject to the fway of Governors or *Bugios*. The tax or tribute is paid in fuch commodities as each country produces. In the fame manner each of the Princes receives tribute from his province, with which he maintains his houfehold, his troops, defrays the expences of keeping the roads in repair, as likewife of his journies to court, maintains his family, &c.

The five imperial crown-lands pay a tax of 148 *mans* and 1200 *kokfs* of rice, which amounts to nearly 44,400,000,000 facks of rice. Each *man* contains 100,000 *kokfs*, each *kokf* 3000 *balis* or facks of rice, and each fack weighs upwards of twenty pounds. The aggregate revenue of the whole empire of Japan amounts at leaft to 2328 *mans* and 6200 *kokfs*.

At the time when KÆMPFER refided in Japan, in the year 1692, the *Dairi* KINSEOKWO TEI, was in the fifth year of his reign, having afcended the throne A. C. 1687. Since that period the following Emperors have reigned.

NAKA *no Mikaddo no Yn*, from 1709 to 1735.
SAKKURA *Matic no Yn*, from 1736 to 1746.
MOMO

THE GOVERNMENT.

Momo *Zon no Yn,* from 1747 to 1761.

Zentoogozio, from 1762 to 1769.

And, since the year 1770, Figasi *jamma no Yn,* who continued to fill the imperial throne at the time of my departure from Japan, in the year 1776.

Of Kubos, or secular Emperors, the following have successively sat on the throne of Japan. In the year 1693, when Kæmpfer took his leave of this country, Kubo Chinayos still reigned. He was then in the 43d year of his age, and had reigned twelve or thirteen years. The whole duration of his reign comprehended a period of twenty-nine years. After him followed:

Ye Nob *Koo,* and reigned from 1709 to 1712.

Ye Tsu Ku *Koo,* from 1713 to 1716.

Yosi Mune *Koo,* from 1717 to 1751.

Ye Siege *Koo,* from 1752 to 1761; at which time the present Kubo

Ye Far *Koo,* ascended the throne, which he still occupied at the time of my departure A. 1776.

The government of each province is intrusted to some Prince, who resides in it, and is responsible to the secular Emperor for his administration. He has a right to all the revenues of his fief, with which he supports his court, his military force, keeps the roads in repair, &c. He is likewise bound, as we said before, to make a journey once every year to Kubo's court, with a degree a degree of pomp suited to the size and dignity of his fief, to take with him considerable presents, and to keep his family constantly at this Emperor's court, as hostages for his allegiance.

The towns, in which these Princes hold their court, are mostly of considerable note, situated near some harbour, or large river, and surrounded with walls and fosses. Most frequently at one of the extremities of the town stands the Prince's castle, which is of a great extent, being likewise surrounded with a wall and fosse, provided with strong gates, and adorned with high towers. These castles are for the most part, like the imperial palace at Jedo, divided into three compartments, each of which is well fortified. The innermost is the residence of the Prince himself; the second is allotted to the superior officers of state; the third and last is destined for his troops, with the rest of his retinue and attendants. Not only are the towns themselves provided with gates, but each individual street has its own gates, which are shut during night, and on some other occasions, so that not a soul can either enter in or go out. The distance between each of these gates is generally from 60 to 120 yards. Each street has its own watch, watch-house, and apparatus for guarding against fire; as likewise an *Ottona*, and other officers, for preserving decorum and good order. For the accommodation of travellers in every town there are a great many inns, which are neat and conveniently situated; by the side of the roads likewise, and near each other, (none of them being more than a quarter of an hour's distance asunder) there are others, which are post-houses, where are always to be found horses, and norimon-bearers, who forward travellers for a certain determined price, proportioned to the length and difficulty of the road: so that the price of travelling is not the same throughout the whole country, but is regulated according to the nature of the roads in each place. Although the regulations here, as well in the towns as in the country, agreeable to the genius of this people, appear sometimes very singular, and frequently even savour of compulsion and constraint, still it cannot be denied, that they are really sometimes both necessary and excellent. Upon the whole, both the supreme government, and the civil magistrates, make the welfare of the state, the preservation of order, and the protection of the persons and property of the subject, an object of greater moment and attention in this country than in most others.

The villages in Japan are for the most part situated near the public roads; they are distinguished from the towns by having only one street, and by being open; but they are otherwise of an extraordinary length, extending from a mile a mile and a half to three miles, and fometimes farther.

The roads are both broad and kept in excellent repair, as they are not liable to be fpoiled by wheel-carriages, in a country where travellers are generally carried by men in a kind of litter, or elfe walk. With refpect to this, they conftantly obferve a moft excellent rule, which is, that travellers fhall always keep on the left-hand fide of the way, fo that different companies, whether great or fmall, may meet and pafs, without in any wife incommoding each other: a regulation, which, in other countries that lie under lefs reftraint, deferves fo much the more to be attended to, as not only in the high roads in the country, but even in towns and cities, every year exhibits in no inconfiderable number, the moft lamentable, and, to an enlightened nation, difgraceful inftances of perfons of every age and fex, but more efpecially children and old people, being rode or driven over by the giddy fons of riot and diffipation; of which broken limbs, if not lofs of life itfelf, is a pretty certain confequence. And as it often happens that bridges cannot be laid down over certain parts of a river, on account of the violent floods, the beft and fafeft regulations are adopted for tranfporting travellers over, either in boats or upon the hands of men. Even in the moft inconfiderable villages there is
a number

a number of petty inns established, where the traveller is sure to find boiling water ready for his tea, with other refreshments.

WEAPONS.

THE arms of the Japanese consist of bows and arrows, scymitars, halberts, and guns. Their *Bows* are very large, and their arrows long, like those of the Chinese. When these bows are to be drawn and the arrows discharged, the troops always place themselves upon one knee; a position which renders it impossible for them to discharge their arrows in quick succession. In the spring the troops assemble to exercise themselves with these bows in shooting at a mark. *Guns* are not their usual weapons: I could only meet with these at the houses of the gentry, where they were displayed upon an elevated stand, appropriated for that purpose in the audience-chamber. The barrels of the guns were of the usual length, but the stock behind the lock was very short, and in as much as I could perceive at a distance, there was a match in the lock; the locks are sometimes made of copper. I never had an opportunity of seeing a gun fired off, although I have
several

several times heard them discharged from the Dutch factory in the neighbourhood of the town of Nagasaki; but the interpreters informed me, that their guns, which, on account of their shortness, could not be placed against the shoulder, were here generally held against the cheek-bone; a position, which, however, appears not a little singular. *Cannons* are not the usual arms of this country; although at Nagasaki, in the possession of the imperial guard, there are some to be seen, which were formerly taken from the Portuguese; but they are never used for saluting the ships; and indeed they are very seldom discharged at all. The Japanese have little or no notion of the proper mode of using them; and whenever they are to fire them off, which is generally done once every seven years, at Nagasaki, in order to cleanse and prove them, the adjutant of artillery provides himself with a long pole, to which he fixes the match, and notwithstanding this precaution, sometimes sets fire to the cannon with averted eyes. The *Scymitar*, therefore, is their chief and choicest weapon, and is constantly worn by every one but the peasants. This scymitar is a yard in length, somewhat inclining to a curve, and has a broad back; the blades are of an incomparably good temper, and such as are old, in particular, are very highly valued. In goodness they far surpass the Spanish blades, which

are

are so much renowned throughout Europe: they will cut a very large nail asunder with ease, and without their edge being turned; and, according to the accounts of the Japanese, will cleave a man asunder from top to bottom. A blade is never sold for less than six kobangs; but these scymitars often fetch from fifty to seventy, and even a hundred rix-dollars, and are considered by the Japanese as the most precious and valuable part of their property. The hilt is furnished with a round and substantial guard, without any bow, and is sometimes full six inches long; the hilt itself is somewhat roundish and flat, is frequently split at the ends, and covered with shark's-skin, which presents a surface replete with knobs of different sizes. These skins have been imported by the Dutch and bought of them at a very dear rate; sometimes from fifty to eighty kobangs, each kobang being valued at six rix-dollars. Round this shagreen silken cords are twisted checkerwise, so that the shagreen appears through; the guard itself is thicker than a rix-dollar, embellished with embossed figures, or curious openwork. The scabbard of the scymitar is thick and rather flat, and cut off square at the end; it is sometimes covered over with the finest shagreen, which is lackered; sometimes it is made of wood, and lackered either entirely black, or variegated with black and white spots, like marble;

marble. Sometimes one sees a silver ring or two encompassing the scabbard; in the fore part on one side there is a small rising prominence with a hole in it, through which a strong silken cord is introduced, that serves occasionally to fasten the scymitar. Near the inner side of the hilt, there is another hole, which contains a knife about six inches in length. This silken cord is sometimes yellow and sometimes green, but more commonly black. They never make use of an appropriated belt, but always thrust the scymitar into the belt upon the left side, with the edge upwards, which to Europeans appears ridiculous enough.

In the figures which Dr. KÆMPFER has given of the Japenese, in his History of Japan, these scymitars are drawn after the European manner, and therefore appear in the very reverse of their real position. Every magistrate, as well as the superior and inferior officers of the army, wear constantly two of these scymitars, one of which is their own private property, the other is what is called their official scymitar, and is farther distinguished by its superior length. Both these scymitars are worn in the belt upon the same side, where they lie a little across each other. On entering a room, and sitting down, they generally take off their official scymitar, and lay it either on one side of them, or before them. The interpreters had only one scymitar, but the banjoses

wore

wore two; and these were always the first that came on board, and the last that left the ship, on those days when any business was to be transacted there.

RELIGION.

PAGANISM is the established religion throughout the whole empire of Japan; but their sects are both numerous, and very opposite to each other in their tenets; notwithstanding which they all live together in the greatest harmony and concord, without disputes or quarrels. The ecclesiastical Emperor, DAIRI, is, like the Pope, the head of the church, and appoints the principal priests. Every sect has its respective church, and its own peculiar idols, which are represented under some determinate, and that, for the most part, very uncouth and hideous form. The number of these fictitious deities is such, that almost every trade has its own tutelar divinity, after the manner of the ancient Greeks and Romans; and consequently they have both their *Dii majorum et minorum gentium*. The Japanese are not, indeed, entirely ignorant of the existence of an eternal, omnipotent Being, fupreme in power and might above all other gods; but their knowledge in this particular is very much obfcured with fable and fuperftition. Notwithftanding this, I have never feen among any Pagans whatever fo large and majeftic a reprefentation of this god, as is to be met with in two of the temples in this country. In the one is feen a wooden image, of fuch an amazing magnitude, that fix men can fit crofs-legged, in the Japanefe fafhion, upon its wrift, and it meafures ten yards in breadth acrofs the fhoulders. In the other, his infinite power is reprefented by a multitude of fubaltern deities, who ftand round him on each fide, to the number of 33,333.

Their temples, of which they have likewife a great variety, are generally built in the fuburbs of the towns, upon the higheft and moft eligible fpots. The priefts in each temple are numerous, although they have little or no employment, any farther than to keep the temple clean, to light the fires and the lamps, and to prefent fuch flowers as are confecrated to the idol, and which they believe to be moft agreeable to him. No fermons are preached, nor hymns fung in the temples; but they are left open all day for the accommodation of fuch as wifh to offer up their prayers, or to leave their offerings. Nor are ftrangers denied admittance to their temples;

not even the Dutch, who are allowed to visit them, and may be accommodated with lodgings in them, whenever it happens that the inns in the petty country towns are bespoke; as was once the case in the course of the journey that I made to the imperial court.

The principal religions of Japan may properly be said to be only two: the *Sinto* and the *Budsdo*. The former is the proper and most ancient religion of the country; though its adherents are not so numerous as those of the latter, which was brought hither from the continent of Asia, and has acquired the greatest number of followers. The doctrine of the *Sinto*, in its original simplicity and purity, was much nobler than it was after it became in process of time adulterated with a great many foreign and superfluous ceremonies. It is even probable that it originated from the Babylonian emigrants, and was in its rise more intelligible and clear, but by degrees became obscured. Its adherents acknowledge and believe in a Supreme Being, who inhabits the highest heavens; but they likewise allow of inferior or subaltern deities. It is by this Supreme Divinity that they swear; and they believe him to be far too great to stand in need of their worship. Their adoration, therefore, has for its object the inferior deities, who, according to their creed, exercise dominion over the earth, the water, the air, &c. and have it in their power to make men happy or miserable. Neither are they without some conception, however imperfect, of the immortality of the soul, and of a future state of happiness or misery after death. According to their tradition, the souls of the virtuous have a place assigned them immediately under heaven, whilst those of the wicked are doomed to wander to and fro under the cope and canopy of heaven, in order to expiate their sins; consequently they place no manner of faith in the metempsychosis or transmigration of souls into animals or other bodies; the whole tenor of their doctrine has no other object than to render mankind virtuous in this life: their chief and universal care is to preserve a clear conscience, to lead a virtuous life, and to shew due obedience to the laws of their sovereign. They abstain from animal food, are very loth to shed blood, and will not touch any dead body. Whenever any one transgresses in any of these points, he is considered as unclean for a longer or a shorter term, as was the case with the Jews, agreeable to the Levitical law. They believe that there are no other devils than those which reside, as souls, in foxes; these animals being considered as very noxious and dangerous in this country.

RELIGION. 21

Although the professors of this religion are persuaded that their gods know all things, and that, therefore, it is unnecessary to pray to them for any thing, they have, nevertheless, both churches and certain stated holidays. Their gods are called *Sin* or *Kami*, and their churches are styled *Mia*. These churches consist of several different apartments and galleries, with windows and doors in front, which can be taken away and replaced at pleasure, according to the custom of the country. The floors are covered with straw-mats, and the roofs project so wide on every side, as to overhang an elevated path in which people walk round the temple. In these churches one meets with no visible idol, nor any image which is designed to represent the Supreme invisible Being; though they sometimes keep a little image in a box, representing some inferior divinity, to whom the temple is consecrated. In the centre of the temple is frequently placed a large mirror, made of cast-metal well polished, which is designed to remind those that come to worship, that, in like manner as their personal blemishes are faithfully pourtrayed in the mirror, so do the secret blemishes and evil qualities of their hearts lie open and exposed to the all-searching eyes of the immortal gods.

I have frequently observed with the greatest astonishment, as well on holidays as on other occasions, the extreme devotion with which the Sintoists approach these temples; they never venture to approach the house of their god, if they are in any wise impure; for which reason they wash themselves first perfectly clean, dress themselves in their very best apparel, and wash their hands a second time just at the entrance of the temple; then advancing with the greatest reverence, they place themselves before the mirror, and after bowing respectfully down to the very ground, turn once more to the mirror, prefer their prayers, and present their offerings. At the conclusion, they ring thrice a little bell which is kept for that purpose in the temple, and retire to spend the remainder of the day in mirth and rejoicing.

The priests in these temples may be divided into two classes; the first, who attend to the domestic business of the temple, are secular priests, and illiterate, in order that they may not be able to reveal the mysteries of their religion. The other class, consisting of those who are in sacred orders, instruct their disciples in the religious mysteries of their sect, who are bound by oath not to reveal any part of them. The secular priests shave their beards, but not their heads; and are habited in a large and loose dress, after the manner of the country; on their heads they wear a lackered hat, with a silken tassel hanging

down

down behind. Since the introduction of *Budsdo*'s doctrine into this country, this sect has adopted a greater variety both of tenets and ceremonies than it originally embraced, and unquestionably merits the preference before all other sects in the island, notwithstanding all the superstition with which it is infected. KUBO professes himself of this sect, and is bound to make a visit every year, either in person or by his ambassador, to one of their temples, and there to perform his devotion, and at the same time to leave behind him presents of great value.

Budsdo's doctrine was originally brought hither from the western coast of the East-Indies; that is to say, from Mallabar, Coromandel, and Ceylon. *Budha*, who without doubt is the same with *Budsdo*, was a prophet among the Bramins, who is reported to have been born in Ceylon about one thousand years before the birth of Christ, and was the founder of that sect which has since diffused itself over every part of the East-Indies, and to the remotest boundaries of Asia. The doctrine, however, did not gain repute in China till a long time after its first introduction; from thence it passed over into Coræa, and from that place into Japan, where it was very generally received, and, being blended with that of the ancient *Sinto*, gave birth to the most monstrous and absurd superstitions. Its principal tenets consist in the following maxims: that the souls of men and beasts are alike immortal: that a just distribution of rewards and punishments takes place after death; that there are different degrees of happiness as well as of punishment; that the souls of the wicked transmigrate after death into the bodies of animals, and at last, in case of amendment, are translated back again into the human form, &c. &c. To the Supreme God they give the name of *Amida*; and Satan is called *Jemma*.

The churches of all the different religious sects are in general built upon the most eligible spots, both in the villages and in the towns; the roads leading to them likewise are frequently adorned with alleys of cypress trees, and handsome gates; most of them have a separate apartment for the idol, who is sometimes exhibited sitting upon an altar, surrounded with incense, flowers, and other decorations.

The churches throughout the whole country are open every day in the year; but they are, as the reader will easily imagine, more generally frequented on the customary festival days, and likewise at other times, by a multitude of visiters, who repair thither in order to amuse and divert themselves.

The usual holidays in Japan are the first day in every month, when they rise early in the morning,

morning, dress themselves handsomely, and go to pay their respects to their friends and superiors, at the same time wishing them joy of the new month. This day is kept as a festival throughout the whole empire; a custom which has been observed from the earliest ages. The full of the moon, or the fifteenth day, is another holiday, on which the people resort to the temples in greater numbers than on the first. The third festival is of less consequence, and falls upon the twenty-eighth day, or the day before the new month.

Besides these monthly festivals, they celebrate five more, which happen but once in the year: the first of these is New year's day. On this day they rise very early in the morning, dress themselves in their best attire, and go round among their superiors, friends, and relations, to wish them a happy new year; the remainder of the day is spent in eating and drinking, visiting the temples, and making merry: some of them make a practice of giving away some trifling present on these occasions; and very often the eldest of the tribe gives a public supper to his kindred. The whole country, at this time, is in a state of busy fermentation, as it were, which lasts for three whole days; after this the whole of the first month is dedicated almost to no other purpose than pastime and pleasure. The *second annual*

annual festival falls upon the third day of the third month; the *third* upon the fifth day of the fifth month; the *fourth* upon the seventh day of the seventh month; and the *fifth* upon the ninth day of the ninth month. These months and days, which make always uneven numbers, are considered by the Japanese as unlucky, and are therefore dedicated (setting all business aside) to mirth and mutual congratulations, and in some measure, though but little, to the service of the divinities. On some of these holidays, in preference to other days, they celebrate their nuptials, give public entertainments and other diversions; as it is a maxim with them, that the gods take delight in seeing mankind joyful and happy.

Some of the churches in the country being more worthy of note than others, it is common to perform pilgrimages thither from all parts of the empire, in like manner as the Mahometans are accustomed to visit Mecca. Among these the temple of *Isie*, which is consecrated to TENSIO DAI SIN, the most ancient of their gods, and supreme above all the other celestial divinities, is particularly remarkable. This temple is the most ancient in the whole empire, and at the same time in the worst condition, being now so exceedingly decayed with age, that it can scarcely be kept together with the greatest care and attention. It has no other ornaments than a mirror,

and

and flips of white paper hung round about on the walls, denoting that nothing impure may approach, or can be pleasing to God; as likewise that nothing can be hid from his all-seeing eye. The Emperor, who cannot personally visit this temple, sends hither every year an ambassador in his stead, in the first month of the year. Every one of his subjects, without any exception of age or sex, is bound to undertake a pilgrimage hither at least once in his life-time, and many perform it every year: people of superior rank, however, go but seldom; as here, as well as in other places, they arrogate to themselves various privileges and prerogatives, in which they consult their private ease and convenience, rather than their duty. These journies may be undertaken at any season of the year, as best suits the convenience of the party, but in general they chuse the pleasantest months, especially the spring. The performance of such a pilgrimage is deemed highly meritorious, and is besides rewarded with an indulgence, granting remission of sins for the whole year. In the course of my journey to the imperial court at Jedo, I saw some thousands of these devout pilgrims, many of whom were so wretched and indigent, that they were obliged to beg their way. These miserable people even carried their beds with them, agreeable to the fashion of the country, consisting of a straw matt,

matt, which they carried on their backs; moſt of them were farther provided with a little bucket, which ſerved them to drink out of, as likewiſe to receive the alms given them. On this bucket I ſaw the name of the owner inſcribed, which ſerved to ſhew who the traveller was, in caſe he ſhould meet with any calamity, or chance to die on the road. On their arrival at *Iſie,* the pilgrims are conducted by ſome prieſt to the temple of the god, where they humbly prefer their prayers, and, in conſideration of ſome preſent made to the prieſt, are favoured with an indulgence; which conſiſts of a few thin laminæ of pewter, kept in an oblong box, made likewiſe of thin pewter.

Beſides the prieſts employed in the ſervice of the different churches, there is another claſs, or a leſs ſacred *Order* of them. The *order of Blind Monks* is, perhaps, one of the moſt ſingular that ever was known, and is not to be paralleled in the whole world, conſiſting of none but blind members, who are diſperſed over the whole empire. The order of *Jammabos,* or Monks of the Mountain, is likewiſe worthy of notice; it was founded about 1200 years ago, and has a General, who reſides in Miaco, and diſtributes titles of honour to his dependants, according to their various merits. Theſe wear, by way of diſtinction, a ſmall cord ſuſpended from the neck,

RELIGION.   29

neck, to which are attached several pieces of fringe, of different lengths, according to the merit of the wearer: they farther wear a scymitar on the left side, and carry in their hands a staff with a copper head to it, and a conch, or *Murex tritonis*, which serves them instead of a trumpet. Their head is covered with a cap, on their back is hung a sack, and a pair of shoes, to make use of when they travel over the mountains, and they are likewise frequently provided with a rosary, or kind of *pater noster*. The monks of this order suffer many hardships, and are in duty bound, once every year, to the great and imminent danger of their lives, to traverse wild forests, and to climb up to the summits of the highest mountains. It is furthermore incumbent upon them to study cleanliness; on which account they bathe very often in cold water, and subsist solely upon roots and herbs which they gather in the mountains; in fine, they wander barefoot over the whole country, and, like the gypsies in the north, cure disorders, restore stolen goods, tell fortunes, &c.

Vows are frequently made by superstitious persons; thus, for instance, one of our best interpreters, a man advanced in years, having made a vow, a long time back, never to make use of shoes, and being this year employed to accompany

pany the Dutch embaſſy to the imperial court in the depth of winter, marched along very patiently upon his bare feet; bore all the inclemency of the weather with the unconcern of a Stoic, and, what was ſurprizing, did not afterwards ſuffer any inconvenience in conſequence of his hard and troubleſome expedition.

Nunneries have been eſtabliſhed in this country upwards of a thouſand years ago, although, with reſpect to number, they fall infinitely ſhort of thoſe eſtabliſhed in Europe.

Every *Order* or ſect has conſtantly its General reſident in *Miaco*; beſides which every church or convent has its own ſuperior: excluſively of theſe, they have likewiſe at the ſecular Emperor's court in *Jedo*, their eccleſiaſtical plenipotentiary; whoſe buſineſs it is to ſettle ſuch diſputes as concern temporal matters in the country, as likewiſe to take cognizance of the miſconduct of thoſe who are in holy orders: but when ſentence of death is to be paſſed upon the latter, the warrant muſt always be previouſly ſigned by the General of the order.

The *Chriſtian* religion was brought into Japan immediately after the diſcovery of this country by the Portugueſe. The firſt Jeſuit Miſſionaries arrived in the province of *Bungo* in the year 1549, and in a ſhort time ſpread themſelves over the

the whole country, where they continued till the year 1638, when 37,000 Chriſtians were maſſacred. In 1549, a Japaneſe youth was baptiſed in *Goa*, who gave the Portugueſe great inſight into the advantages which they might reap in Japan, both with reſpect to commerce and the propagation of the Chriſtian religion. The Portugueſe enjoyed here the moſt unlimited freedom, with liberty to travel over the whole country, to trade and to preach. Their commerce proved very lucrative, and the work of converſion made ſuch a rapid progreſs, that many of the Princes of the empire, as for inſtance, the Princes of *Bungo, Arrina, Emura*, and many more, embraced the Chriſtian religion, which induced the Portugueſe to come over in great numbers, marry, and ſettle in different parts of the country. In 1582, after forty years labour, the Catholic religion was in ſuch high eſteem here, that a Japaneſe embaſſy was ſent to Rome to Pope GREGORY XIII. with letters and valuable preſents. But the incredible profits of this commerce, added to the rapid progreſs of the Chriſtian religion, ſoon puffed up the Portugueſe with pride, and it was not long before their avarice and haughtineſs proved their ruin. In proportion as their riches and credit increaſed, they became inſupportable to the Japaneſe, and were at length deteſted to ſuch a degree, that already in the

year

year 1586 a decree was issued for the extermination of the Christians; in consequence of which, heavy persecutions were commenced against them, and in the year 1590 only, upwards of twenty thousand of them were put to death. Notwithstanding all this, numbers of the Japanese daily became proselytes to the Christian faith; so that in the years 1591 and 1592 not less than twelve thousand were converted and baptised. Even the Emperor KUBO FIDE JORI himself professed Christianity, together with his court and army; and had the Portuguese but conducted themselves with prudence and gentleness, there is every reason to believe, that the persecutions already commenced against them would have ceased. But instead of this, they gave daily greater scope to their haughtiness and ambition, and one of their bishops behaving with unwarrantable rudeness towards a Prince of the Empire, thereby accelerated their final ruin; giving, at the same time, a decisive blow to their lucrative commerce, together with the propagation of the Christian religion. This circumstance took place in the year 1596, when a certain Prince was so grossly affronted by an ambitious Prelate, during a journey to the imperial court, that, on his arrival at *Jedo*, the former laid before KUBO a statement of the whole affair. Hence arose a new persecution against the Christians in the year following; the Priests

being

being forbidden to preach, a great many of the
Clergy banished out of the country, and the
mercantile part of the colony sent to the island
of *Desima*. At this time too a conspiracy was
discovered, which the Portuguese had set on foot
against the Emperor, with an intent to dethrone
him. The Dutch, who happened at that time
to be at war with the Portuguese, having captured one of their vessels, found, among other
papers, a letter from a certain Japanese Captain,
named MORO, to the King of Portugal, containing the particulars of the plot concerted against
the Emperor's throne and person. The actual
existence of this conspiracy being afterwards fully
authenticated by another letter written by MORO
to *Macao*, the Japanese government came to the
final determination to banish all Christians from
the empire, who should refuse to abjure the Catholic faith, or else to put them all to death
without quarter. This persecution was accordingly commenced, and carried on without inter-
mission for the space of forty years, when it ende
in the total eradication of the Christian religion,
together with the final overthrow of the trade
carried on by the Portuguese; after 37,000
Christians, who had taken refuge in the castle of
Simabara, where they sustained a siege, had been
forced to surrender, and were all put to the sword
in one day. The Japanese, who were persuaded

that

that this unwarrantable conduct in the Christians was the inseparable consequence of their doctrines, took from that time forward the most efficacious measures to prevent the Christian faith from being ever re-established in their dominions; and the Portuguese received strict injunctions, under the severest penalties, never to approach their coasts any more. And in order the more effectually to discover whether any Japanese Christians remained hidden and concealed in the country, recourse was had to various institutions, and, among others, to that of trampling upon the images of the saints, a custom which still prevails, and is repeated at the commencement of every year in Nagasaki and the circumjacent country.

Philosophers and moralists are regarded in this country in the same light as priests and sacred persons, and their tenets have been embraced with equal ardour with those of other spiritual sects. The chief, which has obtained estimation and repute in Japan is *Sjuto* or *Koosi*, known in Europe by the name of the Morality of Confucius. This system derives its origin from China, where Confucius was born 400 years after Budsdo. Its followers, though they cannot properly be said to worship any God, place their *summum bonum*, nevertheless, in a virtuous life; and admit of rewards or punishments for man in this life only. They confess that a universal soul or spirit belongs to the world, without acknowledging any other gods, without having churches, and without worshipping any one. Their doctrine, therefore, chiefly inculcates the following maxims; to lead a virtuous life, to do justice to every man, to behave at the same time to all persons with civility, to govern with equity, and to maintain an inviolate integrity of heart. They do not burn their dead, but lay them, like the Europeans, in a chest, and bury them in the earth. Suicide is not only deemed lawful among them, but it is even applauded, and considered as an heroic act.

The difference between this system of morality, which has been introduced among them in latter times, and their most ancient religion, is very great and remarkable. In their modern system we discover the offspring of human wit; whilst their ancient religion exhibits evident traces of the divine Law of Moses.

FOOD, AND THE VARIOUS MODES OF PREPARING IT.

IN the multiplicity of the articles of food to be met with in its islands, and the surrounding ocean, and which both nature and art conspire to furnish and prepare, Japan may, perhaps, be said to surpass most other countries hitherto known to us. The Japanese not only make use of such things for food and aliment, which are in themselves wholesome and nutritive, but take in almost the whole of the animal and vegetable kingdoms, not excepting the most poisonous; which, by their mode of dressing and preparing them, may be rendered harmless and even useful. The meat that is served up in every dish, is cut into small pieces, thoroughly boiled and stewed, and mixed with agreeable sauces. In this manner every thing is served up in the very best order; and the master of the house is not harrassed at his table with the trouble of cutting up great pieces, or of distributing the provisions round to the guests. At meal-time every one seats himself upon the soft floor-mats; facing each guest is placed a small square table, that serves for the purpose of holding the different dishes, which already in the kitchen are portioned out to each person, and are served up in the neatest vessels, either of porcelain or japanned wood. These cups are tolerably large basons, and always furnished with a lid. The first course consists generally of fish, with fish-soup; the soup they drink out of the cup, but eat the solid part, which is chopped into small pieces, with two lackered pegs, which they hold so dexterously

between

between the fingers of the right hand, that they can with the greatest nicety take up the smallest grain of rice with them; and these pegs serve them for the purpose both of fork and spoon. As soon as one course is finished it is taken away, and another served up in its room. The last course is brought to table in a cup of blue porcelain, and this likewise is furnished with a lid. The victuals are carried in by a servant, who kneels down as he places them upon the table, and takes them away after dinner. When several persons eat in company together, they all salute each other with a low bow, before they begin to eat. The ladies do not eat with the men, but by themselves. Between each dish, they drink warm sacki, or rice-beer, which is poured out of a tea-kettle into shallow tea-saucers, made of lackered wood; and during this, they sometimes eat a quarter of an egg, boiled hard, and very frequently they drink at the same time to some body's health. In general they eat three times a day; about eight o'clock in the morning, two o'clock at noon, and eight in the evening. There are some that observe no regular time for their meals; but eat whenever they are hungry; for which reason the victuals are obliged to be kept in readiness the whole day. Rice, which is here exceedingly white and well-tasted, supplies, with the Japanese, the place of bread:

they

they eat it boiled with every kind of provisions. *Miso* foup, boiled with fish and onions, is eaten by the common people, frequently three times a day, or at each of their cuftomary meals. *Misos* are not unlike lentils, and are fmall beans, gathered from the *Dolichos soja*. Fish is likewife a very common difh with the Japanefe, both boiled and fried in oil. Fowls, of which they have a great variety, both wild and tame, are eaten in great abundance; and the flesh of whales, though coarfe, is in feveral places, at leaft among the poorer fort, a very common food. It has a red and difagreeable look, and was often expofed for fale in the ftreets in Nagafaki, when I paffed by, in order to go on board of fhip.

In preparing their victuals, they make ufe of expreffed oils, of feveral different forts. Thefe oils are made chiefly from the feeds of *Sefamum*, of *Tfubaki*, (the *Camellia japonica*) *Kiri*, (the *Bignonia tomentofa*) *Abrafin*, (*Dryandra cordata*) *Azedarach*, and feveral others; fometimes from the *Rhus fucce-danea*, *Taxus baccata*, and *Gingko*. In their victuals they make a very plentiful ufe of *mushrooms*, and the fruit of the *Solanum melongena*, as well as the roots of the *Solanum efculentum*, (batatas) *carrots*, and feveral kinds of bulbous roots, and of *beans*. For the defert, they have *kaki-figs*, *chefnuts*, *water-nuts*, and *pears*, which are poffibly often exported from hence to Batavia; befides *lemons*,
Seville,

Seville and *China-oranges, shaddocks, grapes,* &c. Among their valuable fishes is what they call the *tay,* (by the Dutch called *steen-braasem,*) which is frequently sold at a very high price, and purchased for holidays and festival occasions. The *Perca sexlineata* (*Ara*) ranks among their finest fish, and their *Clupea Thrissa* is so fat, that it is equal to the best herrings that are caught in Europe. *Salmon* is only found near the *Fakonie* mountains, and is neither so large, nor so well-tasted as those of Europe. Of *oysters* and other *shell-fish,* several different sorts are eaten; but always boiled or stewed, as likewise *shrimps* and *crabs.*

DRINK.

TEA and sacki-beer constitute the sole liquors of the Japanese, which fall infinitely short in number of those which the thirsty Europeans can exhibit. Wines and distilled liquors they never make use of, and can hardly be persuaded to taste them, when offered them by the Dutch. Coffee is scarcely known, even by the taste, to a few of the interpreters; and brandy is not with them one of the necessaries of life. They have hitherto never suffered themselves to be corrupted by by the Europeans that have visited them: rather than adopt any practice from others, which might be actually both useful and convenient, they have chosen to retain their ancient and primitive mode of life, in its original purity; into which they would not even insensibly introduce any usage or custom, that in the course of time might become useless to them, or detrimental.

Sacki is the name of a kind of beer, which the Japanese prepare from rice; it is tolerably clear, and not a little resembles wine, but has a very singular taste, which cannot be reckoned extremely pleasant. This liquor, when it is fresh, is more inclined to a white colour, but after it has lain in small wooden casks, it becomes very brown.

This drink is vended in every tavern, in the same manner as wine is sold in all cellars in Europe, and it constitutes their cheer at entertainments, and loofer hours, and is likewise used as wine, by the more wealthy, at their very meals. It is never drank cold by the Japanese, but is warmed in a common tea-kettle, from which it is poured out into flat tea-cups, made of lackered wood, and in this manner it is drank quite warm, which in a very short time heats and inebriates them; but the whole intoxication vanishes in a few minutes, and is generally succeeded by a disagreeable head-ach. *Sacki* is imported to Batavia, as an article of commerce, but is drank out of wine-glaffes before meals, to provoke an appetite, on which occafions the white *facki* is generally preferred, which is lefs difgufting to the tafte.

Tea is drank throughout the whole country, for the purpofe of quenching thirft; for which reafon they keep in every houfe, and more efpecially in every inn, a kettle upon the fire all day long, with boiling water and ground tea; from this the brown decoction is poured out for immediate ufe, and another kettle, filled with cold water, affords them the means of diluting and cooling it. In the houfes of people of diftinction, vifiters are always prefented with *green tea*, with which the Dutch are entertained, whenever they wait upon any of the privy-counfellors or other perfons in office. This tea is frefh gathered, and ground to powder; boiling water being firft poured into a can, they put in the tea in its pulverized ftate, and ftir it round with a ftick, in the fame manner as is ufually done with chocolate, and then pour it out into tea-cups; it muft be drank immediately, otherwife the green powder fettles at the bottom. No perfon of diftinction undertakes a journey of any length, without carrying with him a lackered cheft, which is borne by a man-fervant, and in which water is kept boiling all the way; ground tea, tea-cups, and every other

other neceſſary appendage are ready prepared and at hand.

The tea-ſhrub grows wild in every part of the country, but I met with it moſt frequently growing on the very borders and margins of cultivated lands, or upon ſuch mountains and downs as did not very well anſwer the trouble of cultivation. This plant grows from the ſeed in the courſe of ſix or ſeven years to the height of a man; but already in the third year of its growth it yields ſome produce of its leaves. Thoſe who are ſomewhat accuſtomed to this kind of harveſt, can gather, in the ſpace of one day, ten or twelve pounds weight of them. The older the leaves are, and the later in the year the gathering is made, the greater abundance, it is true, they yield, but then the tea is ſo much the worſe; as the ſmaller leaves, and thoſe which have but juſt ſhot forth, furniſh the fineſt and moſt valuable. The tea, therefore, is gathered annually at three different ſeaſons. The firſt harveſt commences (*at the end of Songvats*) the beginning of March, or the end of February, at which ſeaſon the leaves begin to puſh forth, poſſeſs a viſcous quality, and are gathered ſolely for the uſe of the Emperor, or for people of rank and opulence; whence it takes the name of imperial tea. A month after this, the ſecond harveſt takes place, when the leaves are full grown, but are ſtill thin, tender,

tender, and well-flavoured. Again a month, and the principal harvest commences, when the greatest quantity is gathered; the leaves having all pushed forth completely, and become very thick and stout. Young shrubs always yield better tea than old ones, and some places produce it in greater perfection, and more delicious than others.

The tea-leaves are afterwards, for the sake of drying them, spread upon thin plates of iron, which are made hot. During this operation they must be continually stirred round with both hands, as long as ever the fingers can support the heat. They are next rolled to and fro upon mats, till they grow perfectly cool; and in case they are not then sufficiently dry, they are roasted and rolled over again, once, or as many times as may be requisite.

THE SMOKING OF TOBACCO

Was in former times not customary in this country; but it is probable, that the Portuguese were the first who introduced this practice. The Japanese have no other name for tobacco than *tabaco*, which is smoked indiscriminately by both sexes. The tobacco used for this purpose, is
planted

planted in the country, and is the common *Nicotiana tabacum*. They cut their tobacco into very fine shreds, almost as fine as human hair: the pipes which they use are very short, seldom more than six inches in length, and are made of lackered bamboo, with a copper mouth-piece and bowl; this latter is so small, that it does not contain above a third part or one half of a thimble full of tobacco, which is twisted up and crammed in with their fingers. These pipes are soon smoaked out, in a very few whiffs only, upon which the ashes are beaten out, and the pipe is filled again; which practice they repeat several times. The smoke is puffed out each time both through the nostrils and the mouth. Persons of distinction have always the following apparatus for smoking: an oblong box, eighteen inches long, a foot broad, and three fingers high, lackered of a brown or black colour, is placed before each person; in this box are laid pipes and tobacco, and three cups are placed, which are used in smoking: one of these round cups, which is generally made of thick and stout porcellain, or lackered wood, is lined with brass on the inside, and is filled with ashes, in which a live coal is placed, for the purpose of lighting the pipe: the second serves to receive the ashes of the tobacco after the pipe is smoked out, when this latter is struck with force against the edge; and

sometimes

sometimes it is spit upon, in order to quench the sparks. The third supplies the place of a spitting-pot, during the time of smoking. At visits, this apparatus is the first thing that is placed before the guests. One of these boxes is sometimes furnished with a lid, which is tied fast with a ribbon, and is carried by a servant, whenever they go to such places, where they do not expect to have tobacco presented to them. The poorer class generally carry both their pipe and tobacco with them, when they go out; the pipe is then put into a case, and worn on the right side in the girdle at the back of their loins; the tobacco-pouch is hardly of the breadth of a hand, and somewhat shorter, furnished with a flap at the top, which is fastened together with a little ivory hook; this pouch is likewise slung to the girdle by means of a silken cord, and a bead of cornelian, or a piece of agate: it is made for the most part of a particular kind of silk, with interwoven flowers of silver and gold.

FESTIVAL

FESTIVAL SPORTS AND GAMES.

ALTHOUGH gravity forms the general character of the Japanese nation, this serious disposition, however, does not prevent them from having their pleasures, their sports, and festivities. These are of two kinds, occasional or periodical, and constitute part of their worship: the latter, in many respects, may be compared to our plays. Their chief festivals are the *Feast of Lanthorns*, and what is called the *Matsuri*.

The *Lanthorn-Festival*, or *Feast of Lamps*, is celebrated towards the end of August, and is called by the natives *Bong*. It lasts three days; but the second afternoon, with the following night, are kept with the greatest festivity. It was originally instituted in memory and honour of the dead, who, they believe, return annually to their kindred and friends on the first afternoon of these games; every one visiting his former house and family, where they remain till the second night, when they are to be sent away again. By way of welcoming them on their arrival, they plant stakes of bamboo near all the tombs, upon which they hang a great number of lanthorns, with lights, and those so close to each other, that the whole mountain appears illuminated: these lanthorns are kept alight till nine or ten o'clock at night.

night. On the second evening, when the spirits
of the defunct are, according to their tradition,
to be sent away again, they fabricate a small
vessel of straw, with lights and lanthorns in it,
which they carry at midnight in procession, with
vocal and instrumental music, and loud cries, to
the sea-shore, where it is launched into the water,
and left to the wind and waves, till it either
catches fire and is consumed, or is swallowed up
by the waves. Both of these illuminations, consisting of several thousand fires, exhibit to the
eye an uncommonly grand and beautiful spectacle.

The feast of *Matsuri* is celebrated upon some
certain festival day, and in honour of some particular god. Thus, for instance, in the town of
Nagasaki, where I was present at one of these
festivals, it is celebrated in memory of *Suwa*, the
tutelar deity of the town. It is celebrated on
the ninth day of the ninth month, which is the
day of this idol's nativity, with games, public
dances, and dramatic representations: the festival
commences on the seventh day, when the temples
are frequented, sermons are preached, prayers
are offered up, and public spectacles are exhibited; but the ninth day excels all in pomp and
expensive magnificence, which they vary every
time in such a manner, that the entertainments of
the present year bear no resemblance to those of
the last; neither are the same arrangements made.

The

The expences are defrayed by the inhabitants of the town, in such manner, that certain streets exhibit and pay the expences of certain pieces and parts of the entertainment. I, together with the rest of the Dutch, had an invitation sent me, to be a spectator of this festival, in 1776, which was celebrated in a large open spot in the town of Nagasaki. A capacious house, resembling a large booth, raised upon posts, and provided with a roof and benches, was erected on one side, for the convenience of the spectators. These consisted not only of the magistrates and ecclesiastics, but likewise of foreigners; and a guard was placed to keep off the croud. First of all appeared the priests, carrying the image of the idol *Suwa*, and took their places, habited in black and white. A company of ten or twelve persons played upon instruments of music, and sang the exploits of their gods and heroes; in the mean time that a party of virgins dancing, displayed the most enchanting elegance in their gestures and deportment. The music consisted in a mere rattling noise, which might perhaps found more grateful in the idol's, than in human ears. A large parasol was next introduced, inscribed with the name of the street, and emblazoned with its coat of arms, followed by a band of musicians, in masks, with drums, flutes, bells, and vocal music. These were succeeded

by

by the device itself, which was different for every street; then followed a band of actors; and lastly, the inhabitants of the street, in solemn procession, with an innumerable and promiscuous croud at their heels. This progressive march lasted nearly a whole hour, after which they marched back again in the same order, and a second procession succeeded in its place; this was followed by a third, and so on, during the whole forenoon. The inhabitants of each street vied with each other in magnificence and invention, with respect to the celebration of this festival, and in displaying, for the most part, such things as were characteristic of the various produce of the mines, mountains, forests, navigation, manufactures, and the like, of the province from which the street derived its name, and whence it had its inhabitants.

Plays I had an opportunity of seeing acted several times, both in Nagasaki and during my journey to the imperial court at Osaka. The spectators sit in houses of different dimensions upon benches; facing them, upon an elevated, but small and narrow place, stands the theatre itself, upon which seldom more than one or two actors perform at a time. These are always dressed in a very singular manner, according as their own taste and fancy suggest, insomuch that a stranger would be apt to believe, that they exhibited

exhibited themselves, not to entertain but to frighten the audience. Their gestures, as well as their dress, are strangely uncouth and extravagant, and consist in artificial contortions of the body, which it must have cost them much trouble to learn and perform. In general they represent some heroic exploit or love-story of their idols and heroes, which are frequently composed in verse, and are sometimes accompanied with music. A curtain may, it is true, be let fall between the actors and the spectators, and some necessary pieces be brought forward upon the theatre; but in other respects, these small theatres have no machinery nor decorations, which can entitle them to be put in comparison with those of Europe. I did not observe that public spectacles contributed any more in this country than in other places, to reform the manners of the people; as the design of them appears to be the same here as in other parts of the world, and as they tend rather to amuse the idle frivolity of mankind with jugglers tricks, than to amend the heart, rather to fill the pockets of the actors, than to be of any real benefit to the spectators.

When the Japanese wish at any time to entertain the Dutch, either in the town of Nagasaki, or more particularly during their journey to the imperial court, they generally provide a *band of female dancers*, for the amusement of their guests.

These

These are generally young damsels, very superbly dressed, whom they fetch from the inns; sometimes young boys likewise are mixed among them. Such a dance requires always a number of persons, who turn and twine and put themselves into a variety of artificial postures, in order to represent an amorous or heroic deed, without either speaking or singing; their steps are however regulated by the music which plays to them. The girls are in particular provided with a number of very fine and light night-gowns, made of silk, which they slip off one after the other, during the dance, from the upper part of their body, so as frequently to have them, to the number of a dozen together, suspended from the girdle which encircles their loins. Their dances therefore correspond, in some measure, with our country-dances, although, upon the whole, they widely differ even from these.

Their *weddings* and *funerals* may likewise claim a place among their festivals, although they do not celebrate them with the same pomp as do the Europeans and other nations.

Marriages are solemnized upon a pleasant eminence without the towns, in the presence of the relations and the priests, when the following ceremonies are observed. The bridegroom and the bride advance together to an altar erected for that purpose, each holding a torch in their hand;

whilst the priest is employed in reading a certain form of prayer, the bride, who occupies the right-hand place, first lights her torch from a burning lamp, and then holds it out to the bridegroom, who lights his torch from hers; upon which the guests wish the new-married couple joy. In this country the men are not allowed a plurality of wives, as in China, but each man is confined to one, who has liberty to go out and shew herself in company, and is not shut up in a recluse and separate apartment, as is the custom with their neighbours. Instances of divorces sometimes occur among them, but these cases are not very common. The more daughters a man has, and the handsomer they are, the richer he esteems himself, it being here the established custom for suitors to make presents to their father-in-law, before they obtain his daughter.

Fornication is very prevalent in this country; notwithstanding which, chastity is frequently held in such high veneration, both with married and single, that when they have been injured in this point, they sometimes lay violent hands upon themselves. In this country likewise the dishonourable practice of keeping mistresses obtains with some; but the children they bring into the world cannot inherit, and the mistresses are considered as servants in the house.

The

The Japanese either burn their dead to ashes, or else bury them in the earth. The former method, as I was informed, was in ancient times much more customary than it is at present, though it is still practised with persons of distinction. This ceremony is not always performed on a funeral pile in the open air, but takes place at times in a small house of stone, calculated for that purpose, and furnished with a chimney. The ashes are carried away in a costly vessel, and preserved for some time in the house at home, after which they are buried in the earth. Both men and women follow the corpse in norimons, together with the widow and children of the deceased, and a numerous train of priests, who sing all the time. After one of the priests has sung the eulogy of the deceased, he waves thrice over the corpse a burning torch, and then throws it away: upon this it is picked up by the children or other relations, and the pile set on fire with it. Those who are interred without being first burned, are inclosed in a wooden chest, after the customary manner, and let down into the grave. The children are very much attached to their parents, even after their death. During the interment, and after the same, fragrant spices are cast into the grave, and the finest flowers are planted upon their tombs. The survivors continue to visit the mansions of the dead for several years,

years, and not unfrequently during their whole lives; repeating their visits at first every day, then every week; after that once a month, and at last once a year, exclusively of the Lanthorn Festival, which is celebrated every year in honour of the defunct.

SCIENCES.

THE Sciences in general fall infinitely short in Japan of that exalted pre-eminence, to which they have attained in Europe. The *History* of their own country, may, however, perhaps be deemed more authentic here than that of most other nations, and this, together with the science of house-keeping, is studied, without exception, by them all. *Agriculture*, which the Japanese consider as the most necessary and useful science, for the prosperity and stability of the empire, is in no place in the world so much esteemed as here; where neither foreign nor civil wars, nor emigrations, lessen their population; and where they never think of encroaching upon the territories of other nations; nor yet of introducing the unnecessary and often detrimental productions of other climates: but where, on the contrary,

their

their whole care is directed in the highest degree, that not a single sod of earth shall lie fallow, nor the revenue of the earth be unthriftily employed.

Astronomy is in great favour and repute; notwithstanding which they are unable, without the assistance of the Chinese and Dutch Almanacs, to compose a perfect Calendar, or to compute to minutes and seconds an eclipse of the sun or moon. *Medicine* neither has attained, nor is it likely that it ever will attain, to any degree of eminence. With *Anatomy* they are totally unacquainted, and their knowledge of diseases is very imperfect, involved in error, and frequently in fable: *Botany* and the knowledge of remedies, constitute the whole of their medical knowledge. Of *Natural Philosophy* and *Chemistry*, the Japanese have little more idea than what they have lately learned from the Physicians of Europe. *Law* is not here a tedious and complicated study: no nation upon earth has a smaller code, and fewer Judges. Commentators upon the Statutes and Advocates are here totally unknown; but in no country perhaps are the laws more strictly carried into execution, without any regard to persons, and without partiality, or violence. The laws are severe, and law-suits short. The original *Language* of the country, in opposition to that of all other nations, is at once copious and expressive. Of foreign languages, Chinese is learned by those who devote themselves to study, and read Chinese books and writings. The Interpreters and some of their Physicians even learn the Dutch language, and some of these understand a little Latin; a language which for nearly two thousand years has given more trouble to youth in the schools of Europe, than in general they have derived benefit from it. Their *Morality* does not consist in any curious labours of the brain, but in simple and rational doctrines, which they endeavour to reduce to practice in their conduct by leading a virtuous life. And this morality is preached and enforced by all their religious sects, and is never detached from their divinity, with which it stands in the closest connexion. The *Science of War*, is with these Orientals very simple: courage, fortitude, and love of their country, make ample amends for their ignorance of military tactics; and with these qualifications they have hitherto always proved victorious, and never once been obliged to bow their necks to their enemies. Four hundred and seventy-one years before the commencement of our æra, we find the first mention made of war in the Japanese History. After that period they have been several times disturbed by foreign forces. Anno 1284, after the Tartars had subdued China, Mooku, their General, sent 4000 vessels, and 240,000 men to

conquer

conquer Japan, but without being able to accomplish his aim.

The *Art of Printing* is unquestionably very ancient in this country; but they always used, and still continue to use plates for this purpose, without having any knowledge of moveable types. They print upon one side of the paper only, on account of its thinness, as otherwise the ink would sink through. They have even a knowledge of *Engraving*, although in the *Art of Drawing* they remain vastly inferior to the Europeans, over whom they however boast this decided preference, that they always draw some animal, plant, or other object, that exists in nature, and do not heap together upon tapestry or other kinds of paintings, fantastical figures of things, which have no actual existence; a circumstance, which has hitherto so little engaged the attention of our artists, and which must do no little credit to an enlightened and sensible European. *Surveying* they understand tolerably well, and possess accurate maps, both of their country in general and of its towns. Besides the general map of the empire, I have seen special maps of Jedo, Miako, Osaka, and the town of Nagasaki, which I likewise contrived to carry out of the country with me, notwithstanding the great danger with which this was attended, and the strictest prohibitions

to

to the contrary. Like the Chinese, the Japanese *write* in upright rows, or columns, from the top to the bottom, and then down again, beginning at the right hand and so proceeding to the left, forming their letters with a pencil made of hare's hair, and touche, or Indian ink, which they rub every time with water upon a stone. *Poetry* is a favourite study with this nation, who employ it to perpetuate the memory of their gods, heroes, and celebrated men. *Music* is likewise held in high estimation, but hitherto they have neither been able to bring their musical instruments to any degree of perfection, nor yet have they made any progress in the science of harmony. At festivals, and on other grand occasions, they make use of drums, fifes, stringed instruments, bells, horse-bells, and other musical instruments. The ladies especially are very fond of music, and even learn to perform upon different instruments themselves; but their favourite instrument is a kind of lute with four strings, which they strike with the fingers, and will pass whole evenings at this diversion, although it is not very pleasant. The *koto* bears a strong resemblance to our dulcimers, having a number of strings, which are struck with sticks; and is incontestibly the most agreeable instrument they have.

In several places, for the instruction of children in reading and writing, public *Schools* are established, in which all the children read aloud, and make a terrible noise. The children are in general educated without chastisement and blows; in their infant years songs are sung to them in praise of their deceased heroes, which tend to encourage them in the practice of virtue and constancy. In youth they are admonished with seriousness, and good examples are held up for their imitation.

Arts and *Manufactures* are carried on in every part of the country, and some of them are brought to such a degree of perfection, as even to surpass those of Europe; whilst some, on the other hand, fall short of European excellence. They work extremely well in *Iron* and *Copper*, and their *Silk* and *Cotton* manufactures equal, and sometimes even excel, the productions of other eastern countries. Their *Lacquering* in wood, especially their ancient workmanship, surpasses every attempt which has been made in this department by other nations. They work likewise with great skill in *Sowas*, which is a mixture of gold and copper, which they understand how to colour blue or black with their toufche, or ink, by a method hitherto unknown to us. They are likewise acquainted with the art of making *Glass*, and can manufacture it for any purpose, both

coloured

coloured and uncoloured. But window-glaſs, which is flat, they could not fabricate formerly. This art they have lately learned from the Europeans, as likewiſe to make watches, which they ſometimes uſe in their houſes. In like manner they underſtand the art of *Glaſs-grinding*, and to form Teleſcopes with it, for which purpoſe they purchaſe mirror-glaſs of the Dutch. In the *working of Steel* they are perfect maſters, of which their incomparable ſwords afford the moſt evident proof. *Paper* is likewiſe manufactured in great abundance in this country, as well for writing and printing, as for tapeſtry, handkerchiefs, clothes, for packing of goods, &c. and is of various ſizes and qualities. They prepare it from the bark of a ſpecies of Mulberry-tree, *Morus papyrifera*. The method is as follows. After the tree has ſhed its leaves in the month of December, they cut off the branches about three feet in length, which they tie up in bundles, and boil in a ley of aſhes, ſtanding inverted in a covered kettle, till ſuch time as the bark is ſo ſhrunk, that half an inch of the woody part is ſeen bare at the ends. They are then taken out and left in the open air to cool, cut up lengthwiſe, and the bark is ſtripped off. Upon this the bark is again ſoaked three or four hours in water, and when it is become ſoft, they ſcrape off the fine black ſkin with a knife. The next thing

thing to be done is, to separate the coarse bark from the fine, which produces the whitest paper. The older the branches are, the coarser is the paper. The bark is now boiled again in fresh ley, and the whole continually stirred with a stick, and fresh water added to it, till the fibres separate. The washing of it, which is a nice and delicate operation, is then performed in a brook, by means of a sieve, by stirring the bark incessantly about till the whole is reduced to the consistence of a fine pap, and, thrown into water, separates in the form of meal. It is then further mixed in a small vessel with a decoction of *Rice* and the *Hibiscus manibot*, and stirred well about, till it has attained a tolerable consistence. After this it is poured into a wider vessel, from whence the sheets are taken and put into proper forms, made of grass-straw, and laid one upon another in heaps, with straw between, that they may be easily lifted up. They are farther covered with a board, and pressed, at first lightly, but afterwards and gradually harder, till the water is separated. When this is done, they lay the sheets upon a board, dry them in the sun, and then gather them into bundles for sale and use. An inferior kind of paper is likewise manufactured from the *Morus Indica*.

The *lackered* wood-work, which is executed in Japan, excels the Chinese, the Siamese, and indeed

indeed that of all other nations in the world. For this purpofe they make choice of the fineſt ſort of firs and cedars, and cover them with the very beſt varniſh, which they prepare from the *Rhus vernix,* a tree that grows in great abundance in many parts of the country. This varniſh, which oozes out of the tree on its being wounded, is procured from ſtems that are three years old, and is received in ſome proper veſſel. When firſt caught, it is of a lightiſh colour and of the conſiſtence of cream; but grows thicker and black on being expoſed to the air. It is of ſo tranſparent a nature, that when it is laid, pure and unmixed, upon boxes and other pieces of furniture, every vein of the wood may be clearly ſeen. For the moſt part a dark ground is ſpread underneath it, which cauſes it to reflect, like a looking-glaſs; and for this purpoſe recourſe is frequently had to the fine ſludge, which is caught in the trough under a grind-ſtone. At other times ground charcoal is uſed, and occaſionally ſome blacker red ſubſtance is mixed with the varniſh, and ſometimes leaf-gold, ground very fine, when it is called *Salplicat.* This lackered work is afterwards for the moſt part embelliſhed with gold and ſilver flowers and figures laid on upon the varniſh, which, however, are liable to wear off in time: ſometimes one has an opportunity of ſeeing theſe figures emboſſed upon the varniſh,

and

and more especially in old work, which is greatly esteemed, and being rare, fetches a high price. This varnish, which hardens to a transparent and difficultly soluble gum, will not endure any blows, but flies and cracks, almost like glass; though it can stand boiling water without receiving any damage. With this they varnish over the posts of their doors and windows, their drawers, chests, boxes, scymitars, fans, tea-cups, and soup-dishes, their portable stools, and most articles of household furniture, which are made of wood.

No Japanese is allowed to leave his native land and visit foreign countries; this being prohibited, under penalty of death. So that the long voyages which the people of this nation formerly undertook in their own vessels to Coræa, China, Java, Formosa, and other places, can be no longer performed, and the art of navigation must of course be upon the decline. This, however, does not prevent them from making short *Voyages* between the rocks, with an inconceivable number of trading vessels, of different sizes, as likewise with fishing-smacks. They seldom venture out far enough at sea to lose sight of land, and always take care to have it in their power to run every evening into some port, or else to come into some other place of safety, in case of sudden storms. Yet they are provided with a compass, which

which is not divided into so many points as those which the Europeans make use of, but their vessels are open at the stern, so that they cannot weather the open sea; and their rudders are large and inconvenient.

The Japanese have little *furniture* in their houses besides their apparatus for the kitchen, and what they use at their meals. Of these, however, as likewise of clothes and other necessaries, one sees such an incredible quantity exposed for sale in the shops of their tradesmen, both in town and country, that one is led to wonder where they can find purchasers, and would be apt to suppose, that they kept magazines here to supply the whole world. Here the native may select, according to his varying taste and fancy, all his clothes ready made, and may be furnished with shoes, umbrellas, lackered ware, porcellain, and a thousand other articles, without having occasion to bespeak any thing before-hand.

THE LAWS AND POLICE.

IF the laws in this country are rigid, the *Police* is equally vigilant, and discipline and good order are as scrupulously observed. The happy consequences of this are extremely visible and important; for hardly any country exhibits fewer instances of vice. And as no respect whatever is paid to persons; and at the same time the laws preserve their pristine and original purity, without any alterations, explanations, and misconstructions, the subjects not only imbibe, as they grow up, an infallible knowledge of what ought, or ought not to be done, but are likewise enlightened by the example and irreproachable conduct of their superiors in age.

Most crimes are punished with *death*, a sentence, which is inflicted with less regard to the magnitude of the crime, than to the audacity of the attempt to transgress the hallowed laws of the empire, and to violate justice, which, together with religion, they consider as the most sacred things in the whole land. *Fines* and pecuniary mulcts and amercements they regard as equally repugnant to justice and reason; as the rich are thereby freed from all punishment; a procedure, which to them appears the height of absurdity. Murder is punished with death; and, if this crime is perpetrated in a town, or in the open street, not only the murderer himself, but sometimes his relations and dependants, and even the neighbours, partake in the punishment, accordingly as they have been more or less accomplices in the crime, or have neglected to prevent its perpetration. To draw one's sword upon any one, is likewise a capital offence. Smuggling of all kinds is punished with death without mercy, and the punishment extends to every individual concerned in the traffic, both buyers and sellers. Every death-warrant must be first signed by the National Council in J'edo, before it is carried into execution; previous to which also the culprit has a fair trial before the proper tribunal, and witnesses are heard. The general mode of punishment is private decapitation with a scymitar, in prison, although crucifixion and other painful modes of death are sometimes practised in public. Those, whose crimes do not merit death, are either sentenced to perpetual imprisonment, or else banished to some distant island, when all their property is confiscated. In the towns it often happens that the inhabitants of a whole street are made to suffer for the mal-practice of a single criminal; the master of a house for the faults of his domestics, and parents for those of their children, in proportion to the share they may have had in the transaction. In Europe, which boasts a purer religion, and a more enlightened philosophy, we very rarely see those punished, who have debauched and seduced others, never see parents and relatives made to suffer for neglecting the education of their children and kindred, at the same time that these heathens

heathens see the justice and propriety of such punishment. The *Prisons* are in this country, it is true, as in most others, gloomy and horrid; the rooms are, however, kept clean and wholesome, and consist of an apartment for the trial by torture, and another for private executions; a kitchen, a dining-room, and a bath.

The *Imposts* in the empire are different in the towns and villages, and in different places. Besides the considerable presents which *Kubo* receives annually from all the feudal Princes, and from the Dutch Company, this temporal Monarch has his revenues from certain towns and districts. The Princes derive their revenues, each from his province, and the towns which the same contains; and their revenues differ in value, according to the situation of the province itself, its opulence, extent, population, and cultivation. Each proprietor of a house is assessed in proportion to the breadth of his house towards the street, besides the presents he makes to the civil officers, and the taxes he pays for the support of the temples and idols. The town of Nagasaki contains ninety streets, and sixty-two temples, or thereabouts, and the produce of its taxes amounts to about three *mangokfs*. The country is rated according to its produce, and this consists, for the most part, in rice. Forests and other little cultivated tracts of land are rated lower.

A Receiver General, or *Voigt*, collects this important impost. Arable land is divided into three classes, according to its different degree of fertility. The man that cultivates a fresh portion of land, holds it free of all taxes after the first two or three years. In order to make an estimate of the value of a piece of ground, which, in spring, frequently lies under water, and at the same time of the lord of the manor's income from it, lands of this description are sometimes measured twice a year, viz. in spring and in harvest-time. The taxes levied upon landed estates are extremely heavy, and frequently amount to more than half, or even two-thirds of the produce. In order to calculate them, they measure off a portion of land, of which they cut down the corn, and thrash it for a specimen, and from thence afterwards calculate what may be the amount of the produce of the whole. The land belongs always to the Crown or to the Prince, and the Farmer holds it in fee no longer than while he cultivates it with proper care and attention.

In every town the most excellent *order* is kept up, for the preservation of the welfare, peace, conveniency, and security of the community. For this purpose four Burgomasters are appointed, of which number one presides every year, who is their prolocutor, speaking in his own name

and

and those of his companions, and is called *Ninban*. Besides these an *Ottona* is appointed for every street, who acts in the capacity of Commissary, and is obliged to give in his report to the Burgomaster concerning every thing that happens: this officer has several of the town-officers under him, to execute his commissions. His duty is to set down the names of all that are born or die in his street, or marry, or travel, or remove thence, or arrive there; he likewise promotes union and concord among the inhabitants, and has the power of casting offenders into prison, and even of putting them in irons. This officer is chosen by the inhabitants of the street, and is paid from the private revenue of the street over which he presides. Lodgers have not the privilege of voting. Lodgings are paid for by the month, the rent being in proportion to the size of the room, which is ascertained by the number of mats upon the floor. Each Ottona has three *Assessors* as his coadjutors, a *Secretary*, who sets down every thing that comes under the cognizance of the office, and a *Cashier*. The *Town-officers* act at the same time in the capacity of spies, who give the Ottona accurate intelligence of every thing that occurs. Each street is, as it were, detached from the rest by gates at each end, which being shut on the approach of any tumult, cut off all communication with the other streets, so that no perturbator of the peace can escape by flight.

Most admirable measures are adopted in the towns for the prevention of *fires*. The Burghers, including both house-keepers and lodgers, keep watch themselves. Two keep watch every night, and their persons are considered so sacred, that it is a capital offence to attack them whilst on duty. Of these, one is constantly with the main guard, and whenever any apprehension is entertained of danger, the watch is doubled. The other goes the rounds, and is, properly speaking, the fire-watch; in which capacity he perambulates the streets, and gives notice of the hour by striking two pieces of wood against each other. Ladders are kept in readiness at the gates, and every other apparatus for extinguishing fire is constantly at hand, and in the best order. In the day-time certain officers are stationed at the churches, who strike the clock with a wooden clapper, in order to shew, what hour of the day it is. Besides this, in every tavern and inn such peace and order are observed, that one seldom sees any instance of frays and drunkenness, irregularities which so greatly and so commonly disgrace the Northern part of the Western World.

That they will be trusty and upright, the Officers of Justice take a very strict *Oath*, on

entering

entering on their office, and this is sometimes repeated every year. Sometimes likewise they are changed, in order that they may not be too long in one place, and in the course of time seduced from the paths of probity. And forasmuch as the punishments in this country are exceedingly severe, and the laws at the same time immutable, it may be affirmed with great truth, that fewer crimes are committed, and fewer punishments inflicted, than in other populous countries, where, notwithstanding the number of punishments yearly inflicted, a multitude of criminals remain concealed, or fall upon some expedient to fly from the spot, or in some other manner escape the punishment they so justly merit. I heard the following extraordinary circumstance mentioned by one of the Interpreters, viz. that there were *laws*, which did not make known the punishment, and that for many crimes the punishment was not universally known. They were of opinion, that a person ought not to be the less on his guard against crimes and transgressions, although the Sovereign did not think proper to determine and make known the species of punishment; and probably they have good reason for thinking thus. However, that no man may plead ignorance of the laws, they are promulgated not only once or twice from the pulpit, according to the custom in the Christian churches,

but likewise in every town and village they are
posted up for public inspection and daily perusal,
in large letters, being placed conspicuous in an
open spot surrounded and guarded with rails.
This place, in the towns, is immediately within
the city gates; in the villages, it occupies the
middle. Directions what ought, or ought not
to be done, are drawn up very concise, without
specifying the punishment annexed to disobedi-
ence, or the addition of any menaces, of which
the governments in some parts of Europe, so renowned for its jurisprudence, have such a plentiful store. One sometimes perceives on the west
side of crosses and posts, that are erected without the towns and villages, the places, where
formerly a greater number of criminals than at
this time present made their exit, and migrated
to another world.

PHYSICIANS

Are of several descriptions. Some profess only
Medicine, and occupy themselves with the cure
of internal disorders. Others practise Surgery; others only burn with Moxa; others perform no other operation than that of puncturing
with

with needles, (the *acu-punctura*,) and others again go about making frictions. Those who perform the latter of these operations, may be heard in the evening patrolling the streets, and making a tender of their services with great noise and vociferation. In a country, where colds are so frequent, this chafing of the body is very beneficial. Those who cure internal disorders, are considered as superior to the rest, from whom they are distinguished by their heads being shaved all over. They never make use of any other than simple remedies, and those generally in the form of decoctions, which are either diuretic or sudorific. Sometimes they make use of powders likewise. Of compound medicines they have no knowledge. A great part of these remedies may be procured, it is true, within the precincts of their own kingdom, but a very considerable quantity is sold to them by the Chinese. Their Physicians sometimes feel the patient's pulse; but they take a long time for examination, sometimes not less than a full quarter of an hour, feeling it first in one arm and then in the other; as though the blood did not flow into both arteries from one and the same source. Their knowledge of Fevers and other internal disorders can be no other than very superficial, and their mode of cure very precarious, as their Physicians have no insight into Anatomy and Physiology,

and

and are very little acquainted with the remedies which they prefcribe. The only perfons among them, who have a little more knowledge of thefe matters, are either the Phyficians of the Court, or the Dutch Interpreters, who have an opportunity of acquiring fome degree of knowledge from the European Phyficians.

Burning with *Moxa* and puncturing with needles are two very effential and cuftomary operations throughout the whole empire, and are performed, in fact, as often as ever Phlebotomy is in Europe. *Moxa* is made ufe of, not only for curing, but likewife for preventing difeafes: no exception is here made either for fex or age; every one makes ufe of it, old and young, children, rich and poor, and even the prifoners themfelves. There are few parts of the body which do not allow of this operation, as for inftance, the finews, (*tendines*) veins, &c. but the fleshy parts, and more efpecially the back, are confidered as the propereft places, which are therefore carefully felected by the operators, and of which they have printed tables. It is of ufe in moft diforders, but efpecially in the Pleurify, Toothach, and it proves of the greateft fervice in Gout and Rheumatifms. *Moxa* is nothing elfe than the woolly part (*tomentum*) of the leaves of Mugwort, (*Artemifia vulgaris*) particularly of the old leaves. It is prepared in the following man-

ner:

ner: the leaves are beaten and rubbed with the hands, till all the green separates from them, and nothing but the woolly part remains. Of this there are two sorts, the coarse and the fine. The fine is considered as the best, and the coarse is commonly used for tinder. When it is to be applied, a little ball is made of it, which is laid upon the appointed place, and then set fire to, when the fire gradually consumes it, and at the same time burns the skin, leaving behind it a scar, which some time after breaks, and a humour distills from it.

Acu-puncture, or puncturing with a needle, is generally performed with a view of curing the cholic, especially that kind which here has the name of *Senki*, and is commonly occasioned by the drinking of Sacki. Thus it has the stomach for its object, over which several small holes, often to the number of nine, are made, under the idea of promoting the discharge of wind; but other fleshy parts of the body likewise may be selected for this operation. The needles used on these occasions are very fine, nearly as fine as the hair of one's head, being made of gold or silver, by persons who have the privilege of making them, and who alone understand how to give them the temper, pliability, and fineness, which it is requisite for them to have. While they are passing through the skin,
they

they are twirled round between the fingers, and the bony parts are carefully avoided.

The *diseases*, to which the Japanese are most liable, and which are peculiar to this country, are the abovementioned Colic, which is here called *Senki*, watery eyes, and indurated glands. The *Senki* Colic, which proceeds from the use of Sacki, or Rice-beer, attacks great numbers of people, and likewise strangers, who reside any length of time in the country. The pain is violent and intolerable, and often leaves swellings behind it, in different parts of the body; and is especially productive of the *Hydrocele*. Red and *watery* eyes are very common among the peasants, and the poorer kind of people in the villages, and originate partly in the smoke of the coals, with which they warm their rooms in winter, and partly from the stench which exhales from their privies. Indurated glands were very common in every part of the country, and frequently, I observed, turned to cancers. They happen particularly in the neck, and increase daily from the size of a pea to that of a man's fist. As the heat in the day-time is frequently very intense, and a sudden gust of wind arising is very apt in those circumstances to stop the pores, and prevent perspiration; it follows of course, that the Rheumatism must be very prevalent among them; in like manner, as for the

same

same reason, during the summer months, *Diarrhæas* and *Dysenteries* attack both the Europeans and Japanese. The same is likewise apt to be the case, when they imprudently eat too much of the fruit, the produce of the country, and more especially of the *Haki-figs*, which are very palatable and in high estimation.

The *Small-pox* and the *Measles* have been long prevalent in this country, and are not more dreaded here than in other places. I did not see a great many people that were much defaced by them: they are unacquainted with Inoculation. The *Hydrocephalus*, or Dropsy in the head, I had an opportunity of seeing in a man thirty-three years old, who came to ask my advice during my journey to the court. He related to me, that he had been attacked with this disorder nineteen months ago, in consequence of having received several blows upon his head from a bamboo cane, in a fray with another man, although the cane was covered with linen. From the crown to the back part of the head a tumor was perceived, about the thickness of a finger, and the bones of the scull were elevated to that degree, that the exterior fontanel was felt soft.

A species of *Miliary Eruption*, termed by the Europeans the *Red Dog*, is very rife here in the hottest summer months, viz. in August and September,

tember, particularly among the Europeans. It continues for several weeks and sometimes for months together. The eruption is elevated above the surface of the skin, rough and of a red colour, without fever. Sometimes it partly disappears, and at other times it becomes visible in greater quantity, especially about noon and evening. The disorder is not always attended with an itching; but whenever this concomitant symptom appears, it is most troublesome in the evening and at night, being attended with great restlessness and want of sleep. Sometimes a very singular kind of itching supervenes, which is chiefly felt when the patient is in motion, when he sets himself down in a chair, or leans with his back against a wall, or is lying in bed, or folds his arms. On these occasions a sensation of pricking is felt in the skin, as if it were pierced with a thousand fine needles; and this sensation ceases immediately, as soon as the limb which was in motion is kept still, even if the same position be preserved. The face is free from this eruption, which diffuses itself over every other part of the body, even to the very extremities of the fingers. A person may be afflicted with this disorder several times, during his residence in India.

The *Venereal* Disease was without doubt imported by the Europeans, who have the superlative

lative merit of having diffused this distemper to many parts of the globe. Venereal complaints are at present very prevalent here, and they are hitherto acquainted with no other mode of alleviating them than the use of decoctions, that purify the blood. The cure by salivation, of which they have indeed heard mention made by the Dutch Surgeons, appears to them very difficult to undertake properly, as well as to undergo. They adopted therefore, both with joy and gratitude, the method, which I had the good fortune to be the first to teach them, viz. of curing this disorder with the *Aqua Mercurialis*. Several of the Interpreters made use of this method as early as the years 1775 and 1776, and performed with it, under my direction, several complete cures, both in and out of the town of Nagasaki. And I please myself with the agreeable hopes, that by means of this easier method, in future many thousand unhappy sufferers will be preserved both from fistulas in the neck, and other dreadful symptoms, attendant on this truly foul disease; which I very frequently had opportunities of seeing, with an equal mixture of grief and horror, during my journey into the country.

AGRICULTURE

Is in the higheſt eſteem with the Japaneſe, inſomuch that (the moſt barren and untractable mountains excepted) one ſees here the ſurface of the earth cultivated all over the country, and moſt of the mountains and hills up to their very tops. Neither rewards nor encouragements are neceſſary in a country, where the tillers of the ground are conſidered as the moſt uſeful claſs of citizens, and where they do not groan under various oppreſſions, which in other countries have hindered, and ever muſt hinder the progreſs of Agriculture. The duties paid by the Farmer of his corn in kind are indeed very heavy, but in other reſpects he cultivates his land with greater freedom, than the Lord of a Manor in Sweden. He is not hindered two days together at a time, in conſequence of furniſhing relays of horſes, by which he perhaps earns a groat, and often returns with the loſs of his horſes: he is not dragged from his field and plough to tranſport a deſerter or a priſoner to the next caſtle: nor are his property and his time waſted in making roads, building bridges, alms-houſes, parſonage-houſes, and magazines. His days are not conſumed in journies after poles and ſtakes in winter, nor with the almoſt endleſs occupation of fencing in

his

his grounds, sunk up to the ancles in mire and clay, in spring. He knows nothing of the impediments and inconveniencies, which attend the maintenance and equipment of horse-and-foot-soldiers. And what contributes still more to his happiness, and leaves sufficient scope for his industry in cultivating his land, is this, that he has only one master, viz. his feudal Lord, without being under the command of a host of masters, as with us. No parcelling out of the land forbids him to improve to the best advantage the portion he possesses, and no right of commonage, belonging to many, prevents each from deriving profit from his share. All are bound to cultivate their land, and if a husbandman cannot annually cultivate a certain portion of his fields, he forfeits them, and another, who can, is at liberty to cultivate them. Thus he is enabled to direct all his thoughts and all his time to the cultivation of his land, an employment, in which he is assisted by his wife and children. Meadows are not to be met with in the whole country; on the contrary, every spot of ground is made use of either for corn-fields, or else for plantations of esculent-rooted vegetables. So that the land is neither wasted upon extensive meadows, for the support of cattle and saddle-horses, nor upon large and unprofitable plantations of tobacco, nor is it fown with feed for any other ftill lefs neceffary purpofe; which is the reafon that the whole country is very thickly inhabited and populous, and can without difficulty give maintenance to all its innumerable inhabitants.

There is no part of the world, where manure is gathered with greater care than it is here, infomuch that nothing that can be converted to this ufe is thrown away or loft. The cattle are fed at home the whole year round, fo that all their excrements are confined to the farm yards, and it is a very common fpectacle to fee old men and children following the horfes that are ufed in travelling, with a fhell (*Haliotis tuberculata*) faftened to the end of a ftick, in order to collect the ordure from off the highways, which is carried home in a bafket. Nay, even urine itfelf, which the Europeans fo feldom turn to the advantage of their fields, is here carefully collected in large earthen pots, which are to be found funk in the earth here and there in different parts, not only in the villages, but even befide the highways. Nor is the Japanefe more fcrupulous and exact in collecting every material fit for manure, than his mode of applying it is different from that of other countries. He does not carry out his manure either in winter or in fummer into his fallow fields, to be dried up there by the fcorching heat of the fun, and to

have

have its nutritive qualities weakened by the evaporation of the volatile salts and of its oily particles; but, on the other hand, gives himself the disgusting trouble of mixing up manure of various sorts, the excrements both of man and beast, with water and urine, together with every kind of refuse from the kitchen, till it becomes a perfect hodge-podge; this he carries in two large pails into his field, and with a ladle pours it upon the plant, which has now attained to the height of about six inches, and receives the whole benefit of it, at the same time that the liquor penetrates immediately to the root. By this mode of manuring, and at the same time by the farmer's indefatigable weeding, the fields are so completely cleared of weeds, that the most sharp-sighted Botanist would be scarcely able to discover a single plant of another species among the corn.

The pains which a farmer takes to cultivate the sides of even the steepest hills, is almost incredible. If the place be even no more than two feet square, he nevertheless raises a wall of stones at the bottom of the declivity, fills the part above this with earth and manure, and sows this little plot of ground with rice or esculent-rooted vegetables. Thousands of these beds adorn most of their mountains, and give them an appearance which excites the greatest astonishment in the breasts of the spectators.

Rice is their principal corn. Buck-wheat, Rye, Barley, and Wheat are very little used. Among their esculent-rooted vegetables Batatas (*Convolvulus edulis*) are the most abundant, and the most palatable. Several sorts of Beans and Peas are planted in abundance, as likewise Alliaceous Plants, Turnips, and Cabbages; from the seeds of which they express an oil for their lamps, and whose yellow flowers give to whole fields together a most beautiful appearance in spring.

In the beginning of April, the farmer begins to dig up the land, which he designs for the *cultivation of Rice*. It lies at this time almost entirely under water, with banks raised round the sides. The furrows are made with a rather crooked hand-bill, about a foot long and a hand broad, fastened to a handle. The Rice-grain is always sown first, in a plot of ground very close, like Cabbage-seed, in beds. Afterwards, when it is grown up to the height of six inches, it is taken up, and planted out in a manner similar to Cabbage-plants, in the Rice-grounds, several plants together in bundles, leaving the space of six inches between each bundle. This is always the women's work, who wade about in water, that is at least six inches deep.

In the month of November it is ripe, and is then mown, and, after being bound up in bundles, carried home. The mere striking of the ears against a barrel, or any other hard body, causes the corn to fall from the stalk, so that in this respect no long and tedious threshing is necessary: but before the husk can be separated from the pure grain, a second threshing, or stamping, is necessary, which is seldom set about before the grain is wanted to be used. Thus it is carried to different places, and sold there entirely unstamped. The stamping of it in small is performed in the following manner. A block of wood is hollowed out, and this cavity is filled with Rice, which they pound with a wooden pestle, till it separates from the husk. In the great, this stamping is performed not only by means of a machine, consisting of a number of pestles, which are set in motion by a water-wheel; but likewise by a similar machine, which a man treads with his foot, and during the stamping, stirs with a stick in the hopper, so that the grain can run down. The Rice in this country is accounted the best in all the East-Indies, and is extremely white, glutinous, and more nutritive than any other.

Buck-wheat, (*Polygonum fagopyrum*) is most commonly used when ground to meal, and made into small cakes, which, after being boiled, and

frequently

frequently at the fame time coloured, are baked, and are fold in the villages and at the baiting-places for a mere trifle, to travellers and their bearers.

Wheat (*Triticum æftivum et hybernum*) is fown in the month of November, and cut down ripe in June. It is ufed in general in the form of fine meal; of this they make fmall cakes, which are eaten in a foft ftate.

Barley (*Hordeum*) is fown at different feafons of the year, fometimes in November, fometimes in December, and at times in the month of October. It is cut down, dried, and threfhed, either towards the latter end of May, or in the beginning of June. The fields in this country often refemble cabbage-gardens with their beds, which are frequently no more than a foot in breadth, and feparated from each other by a deep furrow or trench, which is likewife a foot broad. In thefe narrow beds the corn is fown ftrait acrofs in rows, which leaves a fmall empty fpace in the middle. I have fometimes, however, feen the corn fown lengthways in the beds, in which cafe there were only two rows. I have likewife had an opportunity of obferving, that when the corn has grown to the height of about a foot, that before it has put forth the ear, the farmer has dug up, as it were, thefe fmall trenches, and very carefully put earth about the roots, whence the corn has both received manure and
been

been watered. I was informed, that after a certain stated time the trenches are filled up with earth, and what before constituted the beds, is converted into trenches. In some places likewise the corn was found to be blighted, a calamity, to which, however, the seed is more liable in Europe. As soon as the corn is cut down, they frequently sow another kind of corn or even French-Beans, (*Phaseoli*) between the stubble, either acrofs it or in furrows, so that the land is actually sown twice in the year, although upon different places, without fresh carting or other attendance. They use this corn chiefly for fodder for their horses and other animals. It is likewise at times ground down to fine flour, of which they make small soft cakes.

Cabbage-feed (*Brassica orientalis*) grows wild in great abundance in every province. In the month of April, the fields all over the country appear gilt with the flowers of this plant. They make no use of the root; but the seed, which ripens in May, yields, on being pressed, an oil, which is used every where for lamp-oil. The plant the Japanese call *Na Tanne*, and the oil *Natanne Abra*, or *Natanne no Abra*.

Barley, Wheat, and Cabbage-feed are all of them threshed out at times quite in a plain and artless manner, upon straw mats, in the open air, in the villages, and not unfrequently before the doors of their houses, with flails, which have three swingles. And indeed some only beat the sheaves with the ears of corn against a barrel, vat, or the like, which causes the corn to drop out: this must afterwards be purged from the chaff and other impurities.

Of Beans, Peas, and Lentils, many sorts are cultivated, both the larger (*Phaseoli*) and the smaller (*Dolichos*). Of *Daidsu* Beans (Dolichos *Soja*) the meal is used for dressing victuals, and the expressed juice for making Soy; as likewise the whole Beans for the soup called *Miso*, which is a daily dish with the common people. *Atsuki* Beans likewise (*Phaseolus radiatus*) are ground to meal, of which small cakes are made with sugar. The common Pea (*Pisum Sativum*) and the broad Bean (*Vicia faba*) I saw sown and made use of in some places. In like manner divers sorts of grass are cultivated, for the sake of using their seeds for food both for man and beast, as the *Awa* (*Panicum verticillatum*), *Kibi* (*Holcus sorghum*), or Millet; *Ko Kibi* (*Panicum Corvi*), *Nan ban Kiwi* (*Cynosurus Coracanus*) with several others. Turnips (*Brassica rapa*) are sown in abundance, and are much used for food, as are likewise other esculent-rooted and bulbous plants, such as Skirrets (*Sium sisarum*), Carrots (*Daucus Carota*), which here are of a colour very little inclined to yellow; Radishes (*Rapha-*

nus

nus sativus); Batatas (*Convolvulus edulis*); and, in a trifling quantity, Potatoes (*Solanum tuberosum*). In addition to these, Lettuces (*Lactuca sativa*); Melons (*Cucumis melo*), both with white and red pulp, to serve by way of desert at meals, and to refresh and cool the human body, and quench thirst in summer; Pumpkins (*Cucurbita pepo*), which are used in soups; Cucumbers (*Cucumis sativus*) both to be eaten raw, and for pickling; the Conomon (*Cucumis conomon*), for pickling, and by way of desert, as likewise to excite an appetite; *Fokke Fokkes*, or the fruit of the *Solanum melongena*, to put into soups; Calabasses, or Bottle-gourds (*Cucurbita lagenaria*), are cultivated for flasks and vessels of a similar kind. For seasoning are used, and sometimes cultivated, the *Amonium mioga*, a new species of Ginger; the Pepper shrub (*Fagara piperita*), of which both the leaves and fruit are taken, to give to soups and sauces a strong spicy favour; Cayenne Pepper (*Capsicum*), Bamboo roots, and various sorts of mushrooms (*Agarici*), which with these people are in great request, occur common in the shops, dried for sale, and are besides in almost daily use, both for soups and sauces. The desert at table consists of various well-tasted fruits, which are cultivated in the gardens, such as Lemons, Seville and China oranges; Pears, Peaches, Plumbs, Cherries, Medlars (*Mespilus Japonica*)

Japonica) of a very delicious taſte ; Figs (*Dioſpyros Kaki*), Grapes (*Vitis vinifera*), Pomgranates (*Punica granatum*), Spaniſh Figs, (*Cactus ficus*), Cheſnuts, Walnuts, with a multiplicity of others. Hops (*Humulus*), I ſaw in different parts, growing wild, but not cultivated nor made uſe of.

As every one's land lies open, without being fenced in with hurdles and pales, which are unknown in this country, it is very common to meet with a great number of culinary vegetables and kitchen-garden plants, growing wild in the open fields, and conſequently there are no other gardens, than thoſe which are found near every houſe, are of a very inſignificant ſize, and are chiefly intended for the ſake of ornament. In theſe are to be ſeen both trees, which make a ſplendid figure with their beautiful, large, and frequently double bloſſoms, and other vegetable productions, as well herbs as bulbous plants, adorned with the moſt elegant flowers, ſuch as, for inſtance, the *Azalea Indica, Nandina domeſtica, Prunus ceraſus, Gardenia florida, Aucuba Japonica,* the *Spireæ, Magnoliæ,* the *Tagetes patula, Celoſia criſtata, Hovenia dulcis, Aſter Chinenſis, Pæonia officinalis, Chryſanthemum Indicum, Calendula officinalis, Impatiens balſamina, Mirabilis dichotoma,* and an infinite number of others.

For materials for *Dying*, I ſaw them cultivate the *Polygonum Chinenſe, barbatum* and *aviculare:*

culare: all of these produced a beautiful blue colour, much like that from Indigo. The leaves were first dried, then pounded, and made into small cakes, which were sold in the shops. With these, I was told, they can dye linen, silk, and cotton. When they boil them up for use, they add ashes to them; and the stronger the decoction is made, of so much the darker blue is the colour obtained; and *vice versa*.

The *cultivation of Cotton and Silk*, is an object of the greatest importance in this country, and furnishes the cloathing of many millions. For this purpose they cultivate and plant every year the cotton shrub (*Gossypium herbaceum*), which yields a very fine and white cotton, fit for cloths, wadding, and other uses. The cultivation of Silk depends upon the planting and propagation of the Mulberry-tree, by means of which an incredible number of Silk-worms are bred, and the raw silk is produced, of which are made silken stuffs, thread, wadding, and a great many more articles, both of ornament and use.

The Varnish-tree, (*Rhus vernix*), the Camphor-tree (*Laurus camphora*), the Pine (*Pinus sylvestris*), the Tea-tree (*Thea bohea*), the Cedar (*Cupressus japonica*), and the Bamboo-cane, or Reed (*Arundo bambos*), do not only grow wild in every part of the country, but are likewise cultivated in several places, on account of the

great

great advantages which the inhabitants derive from all thefe articles. The Bamboo-reeds ferve them for water-pipes, for levers, for making bafkets and cabinets, for writing pens, fans, &c. Firs ferve to adorn the courts and places in the vicinity of their houfes, and the wood is ufed for building, as likewife in handicraft trades of every kind, even in the fineft lackered work. Cedars are ufed for naval craft, houfehold furniture, and cabinet work, in the fame manner as fir. The *Varnifh-tree* contains a milky juice, which is the beft of all gums for lackering. The *Camphor-tree* grows wild in great abundance in the neighbourhood of *Satfuma*, and on the *Gotbo* iflands. From this tree is prepared the chief part of the Camphor that is ufed in Europe. The Japanefe fplit the wood and roots into very fine pieces, boil it up with water in an iron pot, covered with a wooden lid, which has a deep concavity on the infide. In this concavity they faften a piece of ftraw or hay, fo that the camphor, when it rifes, may adhere to it. The gum camphor, on being feparated from the ftraw, is in grains, and is packed up in wooden cafks, and fold to the Dutch Company by weight.

As in the whole of this extenfive empire, there is neither any tallow to be found, nor any butter churned, the inhabitants have turned their attention to fupply the place of thefe articles, by ufing

fweet

sweet oils, both for dressing victuals, and for burning in the house. The seed of the *Rhus succedanea* yields, on being pressed, an oil which soon congeals to the consistence of tallow, and from which they prepare candles; but these are by no means so much in use as lamps. So they sometimes likewise manufacture candles from the coagulated oil of the *Laurus camphora*, and *glauca*, of the *Rhus vernix*, and the *Melia azedarach*. For burning in lamps again, to light up their rooms in winter, they make use of several sorts of oil, as for instance, that of the *Dryandra cordata*, &c. but especially and most commonly the *Brassica orientalis*. On the other hand, they use in the kitchen the finer oil of *Sesamum*, for frying fish, and dressing other dishes.

The Sugar-maple does not, to my knowledge, grow in Japan, neither have Sugar-canes been hitherto imported for cultivation; the Japanese Interpreters nevertheless shewed me that they had a juice, from which sugar may be prepared. This, they informed me, was made from the juice of a certain tree, which grows upon the islands that surround Japan. It had a sweet taste, but was of a brownish colour, and a disagreeable aspect. So that if sugar is a necessary commodity for a country, it seems to be the only one, which the Japanese need to receive from the hands of foreigners. That besides, they have, and

and that in the greateſt abundance, every thing elſe which is needful both for food, cloathing, and the conveniences of life, reſults from that which was ſaid above. And whereas in moſt other countries complaints are made more or leſs frequently about bad harveſts and ſevere famine, ſuch complaints are ſeldom heard in the populous empire of Japan, where the inhabitants live frugally, and without prodigality or diſſipation, and where they providently blend in the ſoil with their different ſpecies of corn, a conſiderable number of leguminous and eſculent-rooted vegetables. Notwithſtanding theſe precautions, however, it ſometimes happens, that even here famine is felt.

As the Japaneſe have ſuch a variety of ſpecies of corn, ſuch a plentiful diverſity both of roots and pulſe, beſides the large ſupply of proviſions, which they fetch from the rich ſtore-houſe of the circumambient ſea, they neither need nor have any conſiderable ſtock-farms. They have few Quadrupeds; for which reaſon there is no occaſion to lay out the land in extenſive meadows. The ſmall number of *horſes* to be met with in this country, is chiefly for the uſe of their Princes; ſome are employed as beaſts of burden, and others ſerve travellers to ride on. Indeed I do not ſuppoſe that the ſum total of all their horſes amounts to the number of thoſe made uſe of in one

one single town in Sweden. Here one neither
hears mention made of stately chargers, nor of
mettlesome coach-horses, nor of swift sledge-
trotters, nor of the Masters of the Horse so
famous in Europe. Of *Oxen* and *Cows* they
seem to have a still smaller number; and they
neither make use of their flesh, nor yet of their
milk, nor of the cheese, butter, and tallow prepared from them: the sole use they make of them
is sometimes for drawing carts, and for ploughing
such fields as lie almost constantly under water.
A very few *Swine* are to be seen in the vicinity
of Nagasaki; and this mischievous animal, the
most hostile to agriculture, if not confined, of
any, was probably introduced by the Chinese.
Sheep and *Goats* are not to be found in the whole
country; the latter do much mischief to a cultivated land, and wool may easily be dispensed
with here, where cotton and silk abound. During
my stay at the Dutch Factory, it happened that
some Japanese arrived at the island with several
sheep, of which they had had the custody for
many years, having received them from some
Chief for the Dutch trade, who sailed to Batavia,
and did not return again. *Dogs*, the only idlers
in this country, are kept from superstitious mo-
tives; and *Cats* are in general the favourites of the
ladies. *Hens* and common *Ducks* are also kept
tame in their houses, chiefly, it is to be presumed,

on

on account of the eggs, of which they are very fond, and make ufe of them on various occafions, boiled hard, and chopped into fmall pieces.

THE NATURAL HISTORY OF THE COUNTRY.

WERE we to enter into a minute inveftigation of the fubject in its full extent, it would be too voluminous for the narrow limits of a work, which is intended to form merely the Journal of my Travels. The prefent fketch, therefore, is only defigned to give fome faint idea of the different productions of this country in the three grand departments of Nature. As to the vegetables, I have already amply defcribed them in my *Flora Japonica*, publifhed in the year 1784; and have at the fame time indicated the profit and ufe which the Japanefe in every refpect know to make of the various forts of trees, fhrubs, and herbs, and their different parts. The animals, which are either rare, or altogether unknown to the Naturalifts in Europe, I have in part already arranged and defcribed in various Academical Treatifes and Difputations, frequently with the addition of Plates. I am in hopes, in cafe my

time

time of life, health, and leisure will permit, to communicate in the same manner the residue, which I may still chance to have in my possession, and which have hitherto escaped divers wayward persecutions of fate.

The following is a list of the Mammalia, which have come within the reach of my observation.

Canis *lupus:* the Wolf, called *okame,* in the northern provinces.

Vulpes, the Fox; an animal detested throughout the whole country.

Familiaris, the Dog; both in its domesticated state, and, as I was informed, likewise wild, called *Yamma ing,* which, however, was probably confounded with the Jackall, or some other species.

Felis *catus:* Cats are to be found in every house, very variable in colour.

Mus *rattus:* the rat domesticates here, as in other countries.

Lepus *timidus:* the Hare (the grey sort) was brought not unfrequently to our Factory and to our table.

Bos *taurus:* Buffaloes with a bunch on their backs, I saw in the neighbourhood of Miaco, drawing large carts; but the cows, which the country people sometimes made use of in agriculture, were very small.

Equus *caballus*: the Horse is of a middling size.

Sus *scrofa*: the Hog is of the Chinese sort.

Whales I saw in the market and the shops in Nagasaki, cut in pieces, and sold for food. They are caught upon the coast with harpoons; and, besides their flesh, their bones are made use of, as is likewise the ambergrise which is said to be frequently found in their bowels, and which once even was shewn to me quite fresh and in a soft state.

Many species of the Mammalia were indeed mentioned to me, as being found in the northerly and least inhabited tracts of the island, such as Harts, Bears, Monkeys, and several others; which, however, I had not an opportunity of seeing alive, nor even their skins, when dead.

Of the Bird tribe both the common Cock and Hen and Geese occur tame; but a great number live wild in the water, between the islands, frequently in incredible quantities, secured both from the attacks of those that wantonly fire at them, in order to scare them, and of those that pursue them before the due season. Others too live high up in the country and in the fields; nevertheless I had no opportunity to make any collection of them, as I had not the use of any fire-arms, and could not procure them by any other means. Those that I knew with somewhat greater certainty,

certainty, were only the following: the Cock
(*Phasianus gallus*): the Crow, *Corvus corax*, the
Anas anser, galericulata & querquedula (the common Goose, the Chinese Teal, an. the Garganey),
which were brought to our kitchen; the *Ardea
alba & major* (the white and common Heron),
which followed the ploughman in the field; the
Tetrao coturnix, or Quail; the *Loxia pyrrhula*, or
Bulfinch, and *Oryzivora*; the *Colmmba oenas*, or
common Pigeon. Of the Amphibia, very few
are to be met with in this country; those that I
saw were merely a *Testudo japonica*, and a *Lacerta
japonica*. The Interpreters, indeed, affirmed that
Serpents were to be found here; but I had never
an opportunity of seeing any signs of them.

Fish, notwithstanding the extensive space they
occupy in the depth of the sea, are sought after
with greater diligence by the Japanese than any
other kind of animal. A great number of these
I collected, and having preserved them in spirits
of wine, I sent them to Batavia, Holland, and
my native country. Misfortunes that happened
to them in their way home, have deprived me
of a great many of these rare animals, and some
of them are still undetermined. Those among
them that are at present known are the following:
the *Muræna nebulosa, picta, annulata,* and *fasciata*,
together with the *Ophicthus cinereus*, all very
beautiful and singular species of Eel; the *Gobius
patella;*

patella; Silurus *maculatus, lineatus*; Callionymus *japonicus*; the Sciæna *cataphracta*; Perca *6-lineata*, and *picta*; Salmo *falar*; Clupea *thriza*; Fistularia *tabacaria*; Cyprinus *aureus*; Tetraodon *hispidus*, and *ocellatus*; Ostracion *cornutus*; Syngnathus *hippocampus*; Raja *torpedo*.

Of the Insects, which were more easy to be procured, as well during the journey to court, as on the island of the factory, some were known, others entirely unknown before, viz. the Anobium *ruficolle*, Coccinella *japonica, 4-pustulata*; Chrysomela *æstuans, pallida*; Dermestes *violaceus*; Cicindela *japonica, catena*; the Scarabæus *æruginosus*, called *Fama Musi*: the Hister *unicolor*; Mordella *nasuta, aculeata*; Ptinus *fur*; Meloë *proscarabæus*; Cassida *nobilis, vesicularis*; Silpha *æstiva*; Buprestis *rustica, ignita, vittata, elegans*; Cerambyx *rubus*; Lampyris *japonica, compressa*; Staphylinus *erythropterus, riparius*; Forficula *auricula*; Cimex *grandis, guttigerus, hispidus, clavatus, trigonus, unipunctatus, fullo, sordidus, chinensis, brunneus, anchora, cornutus, niger, andreæ, colon, augur, ocellatus*; Blatta *orientalis, germanica, gigantea*; Mantis *religiosa, maculata, nasuta*; Gryllus *nasutus*; Acheta *gryllotalpa*; Papilio *argiolus, rapæ, Calbum, thrax, hecabe, proteus, ascanius, phlæas, cardui, niphe*; Sphinx *atropos*; Bombyx *lubricipeda*; Noctua *serici, chi, paranympha*; Phalæna *nymphæata, prunata, immutata*.

mutata, amatoria; Pyralis *ocellaris;* Tortrix *viridana;* Hemerobius *perla, grandis;* Agrion *puella, virgo;* Panorp.. *japonica;* Apis *mellifica;* Vespa *parietum;* Musca *carnaria, japonica, albifrons, cæsar, mellina, vibrans, domestica, fimetaria, cynipsea, pluvialis;* Stomoxys *calcitrans;* Tipula *phalænoides, ruficollis, femorata;* Culex *pipiens;* Oniscus *oceanicus, asellus;* Monoculus *polyphemus;* Pulex *irritans;* Pediculus *humanus;* Julus *terrestris;* Lepisma *saccharina;* Cancer *diogenes, astacus* and *dorsipes.*

Shells were collected by the Japanese, especially in the more northerly districts, were laid upon carded cotton, fastened to it with rice-glue, and sold to the Dutch that went on the journey to court. These shell-fish were all very elegant, but the smaller specimens were always selected for this purpose. Those which were used more commonly in the country for food, and were sometimes even brought to our table, were the Ostrea *pleuronectes* and *gigas,* a very long and thick species of Oyster, together with the Venus *chione* and *meretrix,* which were either boiled or stewed. Of Worms, Shells, and Corals, I collected the following: the Sepia *octopodia, sepiola;* Asterias *rubens;* Lepas *mitella, balanoides;* Mya *truncata* (*fossil;*) Solen *vagina, legumen, bullatus, strigilatus;* Tellina *solidula, delicatula, lactea, albida;* Donax *scripta, irus;* Cardium *rusticum;* Venus *virginea,*

virginea, decussata, læta, deflorata, tigerina, rotundata, cancellata, verrucosa, pectinata, exoleta, together with *chione,* which is called *hamagai* and *meretrix,* which bears the name of *Sigakf.* The Mactra *violacea, glabrata, solida, lutaria, stultorum;* Arca *antiquata, undata, pella, barbata, noæ;* Spondylus *gæderopus;* Chama *antiquata, lazarus;* Mytilus *hirundo, barbatus, bilocularis, margaritiferus;* Ostrea *lima, pellucens, plica, maxima, folium, fornicata, pleuronectes,* and *gigas;* Anomia *hysterophorus, terebratula, plicatella, lacunosa, cepa;* Pinna *nobilis;* Argonauta *argo;* Conus *spectrum;* Cypræa *mauritanica, serpentis;* Voluta *mercatoria;* Buccinum *galea, spiratum, nitidulum, lapillus;* Bulla *naucum, amplustre, ampulla, physis, spelta;* Murex *tritonis, aluco, saxatilis, antiquus;* Strombus *lubuanus;* Trochus *conulus, vestiarius, pharaonis;* Turbo *bidens, ungulinus;* Nerita *canrena;* Haliotis *tuberculata;* Patella *ungarica, saccharina, unguis, nubecula, barbara, cærulea;* Serpula *arenaria, triquetra, spirorbis;* Madrepora *porpita* petrefied; Isis *entrocha;* Tubipora *musicalis,* which is called *iwa kik* and *teredo;* Umbilici *veneris* were found cast up on the shore, in like manner as *Belemnites* were found on the mountains.

That the precious metals, *Gold* and *Silver,* are to be found in abundance in the empire of Japan, has

has been well known, both to the Portuguese, who formerly exported whole ship-loads of them, and to the Dutch, in former times. *Gold* is found in several parts; and perhaps Japan may in this respect contest the palm with the richest country in the world: but, in order that this metal may not lose its value by becoming too plentiful, it is prohibited to dig more than a certain stated quantity; not to mention that no metallic mine, of any kind whatever, can be opened and wrought without the Emperor's express permission. When this permission is obtained, two-thirds of the produce are the portion of the Emperor, and the proprietor of the land receives one-third for his expences. Gold is found in small quantities in the sand; but the chief part is extracted from cupreous pyrites, dissolved by brimstone. The finest gold, together with the richest gold-mine, I was told, are found on the largest of the Nipon Islands, near *Sado*. The next in quality to this is that which is found in *Surunga*. Besides these places, it is known for a certainty, that several rich gold-mines are to be found in *Satsuma*, as likewise in *Tsikungo*, and in the island of *Amakusa*. It is used for the Mint, gilding, and embroidery; but is not carried out of the country.

Silver must formerly have been found in much greater plenty than at present, as a large quantity

tity of it was then exported from this country. The Japanese consider it as being much more rare than gold, although the latter metal is dearer. They now likewise received in barter a considerable sum of Dutch Ducatoons, from the Dutch Company. It is said to be found in the province of *Bingo*; and in the more northerly parts towards *Kattami*, as I was informed, very rich silver-mines are to be met with. Independently of these places, the two islands, which are called the Gold and Silver Isles (*Ginsima, Kinsima*) are said to contain a great quantity of both of these precious metals. Silver is used for coining and for plating.

Copper is quite common in every part of the empire, and is richly impregnated with gold, constituting the main source of the wealth of many provinces. It was not only formerly exported in amazing quantities, but still continues to be exported both by the Dutch and Chinese Merchants. The finest and most malleable is dug in *Suruga, Atsingo, Kyno Kuni*. The last sort is esteemed to be the most malleable of any, whilst that from *Suruga* contains the greatest quantity of gold. A great number of copper-mines are to be found in Satsuma and at other places. Of this metal are made small pieces of money for change; it is used likewise for plating, for making utensils of Sowas, for pots, kettles, &c.

Iron

Iron seems to be scarcer than any other metal in this country. It is found, however, in the provinces of *Mimafaka*, *Bitffu*, and *Bifen*. This they are neither fond of importing, nor yet of exporting it for sale. Of it they manufacture scymitars, arms, sciffors, knives, and various other implements, of which they stand in need.

Of *Amber* I had a present made me by my friends: they called it *Nambu*. It was of a dark as well as of a light yellow colour, and likewise streakey. I was told also that it is found in this country.

Brimstone is found in great abundance in Japan, especially upon a certain island, near Satsuma. *Pit-Coal*, I was informed, is likewise to be met with in the northern provinces. *Red Agate*, with white veins, I saw several times made use of for the buttons, &c. of tobacco pouches, and medicine chests, which Agate was most frequently cut in the shape of a butter-fly, or some other animal.

COMMERCE

Is carried on either within the empire itself, between its different towns and harbours, or else with foreigners. Their inland trade is in a very
flourishing

flourishing state, and in every respect free and uncontrouled, being exempted from imposts, and having no want of communication between the various and innumerable places of the empire. The harbours are seen covered with large and small craft, the high roads are crouded with travellers, and wares that are transporting from one place to another, and the shops are every where filled with goods from every part of the empire, especially in the principal trading towns. In these towns, and particularly in Miaco, which is situated in the centre of the empire, are kept likewise several large fairs, to which a vast concourse of people resort from each extremity of the land, to buy and sell. If we except Kubo, the merchant is, it is true, the only one in the whole country, who can become rich, and sometimes accumulate very considerable sums. But, notwithstanding his wealth, he cannot here, as in other countries, either purchase great titles, or raise himself to a higher rank in life; on the contrary, a merchant is always despised, and the public at large entertain the most contemptible opinion of him, inasmuch as they look upon it, that he has amassed his treasures in a dishonourable way, and not without doing an injury to his fellow-citizens. In casting their accounts, they always make use of Decimals. For weighing they use a steelyard, to which they fasten a scale, wherein they place their wares.

Upon

Upon this steelyard is hung, by means of a string, a weight, which can be pushed backwards or forwards to ascertain the weight of the commodity. Such small steelyards the merchants always carry about them, either single or else in a box, together with a computing board. The *Tea Trade* is confined entirely to the inland consumption, the quantity exported amounting to little or nothing. The traffic in *Soy*, on the other hand, is more considerable; and as the tea produced in this country is reckoned inferior to that of China, so the soy is much better than that which is brewed in China. For this reason soy is not only exported to Batavia, in the wooden barrels in which it is made, but is likewise sold from thence to Europe and to every part of the East-Indies. In some places of Japan too the soy is reckoned still better than in others; but, in order to preserve the very best sort, and prevent its undergoing a fermentation, in consequence of the heat of the climate, and thus being totally spoiled, the Dutch at the Factory boil it up in iron kettles, and afterwards draw it off into bottles, which are then well corked and sealed. This mode of treatment renders it stronger and preserves it better, and makes it serviceable for all kinds of sauce. The *Silk trade* is indeed in a very flourishing state in the empire; but their manufactured silk cloths, on account of their

their flightness, cannot be exported and used by the Europeans. The home trade in *Porcellain* is very brisk; but the exports are very few; as the Japanese Porcellain, though very good with respect to the materials, is thick and clumsy, and very seldom well coloured, and in general is far inferior in beauty to the Chinese.

The trade with China has probably been carried on longer than with any other nation; it is likewise the only Indian nation, with which they continue to have any dealings. From the remotest times the Chinese traded in raw silk, which they imported: they first landed at Ofacca, and afterwards at the harbour of Nagasaki, where they still continue to anchor, and have a Factory, together with a Temple, and their own Priests. Till the year 1684, there arrived annually two hundred vessels, each equipped with fifty men: but on its being discovered that the Jesuits, who at that time stood in high favour with the Chinese Emperor, had, through the medium of some merchants, smuggled into Japan several Catholic books, originally printed in China; the Chinese were in consequence of this more restricted than formerly, and their capital in trade, which before was discretional, was fixed at 600,000 thayls, and the number of their ships reduced to seventy, equipped with only thirty men each. At present they are confined to a small island opposite the

town

town of Nagafaki: they fend no Ambaffador to
the Emperor; they have no Purveyor, but barter
their own provifions themfelves at the gate; they
have likewife no Director over their Commerce;
but Interpreters, a Guard, and Supervifors are
appointed to attend them, the fame as the Dutch.
They vend their wares at three different feafons
of the year, viz. Spring, Summer, and Autumn.
They fell here raw Silk, and manufactured filken
Stuffs, Sugar, Turpentine, Myrrh, Agate, Ca-
lumbak, Baros Camphor, Ninfi, Medical Books,
and other articles appertaining to medicine: in
exchange for which they take Copper in bars,
lackered ware, &c. Many, who are fond of
pork, bring with them fwine from China. When
a fhip of theirs has taken in its lading, and fet
fail, it is followed to a confiderable diftance at
fea by a Japanefe veffel, in order to prevent
fmuggling on the coaft.

The Portuguefe, who firft difcovered the
iflands of Japan, were likewife the firft European
nation that carried on any trade in thefe parts.
The profits were in the beginning incredible,
infomuch that annually upwards of 300 tuns of
gold were exported from hence. Afterwards,
when they had rendered themfelves detefted by
their haughty conduct, and their trade in confequence of this had fallen off amazingly, yet ftill
they continued to export Anno 1636, 2350 chefts

of

of silver; or 2,350,000 thayls. Anno 1637, they exported 2,142,365 thayls, and in the year 1638, 1,259,023 thayls. After the Portuguese had been expelled from the land, they, as well as the Spaniards, made several attempts to re-establish their trade; but every attempt not only miscarried, but was attended with the most disagreeable consequences among a people, so inflexible in their resolves as the Japanese. Anno 1640, a ship was sent from Macao, having on board two Ambassadors, with a retinue of seventy-three persons. These were all of them immediately made prisoners in Nagasaki, and their arrival signified to the court; upon which they were all, excepting twelve, who had previously set out on their return, sentenced to be put to death, and were all of them beheaded upon one and the same day, and even in one and the same moment, each by a separate executioner. At the same time the prohibition was renewed for this nation ever to come to Japan; and this prohibition contains the following no less arrogant than strange menace, that should even the King of Portugal himself, or the God of the Christians arrive there, they should undergo the same fate.

A large Spanish three-decker, well-manned, and mounting a considerable number of guns, was audacious enough to anchor in the harbour of Nagasaki, and experienced a still more lamentable

mentable fate; which proves how inflexible the Japanese are in their determinations, how pertinaciously they execute the statutes of their laws and supreme magistrate, and do not even suffer themselves to be deterred by the formidable cannon and artillery of Europe. The ship alluded to came from the Manillies, unloaded their cargo in Nagasaki, and took in a heavy lading of silver and other commodities. Meanwhile intelligence of their arrival had been sent to court, upon which the Prince of Arima received orders to burn the ship, together with its crew and merchandise. Accordingly the Prince attacked the ship, in spite of the most valiant resistance. As soon as he had boarded the ship with his forces, the Spaniards retreated under their uppermost deck. The Prince retired in time to save himself, and the deck was blown up into the air. The Spaniards were attacked with equal bravery a second and after that a third time, till all their decks were blown up, when the ship went to the bottom, and not a single man was saved. Upwards of 3000 of the Japanese perished in this attack, and the contest lasted nearly six hours. More than 300 chests of silver have been since got up at different times.

The Dutch trade has experienced many vicissitudes, and has ever, one time after another, both
been

been diminished, and rendered less profitable. As the Portuguese could not by the influence which they had at first acquired, prevent the Dutch from trading here likewise, the latter established a Factory upon an island near the town of *Firando*, which they were in the sequel compelled to abandon. In the reign of the Emperor IYEYAS, Anno 1601, the Dutch first obtained the Royal permission to carry on a trade in any part of Japan, a trade, which flourished till the year 1619, when they had the imprudence to request the renewal of this charter from the succeeding Emperor FIDETADA. Since this period their profits were greatly reduced, and their privileges in many respects retrenched. Anno 1638, they received orders to demolish their warehouse at *Firando*, which was built of stone, with great strength as well as magnificence, and had the letters A : o C. inscribed over the door; a circumstance, which could not fail of alarming a people so extremely mistrustful, and so ill-treated by the Portuguese. Shortly after this transaction, they received orders to abandon *Firando* entirely, and to remove to Nagasaki, and in future to cast anchor only in this harbour, which is situated at the very extremity of the empire. Here they were subjected to the strictest inspection; the rudders being at first taken off from the ships, the powder, balls, cannon, and arms carried into the country, and the

the ship unladen by the Japanese themselves; but some of these precautions have been since gradually omitted.

At first the Dutch imported raw Silk, manufactured Silk-stuffs, and Half-silks, Chintzes, Cottons, Clothes, Sappan-wood, Brazil-wood, Buffaloes-hides, Wax, Buffaloes-horns, Ivory, Shagreen, Spanish Leather, Pepper, Sugar, Cloves, Nutmegs, Baros Camphor, Quickfilver, Saffron, Lead, Saltpetre, Borax, Alum, Musk, Gum Lac, Benzoe, Storax, Catechu, Ambergris, Costus Arabicus, Coral, Antimony, Looking-glasses, Lignum Colubrinum, Files, Needles, Glass, Spectacles, Birds, and other curiosities. The profits of this trade were very considerable at Firando; when, on the lowest calculation, six millions of gilders were exported, and in silver alone upwards of four millions. At the request of the Dutch themselves, the silver trade was afterwards exchanged for that of copper, the profits upon the latter being at that time the most considerable: but from that period likewise the exportation of silver has been strictly forbidden. The worst blow perhaps, which the Dutch trade has received, was in the year 1672, in consequence of the enmity, which the Privy-Counsellor INABA MINO, a favourite of the pious Emperor DAIJOJIN, had conceived against the Dutch. This hatred he gratified by means of one of his relations, who was appointed Governor in Nagafaki. This man ordered famples to be fent him of every kind of wares, which were that year brought in the Company's fhips to Nagafaki. Thefe famples he fhewed to the merchants, and informed himfelf of the price fet upon them, as well as of the quantity, which they wifhed to have. Upon this he proffered the Dutch much lefs for thefe commodities, and left it at their option, to export them in cafe they did not find it anfwer to them. According to this valuation, the price of commodities was reduced every year, and the kobangs, or Japanefe currency rofe in value. This conduct, it is true, gave birth to complaints, and the Dutch trade was fo far free and uncontrolled, that their wares were permitted to be fold by public auction; but the whole amount of their fale was limited in the year 1685, to 300,000 thayls. At prefent the company employs only two fhips, and its profits are very inconfiderable. The commodities, which are now in general imported and exported by it, have been already fpecified by me in the Third Volume of this work.

The Coins current in this country, I have likewife already defcribed in part in the Third Volume; as for inftance, new *Kobangs, Itjibs, Nandiogin, Itaganne* and *Kodama, Seni*, old *Kobangs,* old *Itjibs, Kosju Kin,* and *Gomome Gin.*

The

The Japanese coins in general are very simple, struck plain and unadorned, and the greater part of them without any rim round the margin, and without that decoration which the Swedish coins possess, and most of them without any determined value. For this reason they are almost always weighed by the Merchants, who, at the same time, likewise set a mark upon them, to signify that the coin is standard weight and unadulterated. The *Obang* is the largest gold coin that is to be found in the whole country, and ought rather to be considered as a medal, than as a piece of money. It is not current in trade, and is seldom to be met with among merchants or persons in private life. It is a flat, roundish, oblong plate of gold, nearly of the thickness of a farthing, and is stampt on one side with fine lines, going transversely across the die, but broken off, and four impressions within the margins of the four sides, each impression exhibiting Dairi's arms. On the other side, which is plain and smooth, are inscribed, in the name of the Prince who issues the coin, several large black letters, reaching from somewhat above the middle down to the lower margin. This inscription assures the proprietor of the genuineness of the coin, and therefore, as soon as it is worn off, the same Prince's secretary is bound to renew it, for which an Itjib must at that time be paid. Such a gold coin

coin is of the value of ten old Kobangs. So that the *Obang* is chiefly in the poffeffion of, and iffued out by the Princes of the country and the Privy Counfellors, who prefent one of thefe pieces to thofe who are in their good graces, when they have no other fit prefent at hand. It is then given by way of doing honour to the perfon to whom it is prefented, fince they confider it lefs honourable to beftow in a prefent, though to the fame amount, the common kind of Kobangs.

Among their Silver coins the *Kodama* is the moft variable, as well with refpect to its fhape and fize, as to the impreffion which is ftamped upon it. Of this coin there are fome that are oblong, while others are circular, or fpherical, or convex, or flat. Sometimes they are ftamped with more and fometimes fewer letters, and at other times with the image of Daikokf. By *Daikokf* is meant the God of Riches, or the Merchant's God, in this country. He is reprefented fitting upon two barrels of rice, with a hammer in his right hand, and a fack at his left. The Japanefe believe him to be invefted with the power of producing, on any fpot which he ftrikes with his hammer, whatever he pleafes; as for inftance, rice, food, clothes, money, &c.

Seni, of copper or iron, are ftrung, a hundred at a time, or, as is moft commonly the cafe, ninety-

ninety-six, upon a rush. The former are then called *Metaſtjakf*, and the latter *Kwurok-kuſjakf*. A string of the latter constitutes the value of one *Maas*, five *Konderins*. The coins in one of these parcels are seldom all of one sort; but generally consist of two, three, or more different kinds. In this case the larger *Seni* are strung on first at one end of the rush, and then follow the smaller; the number of *Seni* diminishing in proportion to the number of large pieces in the parcel, which are of greater value than the small ones. Such parcels of *Seni* often lie ready strung in their shops, both in town and country, for the accommodation of travellers, who are thus enabled to exchange their small coin expeditiously, without having occasion to lose any time in reckoning it up. In the town of Nagasaki, Chinese farthings are likewise current in trade: these are distinguished by their yellow colour. They resemble the Japanese *Seni* in every respect, except in the colour of the metal, and the inscription.

RESIDENCE AT DEZIMA, PREVIOUS TO MY
RETURN HOME.

AFTER my arrival at the Factory, from the Court, I spent a very hot summer, and was very busily employed in reviewing and arranging the different collections which I had made in the course of my journey, as well of dried and preserved, as of curious live trees and shrubs, which I intended to send to Amsterdam, by the homeward-bound ships from Batavia. These were in particular several very beautiful species of the Maple genus (*Aceres*), besides others appertaining to those of *Lycium*, *Celastrus*, *Viburnum*, *Prunus*, *Cycas*, *Cypressus*, *Citrus*, &c.

I made likewise at this time several excursions in the vicinity of Nagasaki, and as this was the season of the year most productive of flowers, I had the pleasure to see my heavy expences, in this respect, somewhat better repaid, than in the preceding autumn and winter.

Instead of hemp, I saw white nettles (*Urtica nivea*, which likewise grew very commonly wild), cultivated in some places for the manufacturing of ropes and cloths.

The *Ricinus* I found planted in several places, the seeds of which being pounded with Moxa and

and Touche together, are put into a box, over which a piece of silk is stretched, which is besmeared with oil, in order that the powder contained underneath may be moistened by it. Whenever a Japanese has occasion to put his seal to any thing, which is often very curiously wrought in horn, he first dips the seal into this box, and then impresses it upon the writing that is to be designated by it. Thus this powder supplies the place of Printer's Ink, and it is therefore necessary, that the silk which covers the box, should always be moistened afresh with oil, as fast as it dries.

The mats, with which the floors in general throughout the whole empire are covered, are mostly plaited in the country, and are of different quality in different provinces. The better sort is manufactured from the *Juncus effusus*, which is plaited very close and neatly together, and the interstices are afterwards filled up with ricestraw to the thickness of two or three fingers. In order therefore that this species of grass may grow to a greater height and be more serviceable, it is cultivated in some places which lie low; and for the purpose of giving the mats a whitish, rather than a yellow colour, it is very common to lay the rushes out to bleach.

The *Lilium superbum*, which is one of the most beautiful flowers in the world, I frequently saw hung up in their small vessels in the harbours, as an offering to their Sea God.

The *Uvaria Japonica* is a small shrub, which creeps along the ground, and grows very plentifully in several places round the harbour of Nagasaki. It is remarkable on account of the great quantity of clear mucus which it contains. When the twigs are deprived of their outside bark, and placed in a glass of water, the mucus exsuding, expands itself round them for about the thickness of a line and upwards, and appears as clear as chrystal. This mucus is sometimes used for the manufacturing of paper, instead of that which they extract from the *Hibiscus manibat*, and the ladies likewise use it to render their hair smooth and glossy.

The *Camellia sasanqua* grows very plentifully near Nagasaki. It is a little shrub, so exactly resembling the Tea-tree, both in its leaves and flowers, that it is difficult to distinguish them from each other, except by their size. The leaves have rather a pleasing scent, and are therefore used by the fair sex, after being boiled, to wash their hair. They are likewise sometimes mixed with Tea-leaves, to render the scent of these still more agreeable.

A very small species of China Orange (*Citrus Japonica*), is frequently cultivated in the houses in pots. This shrub hardly exceeds six inches in height,

height, and its fruit, which is sweet and palateable, like China Oranges, is not larger than an ordinary Cherry.

Truffles (*Lycoperdon tuber*), are dug out of the ground in many places, of the size of a plumb: when fresh dug, they are soft and rather of a brown colour: but when salted they turn black. I frequently saw the Japanese eat them, after they had been salted, in soups, in the same manner as Morils.

Soy-sauce, which is every where and every day used throughout the whole empire, I might almost say in every dish, and which begins even to be made use of in Europe, is prepared from Soy Beans (*Dolichos Soja*) and salt, mixed with barley or wheat. For this purpose they cultivate this species of bean in several places, although it grows in great plenty wild. Scarcely any kind of legumen is more copiously used than this. The seeds are served up in soups, once or twice a day all the year round, to people of distinction or otherwise, to the poor and to the rich. *Soy* is prepared in the following manner: the beans are boiled till they become rather soft; afterwards an equal quantity of pounded barley or wheat is added. These ingredients being mixed together, are set in a warm place, and covered up for four and twenty hours, that they may ferment. An equal quantity of salt is then added to the mixture,

ture, and twice and a half as much water is poured upon it. After it has been mixed in this manner in an earthen veſſel, it muſt ſtand well covered two or three whole months together, during which period it is neceſſary however at firſt for it to be ſtirred about ſeveral times in the day for ſeveral days together. The liquor is then preſſed and ſtrained off, and kept in wooden veſſels. Some provinces furniſh better ſoy than others; but excluſively of this, it grows better and clearer through age. Its colour is invariably brown, and its chief excellence conſiſts in the agreeable ſalt taſte which it poſſeſſes.

Myrica nagi is but rarely found at Nagaſaki; the wood is quite white, and is uſed for making combs for the ladies to wear in their hair.

The Fir-tree (*Pinus ſylveſtris*), is that of which the wood is moſt commonly uſed by the cabinet-makers in their work-ſhops: but the wood of the Japaneſe Cypreſs (*Cypreſſus japonica*), which is both ſoft and beautiful, is likewiſe very much uſed, as is alſo that of the *Taxus Macrophylla*, and ſeveral other ſorts.

The *Arum eſculentum* is cultivated in ſmall beds in the fields, not only on account of its eſculent roots, though theſe, unleſs prepared, are very acrid, but alſo on account of its ſtalks, which they cut in pieces and put into their ſoups. In like manner they uſe for food the roots of the

following

following plants, which grow wild, viz. the *Sagittaria sagittata*, *Polygonum multiflorum*, and *Dioscorea Japonica*, the two latter of which serve as fodder for the cattle, and were very frequently brought, together with other grass, to the cattle at the Dutch Factory.

One of the Interpreters, a friend of mine, of the name of KOSAK, often did me the favour to collect for me several different kinds of coin, which were said to be very ancient, and to have been formerly current in the land. These were presented to me as great curiosities. They were all of them *Seni* of red copper, and resembled the others in size, thickness, and the square hole in the middle; but they were marked with different letters.

One of them was reputed to be 1135 years old, and to have furnished the standard for the measure of the country; as the diameter of this coin was required to be just one Japanese inch. It had no letters on the other side.

Another was reported to be 758 years old, without any characters upon the other side.

The third, 748 years old, was likewise without any characters on one side.

The fourth, 718 years old, without any letters on one side, like the foregoing.

The fifth, 651 years old, without any letters on the other side.

The

The sixth, 596 years old, without any inscription on one side.

The seventh, I was informed, was 566 years old; it had two letters on the under side. The ages of all these coins are reckoned only down to the year 1776, when I received them, each with its age set down separate, and folded up in paper. All these, together with the Japanese coins above described, are to be found in his Swedish Majesty's very valuable Collection of Coins, at Drotningholm.

A blackish coloured *Cicada* was called *Semi* by the Japanese, and a *Bombylius* with a white tail, had the name of *Abu*.

July 31, 1776, the *Zeeduyn*, a ship belonging to the Dutch Company, arrived from Batavia; and on the 2d of *August* following, the Admiral's ship *Stavenisse*, having on board M. DUURKOOP, who was to reside here this year in quality of Chief of the Factory.

August 26th, in the evening, the Japanese began to celebrate in Nagasaki and throughout the whole empire, the Feast of Lamps, or Lanthorn-festival, which is kept with great solemnity in Nagasaki.

September 13th, towards evening, intelligence was brought, that the Prince of *Owari*, Cousin-german to KUBO, had died five days before. On account of this event, orders were now given out,

out, that no person whatever should play upon any kind of instrument for the space of five days, which in this country is the ordinary time of the deepest mourning. This Prince was about forty years of age, or rather more. For some time previous to this, he had been made choice of for the Emperor's son-in-law; but his ill stars had decreed, that the day before his arrival in Jedo, his intended bride had paid the last debt of nature.

When Copper is weighed for exportation, it is always done with a large Dutch weighing-machine. In each chest a pickel is put, and on each pickel the additional weight of a catje is allowed, of which the Administrators at Onrust, in Batavia, to whom the copper is consigned, receive a fifth part. Of the remaining four-fifths, the ship's Captain receives two-thirds, and the first Mate one-third, in order that those who are responsible for the weight, may not be losers. However, notwithstanding this precaution, it happens every year, that in carrying the chests of copper to the bridge, the Japanese contrive to steal some of it, so that those who are concerned in them, always lose something. They do not regard it as a crime to rob the Dutch Merchants in this manner; and the stolen copper is afterwards sold to the Chinese, who pay a greater price for it than the
Dutch

Dutch would. The preceding year the Captain was fifty-two pickels too ſhort.

Several of the crew in the Dutch ſhips, who had been attacked very feverely with the fever in Batavia, fpeedily recovered their health here; and others, who had large indurated tumors in different parts of their bodies, and a fwelled abdomen, which is a very common confequence of the malignant Batavian fevers, were here perfectly freed from them.

Unicorns teeth (*unicornu*) were fold this year at a much lower price than the preceding. A maas of it fetched this year only four maas, eight konderyns, and five kaſjes, which amounts to about feventy-eight thayls for each catje.

October 10th, the newly-arrived Governor reviewed firſt of all the Imperial guard in the harbour, after which he paid a viſit to the Dutch Admiral-ſhip, and laſtly proceeded to the iſland of Dezima, accompanied by the Governor, who was now going out of office.

The following Gentlemen were Governors in Nagaſaki during my abode there. Anno 1775, Noto *no Kami* went out of office, and was fucceeded by Nagato *no Kami*: who in his turn reſigned the reins of government in the year 1776 to his fucceſſor Tango *no Kami*.

Of the Fiſhermen who, from the harbour of Nagaſaki alone, go forth to feek their livelihood upon the deep, and who may be seen by their lighted torches, at the distance of four miles or more from the town, the number is almost incredible. The multiplicity of fires which were now seen at this distance, presented to the spectator, in the dark autumnal evenings, the most glorious sight imaginable.

Among other commodities, which private persons exported on their own account, there was likewise this year a parcel of iron carried out by one of the Captains, probably with a view of selling it to some profit to the Chinese in Batavia.

As I foresaw, that were I to prolong my stay in this country to another year, I should still be able to contribute little or nothing more to the advancement of the sciences than I had already done this year, I formed a firm resolution to return to Batavia. On the other hand, our new Chief endeavoured at first to persuade, and at last to compel me, to continue here another year, with a view to his own advantage, as he placed greater confidence in my medical talents, than he expected he should have reason to do in those of my successor. I was, however, fortunate enough to escape from him, and to revisit those places, where I could have greater liberty and a wider extent of country, to collect and examine without control the wonderous treasures of nature.

November

November 23d, I bade farewell to the ifland of Dezima, and failed to the Admiral's fhip Staveniffe, which rode at anchor off Papenberg.

On the 29th following, Commiffaries from the Factory came on board, to deliver letters and other documents to the Government in Batavia.

On the 30th in the morning we weighed our firft anchor, although we ftill ftaid there a couple of days.

December the 3d, about ten o'clock, we weighed our other anchor and got under fail. The *Zeeduyn* failed a-head of us, and fired her guns, as we did ours, at eleven o'clock, directly before Papenberg, and again at twelve, at the laft ridge of mountains called *Cavallos*, at the fame time reciprocally wifhing each other a profperous voyage.

The lading in each fhip confifted now chiefly of 6750 pickels of bar-copper, and 364 barrels of camphor, each barrel containing from 120 to 130 pounds weight.

ARRIVAL IN BATAVIA.

1777. *January* 4th, I landed, after a prosperous voyage, in Batavia, and waited again upon my respectable friend Dr. HOFFMAN, who now likewise made me an offer of his house and table during my stay at this place.

At the mouth of the great river, which flows through Batavia, a considerable way down into the harbour, the current was at this season of the year so violent, that it required no little caution, and was at the same time attended with some degree of danger, to work one's way up to the town in sloops and other vessels.

Among other kind friends, whom I now missed on the island, was Dr. HOFFMAN's lady, who had departed from this world during my absence. This recalled to my remembrance, how I had, shortly before my departure to Japan, sat down to dinner in this very house with thirteen persons; eleven of whom, my friend now informed me, had been carried off by the fevers which usually prevail here, in the space of three weeks, insomuch, that of the whole thirteen, he and myself were at this time the sole survivors. This furnishes an irrefragable proof of the mortality and unhealthy climate of this spot, where a great number of humid vapours fill the heated atmosphere.

mofphere, render the body fluggifh, and apt readily to receive the feeds of putrefaction.

The Governor General, *van der* PARRA, had likewife left this fublunary fphere in the courfe of the preceding year; in whom I loft a real patron. He was incontrovertibly a man of good fenfe, and had rendered effential fervices to the Dutch Company, although he had not neglected, during the great length of time that he continued in office, to confult his own interefts. To his fon, who was his fole heir, he had bequeathed upwards of four millions of guilders. The fupreme authority in all the Eaft-Indies now devolved into the hands of *van* RIEMSDYK, an old and fuperannuated man, who, if we except an unwearied attention to his own intereft, did not feem ever to have been poffeffed of any remarkable qualities. The firft time, after my landing, that I waited upon his Excellency, which is the ufual title of this Chief Magiftrate, I was immediately confulted with refpect to his Lady's illnefs, which confifted in a cancer in one of her breafts, and was beyond all hope incurable.

After I had farther paid my court to my benefactor, M. RADERMACHER, a gentleman, to whom the Sciences at large are greatly indebted, and the active friend of the whole human race, I made it my firft care to infpect the various things,

things, which I had left in charge with my hoſt in a large cheſt, and in a very capacious warehouſe. But how great was my confuſion and ſurprize, when on opening the cheſt I diſcovered, that notwithſtanding it had been placed upon bottles, and in this manner raiſed above the ground, the major part of the Herbs, that I had formerly collected in Java, together with a great number of the books that I had left behind me, were, almoſt to a third of the height of the cheſt from the bottom, entirely rotten and mouldered away with the damp air, which had been pent up in it.

At this ſeaſon of the year it ſtill rained violently, commonly every day, particularly in the morning and evening, beſides flitting ſhowers. The ſky was for the moſt part overcaſt, and the air thick and damp, inſomuch that it was impoſſible for me to dry any of the herbs I had collected, as every thing mouldered away and rotted in rooms that were cloſe ſhut. The rainy months are reckoned from December to March, during which time the air here is cool, and fewer diſorders prevail, and this ſeaſon is what they generally call their winter. After this follows the warmer ſeaſon, when the heat is ſcorching and intolerable, and the ſky clear, with a continual ſucceſſion of dry weather.

The New Year of the Chinese now commenced with the first New Moon in February, and was celebrated by them with great solemnity.

M. RADERMACHER, the State-Counsellor, from whom I experienced extraordinary friendship and protection, insisted on my being his guest once or twice a week at least, and giving him an account of what I had collected and discovered, as well in Japan, as in the vicinity of Batavia; the environs of which, even during the most sultry heat of the afternoon, when others were enjoying a comfortable afternoon's nap, I every day visited and explored. On one of these occasions a circumstance happened, which greatly astonished both him and myself. It chanced that one day M. FEITH, who was lately the Chief at the Dutch Factory at Japan, and whom I had accompanied the foregoing year to the Imperial Court, was questioned by M. RADERMACHER concerning the reigning Emperor in Japan, and whether he was acquainted with his Imperial Majesty's name. This question he was then obliged to answer in the negative, although he had lived at least fourteen years in that country, during which period he had four times had an audience of the Emperor, in the character of ambassador. The following day, when I had the honour to dine at this same Counsellor's house, he imagined that he could

propose

propose a question to me, which I should be at a loss to answer; though he had hitherto seldom found me non-plussed. I was accordingly interrogated with respect to the name and age of the present Emperor of Japan. And as I on this occasion was not only able to answer to these questions, but likewise informed them, that I had procured authentic intelligence concerning the names of the Ecclesiastical Emperor, the Hereditary Prince, and of the Emperors both Spiritual and Temporal, who had died in the course of the present century, both the Counsellor himself and the whole company were greatly amazed, that I should have been able to penetrate into a secret, which was esteemed inscrutable, and which an ambassador in the space of many years had not been able to discover. This list of the Japanese Emperors, which I left with M. RADERMACHER, was since introduced into the Transactions which a Literary Society in Batavia published some years afterwards. The confidence and friendship, which both the Interpreters and Physicians in Japan had conceived for me, were highly instrumental in procuring me the information which I received, in what relates to the Political History of Japan.

KÆMPFER has given in his History a copious list both of the Ecclesiastical and Temporal Emperors in Japan, who had succeeded each other till the year of his departure from that country. The continuation of this lift to the prefent period was a principal object of my wifhes, however difficult the attainment of it was with any tolerable degree of certainty. During my abode in the Metropolis, Jedo, however, I was fortunate enough to procure, by means of the Principal Interpreter, and the Imperial Phyfician, the above-mentioned Catalogue both of the Ecclefiaftical and Temporal Emperors, and the name of the prefent Emperor. And with thefe my Japanefe friends I have in the fequel, for many years after my return to my native country, maintained a very inftructive correfpondence; and I have even afterwards had a moft defirable opportunity, with the kind affiftance of my honoured patron Profeffor BURMANN, of Amfterdam, to recommend and promote one of my friends and beloved pupils, Dr. STUTZER, to India and the remote ifland of Japan.

Although the climate is extremely unhealthy, efpecially in the town, the Europeans, with very little exception, lead here a very irregular life. At dinner they inflame their blood with ale and wine, and after dinner, with fmoking tobacco, drinking ale and wine. At half paft two in the afternoon they go to bed, and take their reft till five o'clock. The evening is fpent in company,

pany, and with ale, wine, cards, and that altogether indispensable article of life, the tobacco-pipe. At half past nine in the evening, they again sit down to table to eat, at the same time that they drink profusely of ale and wine. After supper is finished, recourse is again had to the delicious pipe, which had only been laid aside during the repast, and which is now a second time lighted up, to burn till eleven o'clock, its fires being all the while mitigated with continual libations of ale and wine, till rendered giddy with heat and these liquors, and at the same time half drunk with the smoke of tobacco, weary and drowsy, they at length retire to bed, to enjoy a restless sleep and comfortless repose.

After I had collected in the vicinity of Batavia whatever at this season of the year was to be found there, of the various productions of nature, I wished to inspect the interior of this incomparable island. For this purpose I went on board the *Vreedelust*, and sailed in this vessel along the northern coast of Java to Samarang.

VOYAGE TO SAMARANG.

WE sailed from the road near the town on the 23d of *March*, and on the 31st day following passed by *Cheribon*, one of the principal Factories, where the East-India Company keeps a Governor, whose yearly income was estimated at 70,000 rix-dollars.

The mountain, near the town of Cheribon, has several times been in a state of conflagration. Two years ago a commotion took place, and the ashes, which in consequence of this it vomited up, destroyed several thousand plantations of coffee in the neighbourhood.

April 2d, we sailed by Mount *Tagal*, which is frequently seen burning at the top. At this time we saw only a smoke issuing from the summit about the thickness of a man's body.

In the course of this voyage, which lasted long enough, on account of the shiftings of the wind, that now took place, I several times saw serpents of different kinds come from the land, and swim upon the water; one of these was above two feet long, and sprang to a considerable height out of the water. When the wind shifts, one is frequently becalmed, and the heat is very troublesome. It was also now the season of the year when the westerly winds began to
ceafe,

ceaſe, and the eaſterly trade winds were expected to ſet in again. On this occaſion our Captain informed me, that he, as well as ſeveral other experienced ſeamen, thought they had obſerved with certainty, that the eaſterly winds ſet in later, and that the trade-winds were in general much weaker, ever ſince the dreadful earthquake which deſtroyed Liſbon, and which was felt ſo univerſally all over the globe.

Notwithſtanding that the iſland of Java produces ſugar-canes in abundance, and ſugar of courſe is not extremely dear, we were in our preſent voyage furniſhed with a very wretched commodity indeed, and put off with coarſe brown ſugar inſtead of white. When I, in behalf of the ſick, remonſtrated with the Captain on the ſubject, his reply was, that it was not unuſual for the ſhips to be ſupplied with brown and coarſe ſugar, inſtead of the white powder-ſugar which the Government allowed; and that the difference between the prices of theſe two ſorts went into a common purſe, for the benefit of the Superintendants of the warehouſes, where they were packed up.

April 9th, I landed at *Samarang*, a middle-ſized handſome, and well fortified town, and at the ſame time the principal eſtabliſhment for the whole coaſt of Java, on which all the other

Factories,

Factories, Cheribon excepted, are dependant. It was conquered by the Dutch in 1708.

Immediately upon my arrival, I took up my refidence with the worthy Phyfician of the Hofpital, a man, who had had great experience in Surgery and the practice of Phyfic, and who fhewed me much friendfhip and kindnefs. But I had hardly landed, before I was taken ill, and was obliged to take to my bed, attacked with a tertian ague, an illnefs which I had brought upon myfelf, when on board, by leaving the window of my cabin open at night, whilft I lay afleep, in confequence of which the perfpirable matter was checked and repelled by the coolnefs of the night-air. Although the fever was very violent, I was fortunate enough to get rid of it, by taking the *Extract of Bark*, after I had previoufly purged myfelf, and fuftained feveral febrile paroxyfms. Meanwhile the fhip profecuted its voyage to *Juana*, a Factory a little farther on upon the coaft, in order to take in there its lading of timber and lumber.

Samarang is fituated upon a large river, at no great diftance from the fea-fhore. It is garrifoned with about 150 foldiers, though the Factory was faid, in fact, to have 1000 men belonging to it. The yearly income of the Governor was fuppofed to amount to 80, nay, 100,000 rix-dollars; for which reafon, this lucrative poft was generally

given

given to the relatives or favourites of the Governor-General, who were however seldom allowed to continue in this office above three years, when they were for the most part promoted to the rank of Counsellors of State, and were obliged to leave their place to another.

I had scarcely recovered from my fever, which, however, was not very slight, when I undertook, with the Governor's permission, and in company with Dr. BOENNEKEN, Physician to the Hospital, a journey, above 180 miles into the country, quite up to the mountains. The Governor, on this occasion, did me the favour to furnish me with his passport, directed to all the Commandants at the Company's fortified posts, and requested me to direct my attention likewise in this expedition to all such plants, as either already had been employed as remedies, or else might serve in the stead of these, for the use and behoof of the Hospitals. For this purpose, he likewise commanded Dr. BOENNEKEN to accompany me, in order that he might acquire a perfect knowledge of them.

April 23d, we set out on horseback to one of the Company's posts, called *Unarang*, in which place a Serjeant is maintained with about twenty privates.

On the 24th, we prosecuted our journey to *Salatiga*, where there is another fortification, with
a Com-

a Commandant in it, who is an Enfign, and has fomewhat above twenty men under him.

On the 26th, we rode on to *Kopping*, a Javanefe village, fituated high up on a mountain. The climate is both cold and healthy of this place, which is not the lefs fertile on that account. Among other remarkable circumftances, which I noticed in my journey, was the following, that the Indian Fig-tree (*Ficus Indica*), which grows to a confiderable height in the forefts, hangs its boughs down fo low, that they touch the ground, and taking root there, fhoot forth new fcyons, which in procefs of time become large trees. In this manner a fingle Fig-tree forms with its boughs that have taken root, a great number of apartments or chambers, as it were, and fpreads to a confiderable diftance.

Kamadu is the name given to a kind of leaves, which fting like ftinging nettles, but much more violently, and even to fuch a degree, as to caufe an inflammation in the fkin. On every vein they have fharp-pointed prickles, which are tranfparent, and contain a fluid that caufes this irritation. The kind which it is found to be a fpecies of the nettle before unknown, to which I at this time gave the name of *Urtica ftimulans*. Any one that, unacquainted with its properties, fhould attempt to break off the twigs of this little tree or fhrub with his naked hands, would pay dear for his imprudence and ignorance. The Javanese are very well acquainted with it in general, and the Dutch Colonists call it *Buffel's-blad*, or Buffaloe's leaf. It has ever been customary with the Javanese Princes on holidays, by way of amusement, to let a Tyger and Buffalo fight together in an area, fenced in with planks, near which a great number of spectators can sit in perfect safety. If on such occasions the Buffalo shews himself tardy in attacking his adversary, he is flogged with this plant, which causes such a heat and inflammation in his skin, that he at length becomes quite wild and outrageous. Whenever any one happens to be stung with this nettle-tree, the best remedy is, instead of washing the part with water, which would only render the pain more intolerable, to anoint it either with oil, or else with rice boiled down to a soft consistence.

On the 27th, we turned back again, and went to *Salatiga*.

On the 28th, we departed from this place, accompanied by the Ensign, to a Javanese village, called *Tundang*, where we resolved to pass the night. The village was tolerably large, but the houses were small, formed of bamboo canes, in the stile of those huts that are made of branches of trees, the bamboos not being placed closer together than what would allow of a passage for
the

the air; a circumstance of some importance in this hot climate. We did not take up our quarters with any of the Javanese, but had a hut built for ourselves. This was immediately performed by some of the Javanese, and the business was completed with such incredible dispatch, that before we could alight from, and unsaddle our horses, and unpack our things, not only our house was entirely finished, but it was likewise furnished with a couch to lie upon, three stools and a table, all which were manufactured on the spot. I stood quite astonished at this new edifice, and entered with the greatest amazement under its friendly shade. Some of the Javanese were employed in cutting trunks of bamboos of different degrees of thickness, others made, with two strokes, a hole in each side of them, and others inserted into these holes bamboo sticks of a smaller size. After this twigs with the leaves on them were interwoven between, and the house, in consequence of a great number of hands being employed on it, was completed in a few minutes, as were also the tables and stools in a similar manner, although these were neither smooth nor even, and consequently not calculated for indolent ramblers of quality, but only for weary travellers.

As we arrived in this place early before evening, I took a ramble to the woods and neighbouring

bouring spots, in search of herbs. *Dioscorea* I found both wild and cultivated, twining with their curling tendrils, frequently to the very summits of the trees.

And as we had no access to the light, before the aperture that served for the door, a fire was made, round which we placed ourselves, I, with the herbs I had gathered, and the other gentlemen with their tobacco-pipes. This lasted not long, before a whole troop of Javanese, consisting of the inhabitants of the village, came and pitched their numerous camp facing us. Among these were several musicians, with a large band of dancers, male and female, who had been sent for hither by my companions, for the sake of diverting me, and that I might have an opportunity of seeing the sports and amusements of the Javanese. Stringed instruments, drums, and pipes began to strike up, and the dancing commenced, and continued with various motions and gestures, being mostly kept up by two dancers at a time. Every one that danced, was obliged to pay a trifle for each dance, either to the person with whom he danced or to the musicians. This rendered it necessary for us to supply the slaves we had brought with us with a few small pieces of money, in order that they might take share in the diversion.

I cannot

I cannot deny, but that this jovial scene and spectacle of mirthful amusement was, in fact, extremely agreeable and entertaining; but the persecution which we suffered from the gnats in this low situation, embittered every pleasure, and proved an insurmountable obstacle to our night's repose. Neither yarn-stockings nor boots were capable of keeping the gnats from our legs; and although the smoke of the fire, as well as of the tobacco, in some measure defended our faces from their attacks, yet these preservatives proved to me, who never was fond of smoke of any kind, quite intolerable. At length, after midnight, I laid me down to sleep upon my grass-bed, and buried myself in such a manner under a veil, and some pocket-handkerchiefs, which I spread over me, that the persecuting gnats were prevented from giving me much disturbance, any farther than by the incessant piping noise which they made.

After passing a sleepless night in this place, we continued our journey the next morning to *Samarang*, where we arrived on the 1st of *May*.

I waited on the Governor, a friendly, well-bred, and amiable man, and made my report to him of what I had been able to collect and discover in my journey. The plants which might be applied with advantage to the use of the sick, as well in as out of the Hospitals, were the following, viz.

The

The *Fumaria officinalis*, called by the Javanese *Rumpung*, was found in a small quantity in the mountainous tracts near Kopping.

The *Rubus moluccanus*, and two other species of this genus, were found between Salatiga and Kopping, on the sides of hills, and particularly near rivers, in profusion.

The *Artemisia*, Mugwort, called by the Javanese *Domolo*, and by the Malays *Seroni*, grew between Salatiga and Kopping, in the rivers and plains, in the greatest profusion.

The *Sonchus oleraceus*, called by the Javanese *Dimboring*, was seen near Kopping; as was likewise

The *Lactuca*, or Lettuce, (by the Javanese *Belot*) but in a small quantity, between Salatiga and Kopping.

The *Scolopendrium* had taken up its quarters among the trees between Unarang and Salatiga.

The *Capsicum*, or Cayenne Pepper, to which the Javanese give the name of *Lombo*, was found wild between Salatiga and Kopping.

The *Oxalis acetosella*, the *Samangi Kunong* of the Javanese, occurred every where very common.

The *Chenopodium*, in the Malay language *Paijam china*, grew near Kopping.

The *Sanicula*, in the Javanese language *Spran*, grew near the rivulets between Salatiga and Kopping.

A *Ranunculus* and a species of *Persicaria*, which the Malays called *Dukut Parang*, grew along with the preceding plant.

The *Schœnanthus*, in the Malay language, *Sire*, was seen between Unarang and Kopping.

The *Fragaria vesca*, or Strawberry, the *Manikan* of the Javanese, occurred in this warm country near Kopping and the rivulets in that neighbourhood.

The *Clematis* twined round the shrubs between Salatiga and Kopping.

Agrimony, in the Malay tongue *Upan Upan Karpo*, grew along with the preceding plant.

The *Salicornia fruticosa*, the *Chimbine* of the Javanese, grew on the shores of Samarang.

The *Vitex* was called by the Javanese *Simina*, as likewise *Lagundo*, and was very common in many places.

The *Costus Arabicus*, which I had before found very common and plentiful in the dikes that environed Batavia, was likewise found in great plenty here, from Samarang all the way to Salatiga, growing among the bushes and the high grass.

The *Leonurus cardiaca*, called in the Malay tongue *Klengenlang*, grew near Kopping.

Urtica, or Nettles, grew here and there, in different parts, tolerably common.

The *Hibiscus abelmoschus* made an elegant figure with its leaves and beautiful flowers between Samarang and Salatiga.

The

The *Adiantum* was found in the skirts of woods, and even in the woods themselves, as also near the rivulets.

The *Datura Stramonium*, called *Rotectibung*, grew between Samarang and Undrang.

The *Smilax* in the woods near Unarang, and

The *Solanum nigrum*, or deadly Nightshade, near Kopping.

The *Verbesina acmella*, the *Sironi* of the Malays, was common every where.

The *Amomum Zingiber*, Ginger; which the Javanese call *Chai*, and the Malays *Bangle*, occurred for the most part cultivated by the Chinese; but the *Amomum zerumbet*, which both the Javanese and Malays sometimes call likewise *Bangle*, although most commonly it bears the name of Lampryang, grew in profusion, chiefly on sandy and meagre spots of land, between Salatiga and Samarang.

The *Curcuma*, Turmeric, by some called *Kunir*, by others again *Kunjet*, I found only near Samarang.

The *Kæmpferia*, or *Sempu*, grows near Salatiga, in watery and low vallies.

The *Amomum compactum*, Cardamom, by the Javanese called *Mojei*, and its fruit *Kappologo*, is cultivated near Salatiga.

The *Piper longum*, long Pepper, the *Chabe* and *Dandang Mussu* of the Javanese, grew copiously

piously in the woods near Salatiga, as likewise elsewhere, frequently on the very stone-fences.

The *Piper nigrum*, black Pepper, called Maritio, grows in profusion near Salatiga, in the woods.

The *Piper cubeba*, or Cubebs, which has obtained the name of *Komukus*, abounds in the woods near Tuntang, and is the sort which is sent over to Europe.

The *Melilothus*, both by the Javanese and Malays called *Treba*, I had before observed at Batavia; now it was found near Salatiga.

The *Cannabis sativa*, or Hemp, likewise grew on a spot near Salatiga; it was high, but still remained a shrub, and was called by the Javanese *Ginge*.

The *Cyperus rotundus* grew every where common.

The *Saccharum officinarum*, or Sugar Cane, is called *Tebu*, and was cultivated all over the country, and at the same time grew wild near Salatiga.

The *Mirabilis Jalappa* occurred for the most part cultivated, but was likewise found wild near Salatiga, and is called in the Malay language *Rambal Pokul Ampat*, an expression which answers to the *Vier uhrs bloom* (Four hours Blossom) of the Dutch.

The *Cynoglossum* (Hound's-tongue), the *Upan Upan Sapi* of the Malays, was found between Salatiga and Kopping.

The

The *Cicuta*? (or Hemlock,) was found juſt above Salatiga, in the clefts of mountains, and by the ſides of rivulets.

The *Plantago major*, or greater Plantain, vegetated near the rivulets, and in other places, in abundance.

The *Ricinus communis*, and the *Jatropha cureas*, which in the Malay tongue was called *Jarrak*, were both of them extremely common both here and in other places on the iſland of Java.

Of the *Arum* there were various ſorts, very common, near ponds and in every ditch.

The *Caryota urens*, called the *Saguer* tree, grew between Salatiga and Kopping, and was ſaid to be the real tree of which Sago is made.

The *Ocymum baſilicum* was common hereabouts, in like manner as the *Ocymum ſanctum* was near Batavia and at other places.

The *Tamarindus indica*, a very tall, ſtrong, and handſome tree, was very common every where.

The *Caſſia fiſtula* and *javanica*, called *Dranguli*, the long cylindrical fruit of which is exactly like canes or walking-ſticks, grew common in the woods near Tundang.

The *Acorus calamus*, or Calamus Aromaticus, grew wild near Samarang and in many other places, winding round the trees, and with its prickles impeding the progreſs of the traveller.

The *Crinum latifolium*, which may be used instead of the *Scilla*, or Squills, grew here, near Batavia, and in other parts.

The *Sida afiatica* is called by the Europeans Malva arborea, and grows near Batavia, Samarang, and other places, common.

Of *Gnaphalium*, or Cudweed, two forts are found near Kopping, which the Javanese call *Sombong Madur*.

The *Sambucus canadenfis*, the *Soobo* of the Javanese, grows in the clefts of mountains near the rivulets in the neighbourhood of Kopping.

The *Poterium fanguiforba*? grows between Unarang and Samarang.

The *Ophiorhiza mungos*, or *Lignum columbrinum*, called by the Javanese as well as the Malays *Kajo ular* and *Bidara laut*, is in different parts of the country tolerably common.

Jafminum, or Jeffamine, was gathered near Salatiga.

The *Coriandrum fativum*, or Coriander, called by the Javanese *Katumjar*, I found in fome few places, where fome other plant was cultivated; fo that it appeared to have been brought from Europe with the feeds.

Piper betle and *Areca catechu*, two plants of which the Indians cannot difpenfe with the ufe, are found every where.

A German

A German Surgeon, who had formerly been in the service of the Company, and was greatly beloved by the Governor in Samarang, had been so unfortunate as to have contracted Cataracts in both his eyes, insomuch that he was now totally blind. The Governor, on being informed by the Physician of the Hospital, who was my host, that I thought myself capable of restoring this Surgeon to his sight, made me an offer of a hundred Ducatoons, in case I succeeded in the attempt; and as all my chirurgical instruments had gone in the ship to Juana, he sent off a courier immediately to fetch them. But this man, who was somewhat above the middle age, must himself have had very little confidence in his own profession of surgery, because he was full as obstinate as he was blind, and would in no wise suffer himself to be induced or persuaded to undergo any operation. I enquired therefore, whether no other blind persons could be found, to whom I might administer some relief, and at the same time instruct my worthy host in an operation, which is one of the finest in the whole Art of Surgery. He immediately procured an elderly European man, and a Chinese woman of 70 years of age, both of whom were blind in both eyes; the former being absolutely stone-blind, and the latter only able to walk a little without leading. On both of them I performed the operation with fuccefs, they being both reftored to their full and perfect fight. And indeed I was perfuaded, previous to my departure from this place, to leave to my hoft not only thefe ophthalmic inftruments, but likewife feveral other inftruments, which are but feldom required to be ufed on board of fhip.

The flowers, both fingle and double of the *Nyctantes Sambac*, are often ftrung upon a thread, and are ufed here likewife for garlands for the head by the European ladies. Sometimes at balls the gentlemen receive a fimilar garland, with a *Champaca* flower in the middle to hang round their necks. The fcent of it is extremely agreeable, and the colour likewife, which is as white as fnow, has a very pleafing effect.

Coffee is cultivated in a great many places, and thefe plantations are beautiful beyond defcription. The coffee-tree produces its firft pods in the third year. A hundred trees yield upon an average three or four chefts of beans, each cheft weighing 120 pounds averdupoife, one year more, another year fomewhat lefs. In the beginning the Dutch Company is faid to have paid the Javanefe twenty-five rix-dollars for every cheft of coffee; at prefent they pay no more than fix, of which the *Tommegom*, or Land-Voigt, receives two rix-dollars; fo that the labouring Javanefe, who plants the coffee, does not receive

ceive more than four. The *Erythrina corallodendrum*, which is called *Dadap*, was here always planted between the coffee-shrubs, that stood thin, and at a distance from each other, in order to give the whole plantation a moderately thick shade and shelter against the scorching rays of the sun.

It was inconceivably pleasant to behold such a plantation, viz. a grove of trees in strait rows, consisting partly of tall and thinly-planted trees, and partly of shrubs, the spreading, and somewhat dependent branches of which were covered with a great number of coffee-pods, and at the same time with a cluster of white flowers.

May 3d, the Javanese celebrated their New-Year; when the *Patti*, or High Sheriff of the Province, who resides here, gave a grand entertainment, to which all the Company's servants in Samarang were invited.

May 14th, I sailed in a Dutch ship from Samarang to Japara, where I was inexpressibly well received and much befriended by M. *van der* BEEK, who was Residentiary at this delightful place; a gentleman, who not only possessed great knowledge himself, but likewise protected and encouraged the Sciences and their votaries in this part of the Eastern World. His singular kindness towards me I shall never bury in oblivion; but my destiny would not permit me to make

any

any long stay here; as the ship at Juana had already taken in its lading, and I was consequently obliged to leave this place in haste, in order to accompany it to Batavia.

May 20, I prosecuted my journey on horseback over-land to Juana, accompanied by a Javanese, whom M. *van der* BEEK had given me for my conductor. And as the journey was too long to be performed in one day, during the heat, I received at the same time letters of recommendation to a certain Prince, whom I was to wait upon in my way thither, and who had married the Emperor's sister. With this Prince I took up my night-quarters; after having had the happiness to sup at his table with him alone, and converse with him in broken Malay, upon various topics. The silence of the night, however, was very much interrupted both by screech-owls and other animals, whose cries and shriekings lasted all night long. The following day, towards evening, I arrived in Juana, and went immediately with a sloop on board the ship, which had already got to the distance of several miles from the road.

The coast on the northern side of Java is very low, and the harbours shallow, for the most part muddy: on this account the ships are obliged to lie at a considerable distance in the roads, and if they are heavy laden, they are in several

places

places stranded, and stick fast in the mud. This happened now to be the case with us at Juana, although the ship had already lain at a considerable distance from the shore, in order to take in the remainder of her lading: and notwithstanding that we seized the opportunity and hoisted our sails at high water, yet we were obliged to unload a heap of planks into large boats, in order to lighten the ship. And when at last there blew a favourable wind, yet still we sailed for two whole leagues together so deep in mud, that the water in the wake of the ship was turbid, and of a blueish cast, from the blue clay. And indeed all seamen testify, that the water in these parts is continually decreasing, whilst the strand increases, and the harbours are filled up with shoals and sand-banks. This is said to have happened in so great a degree, since the Dutch Company first sent their ships hither, that the place where they at that time used to lie is now a morass, and they cannot now approach within a considerable distance of it. In fact, this northern side of Java is the most fertile, while, on the other hand, the southern coast is very mountainous, has deeper water, and is more barren.

Between Juana and Japara a promontory extends into the sea, which we now sailed by. There is a rock here, which has received the name

name of the *Devil's Rock*, becaufe Corfairs are faid frequently to harbour here, as well as near the iflands of *Intermaja* and *Boompjes*, who attack and capture every veffel, great or fmall, that is not well-armed, or that does not fail under convoy. Thefe Corfairs are not Javanefe, but come from the coafts of the ifland of Borneo, and the circumjacent ifles, and therefore cannot be extirpated.

Our journey proved very profperous, and we arrived again at Batavia on the 1ft of June.

As foon as I had returned to Batavia, I was called upon to act as Phyfician on board the Hofpital-fhip, that is ftationed in the road juft before the town. Although, on a fhip's arrival in the road, all the fick that are on board, are always removed immediately to the Town-Hofpital, as well as thofe who afterwards may be taken ill; neverthelefs an Hofpital-fhip (as it is called) which is for the moft part an old veffel unfit for any other ufe, is kept here for the reception of thofe, who are taken ill in the night, as the town is fhut up and no one can obtain entrance. This duty, or rather night-watch, is undertaken in rotation by all the Ship-Surgeons, who are in Batavia; but they feldom perform it themfelves, but hire fome old Surgeon for this purpofe in their ftead. Thus I was this time excufed from it for one Ducatoon.

I had

I had now the good fortune to form an acquaintance with a worthy countryman of mine, M. WIMMERCRANTZ, a Captain of Engineers in the Dutch Company's service, in which he was as useful, as he was universally beloved and esteemed. He lived in the suburbs, and not only received me with great friendship, but also afterwards, during my stay in this place, rendered me actual services; and, in short, shewed me much of that favour, which he had before lavishly bestowed upon several of his beloved countrymen.

On the 19th of June, as I had still to wait the arrival of some ship, that should sail to Ceylon, which island I wished to visit, I made, with permission of the Governor, and in company with Baron von WURMB, likewise attended by an officer, whom the Commissary over the natives (for the interior) had sent with us, a journey up the country to the warm Baths, and the (so called) Blue-mountains. For this journey Captain WIMMERCRANTZ had the goodness to accommodate me with the loan of his own horse, of which I had the use both on my journey thither and on my return.

We travelled the first day to *Tanjong,* a place, which at this time belonged to the Privy-Counsellor CRAAN, and is situated about eighteen poles from the capital. The country is here measured

off

off with posts, as in Europe, but however of different lengths.

On the 20th, we travelled in the morning about twenty-five poles, to *Chipinong*, where we dined, and afterwards went farther by *Chimangis* and *Chiluar* to *Buytenzorg*, fifty poles from Batavia. This place is intended for the pleasure of the ruling Governor-General, and has been made choice of and built for this purpose by Governor-General IMHOFF. The building, which is of stone, is very handsome, consisting of two wings and a little citadel, with beautiful gardens between. By reason of its distance from the capital, however, the Governor-General can seldom reside here.

On the 22d, we travelled to *Chiseroa*, and from thence farther over high mountains to *Chipannas*. Both these places, as likewise *Pondogedé* and *Arkidemas* belong to the Governor-General, or rather to the Dutch Company. Here we rested over night, and viewed the warm Bath, which is called in Malay *Chipannas*, and gives its name to the circumjacent country.

The warm Bath springs up almost in the middle between the two large ridges of mountains, in a valley. The water was found not to be boiling hot, but the finger could bear the heat, when placed in it. It bubbled up in several places. A hut was built over the veins, that

conveyed

conveyed the water into the Bath. The hole itself was not deep, and the force of the spring not very great: the earth around it was of the colour of iron-rust, and on the sides of the water a thin crust of a deep green hue had settled, that perfectly resembled verdegrife. The house, which was built for those that used the Bath, consisted of two parts: one chamber was very large, through which the water was conducted to the other: here were two drains in the floor, to purify the water from its filth: the other chamber had a large, square hole in it, lined with boards, and furnished with stairs. To this room ran two pipes of metal, out of which either cold or warm water could be let in at pleasure to any height one chose, during bathing. At the top of the water a crust was formed, nearly of the thickness of a farthing, and of a saltish taste. I was informed, that if the water were used for drinking, it opened the body, and therefore was seldom applied internally, but for the most part externally. Some time ago a great number of sick persons, some of them even from the Hospital, were sent hither from Batavia, to use the Bath, and for this purpose an Hospital was instituted here, which at this time stood unoccupied and useless. A European Farmer now lived here, and had the care and inspection of the Bath and several gardens.

The

The climate is very healthy and refreshing: indeed the air, especially in the morning and evening, was not only cool, but absolutely cold, insomuch that I, who had not brought a great coat with me, was chilled and perfectly shivered with the cold evening air, in a country, that lies almost directly under the Æquator.

Cabbages, esculent-rooted plants, greens, and fruit-trees, from Europe, are cultivated here, and thrive greatly; as also at *Arkidomas*, *Chiseroa*, and *Pondogedé*, from all which places refreshments are sent three times a week to the Governor-General's table, in Batavia. Oranges ripen, and are much more delicious than those, which grow nearer to Batavia.

The Javanese reported, and endeavoured to persuade the Europeans to believe, so ridiculous a story, as that on the mountains of *Chipannas* a species of Monkey was found (*the Orang Outang*) which had curling hair, and retroverted feet. No European had ever seen any such here.

The Javanese, and those Chinese that lived among them, had their roofs covered with cleft bamboos, which were laid one upon the other, almost like tiles.

I saw a species of *Ardea* in this place, which resembles the *Antigone*: the *rostrum* is *albo-flavescens*; *gula nuda, flava*; *caput calvum, albidum*;

dum; *pedes cærulescentes*; *remiges cinereo-nigri*; *dorsum et cauda nigra*; *abdomen albidum*.

The Turtle-doves (*Columba risoria*), which at the Cape of Good-Hope are always blue, are here of a paler colour, and for the most part white.

Kadondon is a wood that is used for quickset-hedges.

Andewala is the name given to a climbing plant with tripartite leaves, which was reported to be a good antidote against poison.

Korang garing and *Tampal utan* are two plants, with which the Javanese dye blue.

Boa kirai is the name of a fruit, which is very astringent and austere.

Tingling mintik is said to be a good and cordial remedy.

On the 24th, we went back again over the mountains to Pondogedé. At the summits of the mountains, which were covered every where with woods and bushes, we left our horses and the road, in order to climb still higher towards the top, and to see the extremely well-known and much celebrated pool of water near *Mebe-medon*. I here met with the climate of the north of Europe, and among other plants, various kinds of Moss likewise, (*Musci*) and Lichens, which otherwise are so uncommon, and indeed scarcely ever to be seen in the warmest climes of India.

We staid over night in *Pondogedé*, and the following day travelled to *Arkidomas*, to take a view of a place, which was very remarkable on account of various small images hewn in stone, which were placed in different parts of the wood, three or four together. The Javanese have a great veneration for them, and both Javanese and Chinese sacrifice to them. In our way we saw the wild Peacocks, which are kept tame, as being rarities in Europe, flying up and down in the woods, and perching at times upon the boughs of the trees, to shew themselves in all their glory, and make an ostentatious display of their long, depending, and magnificent tails. I shot one of them, which we roasted in the evening; but found it very dry and insipid. A commandant from a small fort had borne us company the whole day, and had brought with him two soldiers, who blew incessantly two small French-horns, in order to frighten away the Tigers. These animals were said to be very dangerous here, insomuch that they frequently carried off travelling Javanese, and not to be able to bear in any wise the sound of powerful wind-instruments. We came towards evening to *Buytenzorg*, which place the Javanese call *Bogor*; but previously to our arrival there, we went to a place near *Paditulis*, to view a stone of great antiquity, in which certain characters were

were hewn, that no one hitherto had been able to read or interpret. The stone is nearly of the height of a man, and about two feet in breadth. The characters appeared to me to be written from the left to the right, and consisted of eight lines and a half.

On the 26th, we made another short excursion from the strait road to Mount *Cherroton*, which is worthy of notice in many respects. It stands quite detached almost in the middle of the country. Our chief view in going thither was to see its singular cavities, in which the Swallows (*Hirundo esculenta*) build their nests, that are of a gelatinous nature, and are used as food. We ascended on foot within a short space of time, to the summit of the mountain, and found that these cavities were, strictly speaking, on the southern side of the mountain, and quite covered at the top. They did not appear to have proceeded from a splitting or separation of the parts, as no fissure was discoverable at the top; but it rather seemed to me that they originated from the air by a gradual mouldering, because they constantly reached to a considerable depth, and had water at the bottom. I entered into several of these, and descended likewise a good way into them, by means of a bamboo-ladder, without however finding any thing else than danger, darkness, and subdivisions, as it were, into several distinct apart-

ments.

men s. The Javanese would not allow us to take any nests away with us; but had nevertheless the politeness, not only to give us some which were undamaged, but likewise to present us, at our request, with two Swallows, of the species that built here, and which were small and quite black.

My fellow-traveller and myself were entertained in a very superb and costly manner by the Javanese Governor of the province, at dinner. The Governor himself, together with his cousin, and we two travellers, formed the whole company. Our host could both talk and understand in some measure the Malay language, which we spoke. The victuals were placed separately before each of us upon small plates of porcellain. Of each dish consequently there was no great quantity, but the number of dishes for each of us amounted to ninety, so that we were hardly able to have a taste of each.

On the 28th, we travelled to a country-seat belonging to M. Duurkoop. It was exceedingly elegant, and contained a remarkable tower, which echoed back nine syllables with distinctness. From this delightful place we returned at length to Batavia.

In the course of this journey I had observed, that the Chinese had settled in great numbers, and that even in the heart of the country; but that

that they neverthelefs did not live together with the Javanefe. This, I was told, was forbidden, in order to avoid difcord and contention, to which the Chinefe were faid to be very prone, if they did not change their religion, and fuffer themfelves to be circumcifed. This, however, did not prevent numbers of the Chinefe from efpoufing the daughters of the Javanefe; although the daughters of the Chinefe were not allowed to marry with Javanefe. And indeed the Chinefe here are not fuffered to fhut up their wives, or disfigure their feet, as they do in China.

I was afterwards very affiduous in my vifits to the Hofpital, where the fick were properly treated, but died neverthelefs in great numbers. The number of deaths was computed to have increafed almoft yearly, efpecially of late, in confequence of the canals, which fupply the town with water, not being kept fufficiently clean. To the truth of this I was frequently a witnefs, when both culinary vegetables and dead animals were thrown into the river by the Chinefe, and afterwards floated down into the harbour and road. Since the gentlemen of rank have begun to erect country-feats and pleafure-grounds without the town, this pernicious cuftom has obtained the afcendency. From the Public Regifters I informed myfelf accurately of the number of Europeans, that died in the Hofpital.

This list, from the year 1714, quite down to the year 1776, I shall now lay before the Reader.

Year.	Dead.	Year.	Dead.	Year.	Dead.
1714	459	1735	1568	1756	1487
1715	469	1736	1574	1757	1441
1716	453	1737	1993	1758	1638
1717	494	1738	1776	1759	1373
1718	591	1739	998	1760	1317
1719	660	1740	1124	1761	1000
1720	750	1741	1075	1762	1390
1721	614	1742	1082	1763	1750
1722	730	1743	1283	1764	1757
1723	657	1744	1595	1765	1754
1724	769	1745	1604	1766	2039
1725	925	1746	1565	1767	2404
1726	904	1747	1881	1768	1831
1727	676	1748	1261	1769	1740
1728	656	1749	1478	1770	2706
1729	626	1750	2035	1771	2316
1730	671	1751	1969	1772	2305
1731	780	1752	1601	1773	1187
1732	781	1753	1618	1774	1957
1733	1116	1754	1517	1775	2788
1734	1375	1755	2109	1776	2877

Hence may be seen that the number of the dead increased almost from year to year; but this augmentation was particularly considerable, after three remarkable changes. From the year 1714 to 1733, the number of the dead was least. In the year 1733, they began out of the town to make a dyke or canal leading to Batavia, on which

occasion

occafion great numbers both of the Javanefe and people of other nations died; from this time alfo the number of the dead has conftantly increafed. In the year 1761, they began to ftow in the Hofpital without the city more fick people than the two hundred convalefcents, which were formerly attended there; and from this time forward the number of the dead increafed ftill more. In 1775, an Hofpital-fhip was laid up in the road; in confequence of which, as well that year as the following, the number of the dead was the greateft of all.

At my own defire, I was taken on board a fhip, that was at this time bound for Ceylon, in the capacity of firft Surgeon; notwithftanding that M. RADERMACHER, as well as my landlord Dr. HOFFMAN, had made many attempts to detain me in this country, by means of fome advantageous employment. Although I was able to bear heat extremely well, and found myfelf very well in other refpects in this hot climate, yet it was both difagreeable and difficult, to tranfact one's bufinefs here; and attachment to my native country rendered me deaf to every reprefentation of advantage from other quarters, even at a time when I could not in the leaft forefee any good fortune accruing to me in the country which gave me birth.

Before the ship had taken her cargo in for the impending voyage to the western coast of India, I made several other excursions in the environs of the town of Batavia.

Jaccatra is a tolerably handsome spot, a little way out of Batavia; it was formerly the metropolis of this part of the island, and was conquered by the Dutch in the year 1619. Here is now kept a small number of soldiers, to defend the citadel, and to be, as it were, a bulwark to Batavia.

The Portuguese came, it is true, to Java long before any other Europeans, and indeed already in 1510; but never could make a firm and lasting settlement here. After them came the English, and soon after that the Dutch, in 1596.

The island of Java is long and very narrow, in length at least 140 German miles, from east to west, and in breadth 30, from north to south.

Three religions are common in Java, viz. the Pagan, with part of the Javanese and Chinese; the Mahometan, with a great part of the Javanese; and the Christian, with the Europeans, and at the same time with some of the Javanese, Malays, and other Indians.

The articles of traffic which Java produces, consist chiefly of Rice, which is excellent, and is exported to many parts of India for sale; *Cardamoms*, of that species which has rounded seed-vessels (*Cardamomum compactum*); *Sugar*, which has been introduced into the country, with a view to its cultivation, grows in abundance, and is exported in the state of brown sugar, not only to all the Indian markets, but likewise to Europe. *Salt*, which is exported to several parts of India, and is exceedingly dear in the Molucca islands in particular; *Pepper*, which is mostly sent to Europe; *Indigo, Callicoe*, and no very inconsiderable quantity of *Cotton-thread*; *Bird's-nests*, which are for the most part, and that with considerable profit, sold in Canton, in China.

The *Loxia oryzivora* is found in abundance in Java, and does frequently considerable damage to the rice-fields.

For change, two small sorts of copper coin were current. One sort was an ordinary farthing, which the Dutch Company had struck, of the common Swedish copper, in Europe, and afterwards imported hither. Of this there are two sorts, perfectly alike, excepting as to size, in which point they differ, the one being twice as large as the other. The largest of these approaches nearest in size to the Swedish farthings. On the one side appear the usual arms of the Company, together with the date of the year, on the other the arms of the Province in which the piece was coined. The worth of each is estimated at double what it would pass for in
Europe,

Europe, so that the Company gains by this mode about one hundred per cent. The other sort is a Javanese coin, stamped on one side with Javanese characters, and upon the other with a wreath of flowers, within which stands *Duyt Javas*, and the year of the Christian æra, in which it was struck.

In like manner I saw several Dutch ducats in the hands of the Chinese and Javanese; but these had been stamped on the upper side with a little round die exhibiting certain Javanese characters, which gave them value and currency among that people.

The Chinese wear slippers with hind-quarters and stout soles, within which are several layers of felt, to prevent them from drawing water and occasioning wet feet to the wearer; but these, as well as their boots, which are made on the same plan, are heavy and clumsy.

VOYAGE TO CEYLON.

JULY 5th, 1777, I embarked, with the blessing of Almighty God, on board the ship *Mars*, in order to sail in the same to Ceylon, being furnished with several letters of recommendation to the Governor and other public Functionaries there.

On the 7th we weighed anchor, and got under sail, with a calm and prosperous wind, leaving behind us one of the finest countries in the world.

On the 11th following, we cast anchor again off *Anjer*, where we proposed to continue a few days, and take in some casks of water, for our impending voyage. The Swedish East-India ship the *Stockholm's Slott*, bound to China, lay in the road already, where she had arrived before us, in order to take in a supply of water, and I had in consequence the pleasure to meet with here and embrace several of my dear friends and countrymen; as, for instance, Captain PETTERSEN, the Supercargoes ALNOOR and BLADH, &c. The water, which was taken in at this place, from the rivulets that ran down hither, was, it is true, sweet, and in some measure good, but exceedingly turbid: and from the circumstance, that the landing here was very difficult, and that the casks were rolled in the water on shore, this turbidity was increased still more. The water likewise conduced greatly to increase and keep up the Diarrhœa, which was rife among the crew; nay, it was almost impossible to drink a single glass of it, unless Tea or Coffee had been previously mixed with it, without occasioning the inconveniencies abovementioned.

The

The larger species of *Pisang* (*Musa Troglodi-tarum*), I observed here to have tolerably distinct seeds, flat, and almost as large as lin-seed.

Canes were sold in great quantities by the Javanese that lived in the villages; and the Swedes bartered for several of the better sort, in which traffic, with what little I understood of the Malay language, I had the pleasure to serve my countrymen, in the capacity of Interpreter.

After this we prosecuted our voyage with success and with favourable winds, so that we crossed the Line on the 9th of August, and on the 28th of the same month, came within view of the Malabar coast, along which we sailed, passing by *Porca, Coilan,* and *Cape Comorin.* Notwithstanding this, the ship was very deeply laden, and without any regard to propriety or moderation, so that it would certainly have been in a very disagreeable situation, had any violent storm sprung up. The cause of this, as well as of a great many other disorders, inconveniencies, and calamities, originated in the insatiable avarice, which prevails among the people in the Company's service. The Captain and all the Officers have the privilege of trafficking with certain commodities, for which purpose a certain space is left them in the stowage of the ship; under cover of this privilege, they introduce and burden the ship with many times as much as the weight

allowed

allowed them, in order to fwell the amount of their profits. It is more particularly the Captain and Chief Mate, who fet themfelves no bounds in their abufe of this privilege. The commodities, which were taken out by individuals in the prefent voyage, confifted of a confiderable quantity of Rice, foft Sugar, and Arrack.

On the 29th, we came within fight of the ifland of Ceylon, and the day following came to our moorings; but we were within a hair's breadth of fuffering fhipwreck, through the ignorance and cowardice of the Mafter. Whilft we continued conftantly to heave the lead, it was perceived that we drove too much againft the fhoals which lie in the mouth of the channel, which feparates the ifland from the continent, and our fhip threatened to run a-ground, when the Second Mate, a bold and enterprizing mariner, obferving the too vifible terrors and faint-heartednefs of the Captain, laid hold of the trumpet, and gave orders to tack about, which in a few minutes brought the fhip, that dragged very heavily, into deeper water, and all of us fafely out of all danger; fo that we could very foon afterwards caft anchor, and return thanks to God, who had fo miraculoufly delivered us from imminent danger.

The following day arrived from Europe the Zeeland fhip *William V*, and at the expiration of a few days more the fhip *Loo*, from Amfterdam.

I forwarded my letters to Columbo, and had soon after the honour to wait upon Governor FALCK, a very learned and sensible man, and at the same time the most disinterested of all the Company's Officers I ever met with. He was born in Ceylon, and had studied in Utrecht. The Governor-General, van der PARRA, had been the chief instrument of his promotion, of which he rendered himself in every respect truly worthy and deserving.

Besides many others, who honoured me in this place with their friendship, I enjoyed also a considerable share of the favour of M. van SLUYSKEN, who went in general by the name of Captain *Cinnamon*, and was inspector over those that barked and delivered in the Cinnamon. I was a regular guest at his table once or twice a week, where I always met with cheerful and instructive company. I contracted likewise an acquaintance here with two worthy countrymen of mine, Baron ALBEDYL, who was an officer, and Monf. von KEULEN, or KJELLIN, who had settled here as a Burgher, and carried on a lucrative and extensive trade to the coast of Coromandel. I further augmented the circle of my acquaintance with an honourable veteran, Captain HOPNER, who had sailed originally from Sweden, in the capacity of a young tar, in a trading vessel, which being attacked by a Turkish corsair, he lost one of his thumbs by a musket-ball, and afterwards advanced himself in the service of the Dutch Company, especially by his knowledge in Engineering and Fire-works. This worthy veteran treated me not only as a friend and beloved countryman in his house and family, but made me likewise an offer of his table, with the use of an apartment during my abode in this place; an offer which I however did not accept, but preferred residing at the ordinary inn, that I might, more uncontrolled, make my little excursions, and collections of the natural productions of this island.

Columbo, which is the capital town for the Dutch trade on this island, is large and handsome, surrounded on all sides with walls, and very strongly fortified.

The Governor's *palace* is very elegant, although it is only one story high. The balcony is of equal length with the house itself, and forms a pleasant and cool apartment, from which there is an entrance to several chambers on the other side.

The *air* is indeed as sultry here as in Batavia, but as the coast itself does not lie so low, but the country is more elevated, and winds more frequent, the heat proves more tolerable, and the climate is more healthy.

Bathing in cold water, and particularly in the open sea, near those coasts which are not infested
with

with crocodiles, is a very common practice, both with the Europeans, and still more so with the Indians. When one takes an afternoon's walk out of the town, one may see hundreds, both black and white, young and old, free and slaves, and indiscriminately of both sexes, sporting in the water, and by these means cooling their bodies, and bracing their fibres, which have been relaxed and debilitated by the scorching rays of the sun.

In company with a Ceylonese, whom the Governor had graciously appointed to attend me, I made daily excursions in the vicinity of Columbo, and collected diligently, with the sweat of my brow, in the circumjacent districts, the various productions of the land, during the time that some of my ship's comrades at the Inn exposed their commodities to sale, and carried on their traffic in a manner much more beneficial to themselves. The fellow-traveller appointed me was one of the most skilful Physicians of the country, who communicated to me always both the Ceylonese and Malabar names of each plant, as well as the manner in which it was used in different diseases. His medical knowledge was very small, preposterous, and for the most part absurd, so that I could not derive much benefit from him in this respect.

The *Barringtonia*, with its large and beautiful bloffom, grew always by the fide of rivulets and near water; and in a very fhort time let its numerous ftamina fall out of its bloffom.

In like manner the *Dolichos pruriens* grew here tolerably common, with its hairy pods, the hairs of which attaching themfelves to the hands, occafion much itching, which is allayed by oil, or decoction of rice, and are celebrated as a Vermifuge.

The Company has a Printing-prefs in the town, which has given birth to various publications. Of the Books that have been printed here, I procured the following, for the Library at Upfal:

Kort Begryp der Chiftelyke Religie, in de Tamulfche Spraak, door SIGISBERTUS ABRAHAM BRONSVELD. Columbo, 1754, 8vo. i. e. A Compendious View of the Chriftian Religion, in the Tamul Language.

Tamulfch Kinder-Catechifmus, door SIGISB. ABRAH. BRONSVELD. Columbo, 1776. 8vo. i. e. The Tamul Catechifm, for Children.

Evangelium Jefu Chrifti von Matthæus, in de Mallabarfe Taal. Columbo, 1741. 4to. Or; The Gofpel according to St. Mark, in the Malabar tongue.

Evangelium Jefu Chrifti von Matthæus, Marcus, Lueds, ende Johannes; ende de Handelingen der Apoftelen,

Apoſtelen, in de Tamulſche Taal. Or; The Four Evangeliſts and the Acts of the Apoſtle, in the Tamul language, printed at Columbo, 1748. 4to.

The Four Evangeliſts, in the Cingaleſe language, in 4to. I procured, without any title-page.

Seſtien Predikatien in de Tamulſche Taal. Or; Sixteen Sermons in the Tamul language, by PHILIPPUS DE VRIEST, Columbo, 1747. 4to.

Grammatica of Singaleeſche Taal-kunſt. Or; A Grammar of the Cingaleſe language, by JOHANNES RUELL, printed at Amſterdam, 1708. 4to.

Manis (*the Ant-eater*) is found much in Ceylon, eſpecially near *Negumbo*. The Dutch call it the *Negumbo Devil,* and the Cingaleſe *Caballe*. Its fleſh is given to the ſick to eat, by way of a remedy. The inhabitants have a method of making a hole in its ſkin with a knife, and thus of guiding and governing the animal at pleaſure, the point of the knife, which is kept in the hole, goading and irritating him.

The fruit of the *Solanum melongena* is in general uſe both among the Europeans and the Indians. It is ſuppoſed to expel urine, and diſſolve the ſtone in the bladder.

The fruit of the *Cherimelle* is ripe in October and November, and was made uſe of pickled in a ſtrong brine.

The *Marmelle* is likewife ripe in October; the internal pulpous part of the fruit is eaten both with and without the addition of fugar. The fruit is of a very flimy or mucilaginous nature, and hence is called (*Slym apel*, or) Slime-apple.

The *Bolange* is eaten in its ripe ftate with a little fugar, and unripe, with falt. It is of the fize of a China orange.

Panningai is the fruit of a palm-tree, which grows in great abundance, and particularly near Jafna. It is of an oblong, femilunar fhape, nearly as yellow as a *Pifang*, but feveral times larger. It has two, three, or more very hard nuts within it. When dreffed, it has a fweet tafte to thofe who are accuftomed to it, but ftrangers do not find it very pleafant. On being opened, it yields an offenfive fmell. When the nuts of it are fown, and the fpring-leaf comes up, this is cut off clofe, and eaten either boiled with falt and rice, or by itfelf, or is pounded to meal, which can be ufed like any other meal. This fpring-leaf is called by the Cingalefe *Kellingo*. From the month of May to the end of the year this fruit is eatable, and conftitutes the chief nourifhment of the Malabars. The *Kellingo* may likewife be dried for future ufe. The meal made from it is ufed particularly in foup with fifh.

On the 28th of *October*, and the following days, I was requested, together with several Physicians, to examine a large quantity of Cinnamon, which had been furnished by the King of *Candi*. Half of it was found to be adulterated and spoiled, tasteless and bad. The best of it, which could be selected from the mass, was forwarded to Batavia.

In like manner five parcels were examined of a new kind of Cinnamon, but lately planted, which had been sent in 1775, as a sample, to Europe, but on their arrival were found not to possess the proper flavour, although before, at the time of its being shipped at Ceylon, it had proved fine and good. The scent of them was now found to be both fine and pleasant, but the flavour was very weak, or next to none at all. So that it is hardly to be doubted, that they had lost their flavour during the voyage; the cause of which was probably this, that the oil contained in them was too volatile, and not sufficiently concentrated in these young branches, the root of which was not more than three years old. Branches of three year's growth, are fit for decortication, it is true, but yet the root and trunk ought to be more aged. And in the very shipping and transporting of it, a fault had likewise been committed, which may have contributed much, if not totally, to the loss of its

flavour,

flavour, for these parcels had been packed up in one sack, and laid in the cabin. Thus the Cinnamon was neither put into two sacks, nor yet laid among Pepper, as is the usual practice. And indeed, in 1776, forty-seven parcels of this same sort of Cinnamon were sent to Europe.

Cinnamon is the chief commodity which the East-India Company fetch from this island, and the bark of this Spice is here finer and more valuable than in any other place in the world. All prime Cinnamon is taken from the *Laurus Cinnamomum*, a tree of a middling height and size. It is distinguished by broader and more obtuse leaves from the *Laurus Cassia*, which yields a coarser kind of Cinnamon, and seems to be merely a variety of the former. It is so much the more probable, that the coarser and finer Cinnamon, or the *Laurus Cinnamomum* and *Cassia*, are merely different varieties, arising from the climate, and especially from the soil; as Ceylon itself does not commonly yield Cinnamon of an equally good quality, throughout the whole island, and in all its various tracts. The south-west angle of the island is the only part which produces the finer sort of this pleasant and excellent cordial spice, and the places, whence it is chiefly procured, are near *Negumbo*, *Columbo*, *Caltere*, *Barbary*, *Gale*, and *Mature*, all which lie along and near the sea-coast. The Cinnamon, which the more inland parts produce, is always coarser, thicker, more pungent, and biting to the tongue.

I visited, out of the town, the Governor's villa, which is called *Pass*, and consists of an elegant house, and a large pleasure-garden, in which Cinnamon has been planted for several years back. The Cinnamon-tree grows in abundance in the woods, and has been propagated without the adventitious aid of art. The Europeans have believed, and the Cingalese even maintained, that Cinnamon, to be good, must always grow wild, and be left to itself, and, that when planted, it neither thrives nor continues to be genuine. The tree is propagated in its wild state by birds, which eat the soft berries, (the kernels of which do not dissolve in their gizzards,) and afterwards disperse and plant them up and down in the woods. This prejudice prevailed till the end of the sixteenth century, when the Governor, *Yman Wilhelm Falck*, first made the attempt, in small, to rear Cinnamon-trees by art, in this garden at *Pass*. The berries were then sown, which grew up well and quickly, but had the untoward fate, that the plants some time after withered and died. On accurately investigating the cause of this, it appeared, that a Ceylonese, who earned his livelihood by barking Cinnamon in the woods, and

saw

saw with vexation the planting of it, which, in time, would render the gathering of it more easy and convenient, had secretly besprinkled them in the night with warm water. After the discovery of this stratagem, the Governor caused again, in the beginning of the Seventeenth Century, several berries to be planted, and in several places, both upon a small and large scale, which grew up, throve well, and had already yielded several crops of Cinnamon. Thus several thousand Cinnamon-trees were now seen in this garden, and in this garden alone, to thrive and turn out to be of a good sort.

In it also I saw an Areek-tree, which was very tall, but uncommonly slender, and at the same time, which is very singular, divided into two branches, each furnished with its respective crown.

Here is seen likewise a *Borassus*, or *Sea-Cocoa*, brought from the Maldive islands, which had been set in earth, had grown up, and was now in the third year of its growth, having only three leaves. The nut had lain eight months in the ground, before it put forth the first leaf. The leaf was *multipartito-pinnatifidum; pinnis bipartitis.*

Marendan is the name given by the Cingalese to the sandy downs along the sea-coast. The Cinnamon which grows in these sandy plains, is accounted the best and most delicate. When the tree is cut down here, and fire afterwards made

made on the spot, the roots shoot up again in long, strait shoots, which yield an incomparably fine Cinnamon-bark. And from these shoots come the so called Cinnamon walking-sticks, which in appearance resemble those from the Hazel-treee, but of which the bark has a cinnamon-smell, whenever it is rubbed. I several times received such sticks, by way of presents, although it is said that they are scarcely allowed to be exported.

The Cinnamon-leaf has a strong scent of Cloves; the root, on the other hand, which, by means of sublimation, yields Camphor, smells altogether like Sassafras. Cinnamon is generally called by the Cingalese *Kurundu*, and is said now to be greatly diminished in the woods, compared to what it was in former times, so much indeed, that the Cinnamon-barkers, for several years, have not been able to procure the quantity required.

The coasts around the whole island of Ceylon, to the distance of six or more leagues inland, belong entirely to the Dutch East-India Company, and are under the jurisdiction of its Governor; although the country is inhabited by Cingalese, who at the conclusion of the war became subjects to the Company. The interior, middle, and mountainous parts of the island, belong to the King or Emperor in Candi, who is now so completely hemmed in on every side, that he can neither smuggle, nor sell any Cinnamon to foreign nations.

Jacberi is the name given to two sorts of *Crotalaria*, which grow here pretty plentifully, viz. the *laburnifolia*, and *retusa*, both with yellow flowers. Neither of these, nor yet the *Menispermum cocculus*, can be what is called the *Radix Colombo*, or Columbo-root, which for some years past has been introduced into Europe, and recommended as a good medicine. It derives its name from the town of Columbo, from whence it is sent with the ships to Europe; but it is well known that this root is neither found near Columbo, nor upon the whole island of Ceylon, but is brought hither from the coast of Malabar. The *Crotalaria retusa* is an annual plant, whose root therefore cannot possess any medicinal virtues. The *Menispermum cocculus* is a common climbing plant in the woods, the root of which I had several times caused to be dug up, and found it bore no resemblance to the Columbo-root, either in its virtues, taste, size, or external appearance, being exceedingly thin, with elevated ridges, and very long.

Sacsander and *Iremus* were two very celebrated plants with the physicians of this place. The former differs in several respects from the latter. The former is an *Aristolochia indica*, the root of which,

which, steeped in brandy, is bitter, a strengthener of the stomach, and carminative. The latter is found in great profusion, as well in the sandy downs near Columbo, as near Mature, and in other places. Its appearance sufficiently indicates, that it belongs to the *Contortæ*, and is, according to every conjecture, a species of *Periploca*, whose root is poisonous and a purifier of the blood.

Binnuge is the name given by the Ceylonese to a species of *Ipecacuanha*, because the root of it is a very good emetic, although it differs from the American. I was informed, that it is used with success in the Hospitals at Columbo, Gale, Mature, and Jafna. It must be given in rather larger doses than the common sort. I was shown two sorts of it: the one was white, and is called *Elle Binnuge*, the other, which is red, is called *Rat Binnuge*. The red is reported to be the best. The white has fine stringy roots, and the red is somewhat thicker. Both are species of *Periploca*, both creep on the sandy downs, or twine round the bushes which grow in the loose sand.

The Portuguese have here, as well as elsewhere, during their residence, introduced both the Christian Religion and their own language, of which many remains are still to be met with in every part. Portuguese, though corrupted, is still spoken very universally, both among the

Malabars

Malabars and others, on the whole of this western side of India; and it is almost equally incumbent upon a traveller in these parts to learn this Portuguese dialect, as it is to learn Malay in the eastern part of India. The Dutch, since their arrival, have endeavoured to preserve the light of the Christian Religion, and for that purpose the Company maintains both Churches and Schools for the natives and slaves, and Priests to instruct them, and perform divine service.

Otherwise the heathens upon the island, like other East-Indian nations, pay great adoration to their Idol *Budha*, or *Budso*, whose image may not only be seen in the churches, but likewise often in their houses. They intitle him *Deant Budu hamdrue*, i. e. *Lord God Budu*. In the churches offerings of all kinds are laid before him, which serve the Priests for an income, and with these offerings they frequently designate their wants and necessities. When one or more lie sick in a house, they forge thin plates of silver, and form of them on a small scale one or more human figures, which they present on *Budha*'s altar. When any one has a disorder in their eyes, they make a pair of eyes of silver, and so in other cases; but when they in general invoke his assistance in any thing, they make a representation either of the leaf of the *Ficus religiosa*, or of the fruit of the *Anacardium*, which they believe

to

to be acceptable to this their deity. When the Priests have collected a number of these offerings, they melt them down again, or sell them by weight to the Goldsmiths. I had an opportunity of procuring by traffic several of these offerings, as also a small one of pure silver, representing the household god *Budba*, whose unlucky fate it was to be pawned by the proprietor of him to a European. It sometimes happens that urgent distress compels them to this measure, but afterwards, as soon as ever they are able, they punctually redeem such pledges. The Idol is always represented sitting with his feet across, after the Indian fashion, with one hand passed over his head and both hands clasped together forwards, and with long ears, which reach down to his shoulders. In the Churches I saw this Image made partly of stone, partly of wood, and of various sizes.

The *Moors*, who come hither from the coasts of the Continent, are tolerably numerous in Columbo, and carry on an extensive trade. They are for the most part tall of stature, darker than the islanders, and well clad. Their dress resembles nearly a lady's gown, is most frequently made of white callicoe, very wide, and gathered up at the waist, and is bound round the body with a girdle of white cotton, tied on the right side. On the head they wear a turban. Their ears are commonly decorated with long ear-rings of gold, of various patterns, some being plain, others twisted, others set with precious stones of a red, blue, or green colour. Some are very large, being a full finger in length; others again are smaller. Sometimes one of these only is worn in the ear, sometimes more, even five or six together, so that with their weight the foramen and tip of the ear are lengthened amazingly, insomuch that the ear reaches down to the shoulders. Many have a small round knobby fruit, which is said to grow upon a holy mountain in the land of *Kaschi*, set in these ear-rings. The fruit is called *Uteratie*, and is most commonly of the size of a small pea, and sometimes as large as a musket-ball. Some fancy that they discover in the holes and creases of this fruit the resemblance of seven faces, in which case it is said to be very much valued, and is purchased by the Moors of quality and opulence, at the great expence of two hundred rix-dollars. As soon as the children are three years old, one of these ear-rings is given them by way of ornament. It is properly the rich, who wear a number of rings in their ears, so that from the condition, size, and number of the ear-rings, one may form an estimate of the wealth and opulence of the wearers.

Persons

Persons of rank among the Cingalese, such as Ambassadors and Officers belonging to the Court in Candi, wear long gold chains round their necks, which hang down upon the breast and stomach. Such had the Ambassadors who now came to Columbo, and similar ones are likewise given to the Dutch Ambassador and his Secretary, by the King, on their arrival at Candi. These chains do not consist of links, but of globules, which are hollow within, and pierced through in every part of their surfaces, and woven round with gold-wire, like fillagree-work. These balls are afterwards strung either upon a silken cord or gold-wire to any length that is desired. One of these chains, which is very light, well executed and ornamental, costs, on account of the smallness of its weight, little more than from twenty or thirty to forty pagods, each pagod being valued at a ducat.

November 4th, I set out from Columbo on my road to *Mature*, in company with M. Frobus, who was to perform the journey thither on the Company's account, in order to see after the packing up of Cinnamon at *Barbari*, *Gale*, and *Mature*; in the mean time that M. Sluysken made a journey to *Negumbo*, in order to superintend the packing and exportation of Cinnamon to Europe by the returning ships.

The

JOURNEY TO MATURE. 191

The journey was performed in a palanquin, which is more open, and differs in some respects from the Japanese norimon, though in most particulars it agrees with it. It has a bamboo-pole over the roof, and is carried by several Moors, who relieve each other on the road. One may both sit and lie in one of these portable chairs. It has at the ends and sides curtains to keep off the heat of the sun. It is for the most part usual to travel with six or twelve bearers.

Our rout went from Columbo to *Panture*, five miles; from thence to *Kaltere*, three miles; to *Barbary*, two miles and a half; to *Wellotte*, one mile; to *Amlagotte*, five miles; to *Hekkede*, three, and the same to *Gale*; from thence to *Belligama*, five miles, and to *Mature*, three miles and a half. The road extended along the coast, and was often incommodious and sandy.

One sees every where along the coast on this side, forests of Cocoa, which extend as far as from *Negumbo* to *Mature*, and beyond, with trees in the greatest abundance, and of incredible service to the natives, who make use of their fruits. These Cocoa-woods do not however reach far into the interior of the country, but confine themselves to the coast, and love a sandy-soil and the sea-air; insomuch, that I have often seen Cocoa-trees grow so near the strand, that they over-hung the salt billows of the sea, which
watered

watered their feet, and in fuch bare and naked fand, that not a fingle blade of grafs could grow there.

I obferved in feveral places Cocoa-leaves tied round the trees, and in this manner fupplying the place of ladders, by means of which the natives could climb up, and gather the fruit. Upon fome trees, one, upon others two of thefe ladders were tied. The fide-branches of each leaf, which were tied together, made from ten to twelve fteps. I alfo faw in fome places a rope tied between two Cocoa-trees, upon which the Cingalefe were able to pafs from one tree to another.

Oxen were ufed in carts, and were very fmall and lean. Some of them were very little larger than a European calf of two months.

There were no bridges over the rivers, fo that we were fain to crofs them in boats, which were fmall, and for that reafon were tied three together, and covered with planks, fo as to form a floating-bridge. The rivers were of confiderable breadth, very deep, and frequently had a ftrong current.

Jarrak-trees (*Jatropha Curcas*) were planted in feveral places, for quickfet hedges.

On the road we met with feveral houfes built at the Company's expence, for the purpofe of baiting and lodging at, and fometimes thefe

houfes

houses were both large and handsome. These were covered on the inside under the roof with linen, with which likewise the chairs as well as the table were covered on our arrival. Exclusively of this, the room was ornamented with various elegant flowers, such as the *Gloriosa*, *Areca*, *Lycopodium cernuum*, *Ixora*, &c. Before the house itself likewise divers pillars were erected in two rows, entwined with young Cocoa-leaves, decorated with flowers, and covered with linen. On our arrival before the house, a piece of linen was spread on the ground, and the palanquin set down upon it. After this linen was spread out for us to walk upon all the way to the house. This honour is commonly paid to the Europeans, when they travel in the Company's service and on its concerns.

On the 5th we arrived at *Caltere*, where a fort is built, in which a Lieutenant commands.

In the afternoon we travelled farther to *Barbary*, whither the Cinnamon is delivered in from all the circumjacent tracts, and where there are several warehouses built of stone, as well for the purpose of storing it, as for the preparation of *Cair*, or a sort of Cloth, made of the fibres of the Cocoa. Just before them, in the harbour, the ships are able to anchor and ride in safety, at this time, for the purpose of taking in Cinnamon.

On the 6th, 319 bales of Cinnamon were shipped, among which were some of cultivated Cinnamon.

On the 7th, we prosecuted our journey, and arrived *on the* 8th in the evening, at Gale, a handsome town, which stands upon a projecting angle of a rock, and is strongly fortified.

The water for drinking here is not very salutary; it greatly inflates the stomach, and occasions in all probability the disease in the testicles and feet, called the Malabar disease, which is very prevalent in the town, but rarely met with out of it.

On the 9th, we took in our lading of Cinnamon at this place, and in the afternoon prosecuted our journey to *Mature,* where we arrived on the following morning. Here we shipped the same day 326 bales of Cinnamon in woollen sacks, over which was afterwards sewed a cow's hide.

Before the Cinnamon is packed up, it must always first be examined by Surgeons appointed for that purpose, as well by the Surgeon who resides at the place where the package is made, as by him that accompanies the ship. I had very frequently an opportunity, in the course of this year, to assist at this employment, and was obliged afterward, in conjunction with the others, to be responsible for the goodness of the Cinnamon. From each bundle a few sticks are

are taken out, which are examined by chewing, and by the taste. This office is very disagreeable and troublesome, because the Cinnamon deprives the tongue and lips of all the mucus with which they are covered, and causes afterwards an intolerable pain, which prevents one from going on any farther with the examination. So that one must perform this business with great caution, and at the same time eat a piece of bread and butter between whiles, which in some measure mitigates the pain. It is but seldom that one is able to hold out two or three days successively.

The superfine Cinnamon is known by the following properties, viz. in the first place, it is thin, and rather pliable; it ought commonly to be about the substance of Royal Paper, or somewhat thicker. Secondly, it is of a light colour, and rather inclinable to yellow, bordering but little upon the brown. Thirdly, it possesses a sweetish taste, and at the same time is not stronger than can be borne without pain, and is not succeeded by any after-taste.

The more the Cinnamon departs from these characteristics, the coarser, and less serviceable it is esteemed; as for instance: in the first place, if it be hard and as thick as a half-crown piece: secondly, if it be very dark or brown: thirdly, if it be very pungent and hot upon the tongue, with a taste bordering upon that of cloves, so that one cannot suffer it without pain, and so that the mucus upon the tongue is consumed by it, when one makes several trials of it: fourthly, if it has any after-taste, such as to be harsh, bitter, or mucilaginous.

Such are the sorts of Cinnamon, when they are selected from the store-houses, and sorted for exportation; but the barkers, who examine the Cinnamon-trees in the woods, and strip off the bark, speak of more and different sorts of Cinnamon, the leaves of which, in their external appearance, bear some resemblance to each other, and are not all used indiscriminately for barking, but are picked and pointed out by those that are judges of the matter. These Cinnamon-barkers are called in the Cingalese language *Schjalias*.

The sorts of Cinnamon which the Schjalias reckon, are the following ten:

1. *Rasse Curundu*, or *Penni Curundu*, i. e. Honey-Cinnamon, which is the best and most agreeable, and has large, broad, and thick leaves.

2. *Nai Curundu*, or Snake-Cinnamon (*Slange-Canel*), which approaches nearest to the former, in deliciousness of flavor, (although it does not absolutely arrive at the same degree) and has also large leaves.

3. *Capuru*.

3. *Capuru Curundu,* or Camphor-Cinnamon; this sort is only to be found in the King's lands, and from its root Camphor is distilled.

4. *Cabatte Curundu,* that is, astringent or austere Cinnamon; it has rather smaller leaves than the former sorts. These four sorts, which are all together from one and the same species of *Laurus cinnamomum,* are nothing more than varieties, nearly resembling each other, which are distinguished by the *Schjalias* merely by the taste, and are the only ones, which ought to be barked, and indeed can be barked, for good Cinnamon.

The following sorts, on the other hand, are never barked at all:

5. *Sævel Curundu,* that is, mucilaginous Cinnamon, the bark of which, when chewed, has a mucous slimy after-taste, like a Mucilage. The bark of this is soft, and of a fibrous, or stringy texture, and not so compact nor firm as that of the others: it is likewise tough, and bends easily, without immediately breaking. This is likewise a variety of the *Laurus Cinnamomum.*

6. *Dawul Curundu,* that is flat, or board Cinnamon; which name it bears, because the bark, in drying, does not roll itself up together, but remains flat. This sort is from the *Laurus Caffia.*

7. *Nica Curundu,* i. e. Cinnamon with leaves which resembles the *Nicacol,* or *Vitex negundo,* viz. in being lanceolate, or long and narrow.

This seems to be a variety of the *Laurus Camphora*.

Besides these seven sorts, they reckon yet three more, which obviously differ from the genuine Cinnamon. And indeed one may immediately see, that they can in no wise with justice be reckoned among the Cinnamon-trees. Of these I have seen one sort only, viz. the *Thorn-Cinnamon*: the other sorts are very rare, and are found only in the Emperor's domains.

8. *Caturu Curundu*, i. e. Thorn-Cinnamon (*Dorn Canel*): this is of a quite different genus from the *Laurus*, and the bark has not the least taste of Cinnamon. The leaves bear no resemblance to the *Laurus*, and the branches have thorns (*spinæ*) upon them.

9. *Mal Curundu*, or Bloom-Cinnamon, and

10. *Tompat Curundu*, i. e. Trefoil-Cinnamon: because the leaves are said to divide towards the top into three laciniæ.

Cinnamon is barked in the woods at two different seasons of the year. The first is termed the *Grand Harvest*, and lasts from April to August: the second is the *Small Harvest*, and lasts from November to the month of January.

It is in the woods on the Company's own domains, that the Schjalias seek and peel the Cinnamon bark; although it sometimes happens that they steal into the Emperor's woods, and at times go as far as within half a league of Candi, in order to fetch it; but if they chance in the latter cafe to be difcovered and taken, they muft expect to have their nofe and ears cut off.

Each diftrict or hamlet in the Company's dominions, is bound to bark and furnifh yearly a certain ftated quantity of Cinnamon; whereas the Cingalefe there have a certain portion of land rent-free, to cultivate and inhabit, with other privileges. Over a certain number of Schjalias are placed other fuperior officers, who have the infpection over them and the Cinnamon, and are likewife authorized to punifh fmall offences. Over all together is placed a European, who is called their Captain (*Hoofd der Mahabadde*, or frequently in common difcourfe Captain *Cinnamon*), who receives and is anfwerable to the Company for all the Cinnamon. He is likewife vefted with authority to try and punifh offences of a deeper die.

The barking of Cinnamon is performed in the following manner: Firft, a good Cinnamon-tree is looked out for, and chofen by the leaves and other characteriftics: thofe branches which are three years old, are lopped off with a common crooked pruning knife. Secondly, From the twigs that have been lopped off, the outfide pellicle (*epidermis*) of the bark is fcraped off with another knife, which is convex on one edge, and concave on the other, with a sharp point at the end, and sharp at both edges. Thirdly, After the bark has been scraped, the twigs are ripped up longways with the point of the knife, and the bark gradually loosened from them with the convex edge of the knife, till it can be entirely taken off. Fourthly, The bark being peeled off, is gathered up together, several smaller tubes or quills of it are inserted into the larger, and thus spread out to dry, when the bark of its own accord rolls itself up still closer together, and is then tied up in bundles, and finally carried off. All these offices are not performed by one single man, but the labour is divided among several. The Schjalias afterwards deliver the Cinnamon into store-houses, erected in several places by the Company, for that purpose, whither it is either carried by porters, or, where there are any rivers, transported in boats. Each bundle is at this time bound round with three slender rattans, and weighs about thirty pounds. In the store-houses these bundles are laid up in heaps, a separate heap for each village, and covered with basten mats.

When the ships are afterwards ready to take in their lading of Cinnamon, it is packed up, after having previously undergone an examination. Each bundle is then made nearly of the

length

length of four feet, and is weighed off to eighty-five pounds neat: although it is afterwards marked and reckoned for only eighty pounds; so that five pounds are allowed for loss by drying during the voyage. Subsequently to its being well secured and tied hard round with cords, the bundle is afterwards sewed up in two sacks, the one within the other, on which latter are marked its weight and the place where it was packed up. These sacks ought not to be made of sail-cloth, or linen, but of wool, or such as in India bear the name of *Gunjesakken*, from which the Cinnamon receives no injury in the transportation.

From the store-houses the sacks of Cinnamon are carried to the ships, and after they have been stowed in there with other goods, loose black pepper is sprinkled over them, to fill up every hole and interstice. The pepper, which is of a dry and hot quality, attracts to itself, during the voyage, the moisture of the Cinnamon, and has been found, by these means, not only to preserve the Cinnamon in its original goodness, but even to increase its strength.

Cinnamon-plantations, towards the end of the sixth, and beginning of the seventh decennium, of the present century, have, by the wise, provident, and unwearied exertions of Governor FALCK, been established in several places, where many thousands of trees have been reared in sandy fandy ground, which is the foil the beſt adapted of any to Cinnamon. At *Situwaka*, which lies on the boundaries between the Emperor's domains in Candi and the territories of the Company, there are very large Cinnamon-grounds, from whence Cinnamon has been already three times barked, and from which likewiſe this year a quantity was ſent to Europe. At *Paſs*, which is a country-ſeat belonging to the Governor, not far from Columbo, and even out before the town and fortreſs of Columbo itſelf, one may ſee ſimilar plantations. At *Kalture* and *Mature* I had now an opportunity of ſeeing with my own eyes exceedingly large plantations of Cinnamon, which had been eſtabliſhed two or three years before. When all theſe and ſeveral more of the ſame kind ſhall have attained their full growth, it will be inconceivably more convenient for the Dutch Eaſt-India Company to fetch their Cinnamon from a garden, where the trees ſtand at proper diſtances and in rows, than for the Sehjalias to creep about far and wide in the pathleſs woods to ſeek and procure it. Add to this, that the Cinnamon in the woods is greatly reduced in quantity, compared to former times; which is partly owing to this, that the portions of land which yielded the beſt Cinnamon have been taken for other uſes, and partly, that the

Cinnamon-

Cinnamon-trees in the wild forests were left without any guard.

November 13th, We set out from *Mature* on our return home, and arrived on the 14th, in the morning, at *Gale*.

On the 16th, setting out from Gale, we travelled farther on our road homewards, and arrived at Columbo on the 19th following.

After the Cinnamon in Columbo has been packed up, the distilling of the oils commence. Oil of Cinnamon, the dearest and most excellent of oils, is distilled no where but in the Company's Laboratory in Columbo, from the fragments and small pieces of Cinnamon, which break off and fall from it, during the packing of it. This dust and refuse is laid in large tubs, and a quantity of water is poured upon it, sufficient to cover it completely. In this manner it is left in several different tubs, which are got ready in daily succession, for six or eight days together, to macerate. One of these tubs commonly holds one hundred pounds weight of Cinnamon-dust. All this is poured, a little at a time, into a copper alembic, and drawn off with a slow fire. The water, called *Aqua Cinnamomi*, then comes over quite white, nearly of the colour of milk, together with the oil, which floats at top in the open glass-recipient placed underneath. A tub is distilled off every four-and-twenty hours.

During

During the whole time of distilling, two Commissaries, or Members of the Council of Justice, are appointed to be alternately present, although this is not precisely the case: but they come mostly every time that the oil is to be separated from the water. Upon this the oil is poured into a bottle, which the Commissaries seal, and keep in a chest, which is likewise sealed by them. In this manner the Apothecary cannot have access to embezzle any, unless he takes care to provide himself with some out of the recipient, before the Commissaries attend. I was at great pains to ascertain, how much oil is procured from a hundred weight of Cinnamon-dust, but constantly without effect; as it is against the Apothecary's interest to let this be known. Thus much however is certain, that Cinnamon does not yield much oil, in proportion to other spices, and that therefore such Cinnamon as is useful, cannot be employed for this purpose; but only the refuse, that cannot be sent to Europe. The oil was sold here on the spot for nine and three-fourths of a Dutch ducat per ounce. It is in the present case of a pale yellow colour, and not of a dark brown, which it generally is, when extracted from the coarser kind of Cinnamon. The other parts of the Cinnamon-tree, besides the bark, are neither used for Cinnamon, nor yet for Oil. The wood of the tree is of a loose and porous

texture,

texture, and handsome enough: when sawed into planks, it is sometimes manufactured into Caddies, and the like; but its scent does not secure it from the attacks of worms.

Jan Lopes was the name given to the *Boerhavia diffusa*, that must not be confounded with the *radix Lopes*, which is brought hither from the Coast of Malabar, and of which this year was sent to Europe by the homeward-bound ships, for the first time, on the Company's account, about three hundred pounds weight.

Moringa-root, with Long Pepper (*Piper longum*) pounded and laid on the part affected, was made use of here as a vesicatory, to raise blisters.

Calaminder was the name given to a sort of wood, which has a very handsome appearance, and of which I saw among the Dutch several elegant pieces of household furniture; as, for instance, Bureaus, Chairs, Tables, Sofas, Boxes, Caskets, &c. These took a polish as smooth as a looking-glass. The wood is so hard, that edge-tools cannot work it, but it must be rasped, and almost ground into shape; and indeed it very rarely holds together with any kind of glue. It is exceedingly fine, and at the same time brittle. In the Cingalese language, Calaminder is said to signify a black flaming tree. The heart, or woody part of it, is extremely handsome, with whitish or pale yellow and black or
brown

brown veins, streaks, and waves. In the root these waves are said to be closer and darker; for which reason the nearer a piece is taken from the root, the more valuable it is deemed; since higher up in the stem of the tree, the waves are thinner and paler. The extremities of the tree, to within one-third or half of it, are said to be fit for nothing, but to be thrown away. Ants are said not to damage it at all. I could not get to see the tree myself; but from the description I received of it, it is very tall, and sometimes so thick that three or four men cannot encompass it. From a specimen of the twigs which I sent some Cingalese to gather for me in the forests, I saw that it was a *Diospyrus ebenum*, or the same tree from which black ebony is procured.

Tame serpents are carried about by the Malabars, or Snake-Enchanters, as they are called, who, for a moderate gratuity, make them dance and play all manner of tricks. The owner caresses them, and often takes them up in his hands, and sometimes provokes them to bite. When the master plays upon a little pipe, the serpent rears its head, and twists it about in various directions to a regular tune and measure. These conjurors stroll about the country and in the towns, in the same manner as the Germans and Savoyards do in Europe,

Europe, in order to pick up a livelihood with bears and monkies.

Serpent-stones, which were in great repute, as infallible antidotes againſt the bite of Serpents, I made diligent enquiries after, in order to learn the mode of preparing them. Such were frequently brought me, and were kept up for a ſufficient length of time at a high price; ſo that thoſe which I bought up at firſt were well paid: at laſt, after I had reſolved not to purchaſe any more, and other cuſtomers were become ſcarce, I procured them a very cheap bargain; inſomuch that I was afterwards enabled, on my arrival at the Cape of Good Hope, to let my friends have them at a rix-dollar a piece. The ſtone is prepared by art, large, and nearly of the ſame ſhape as a bean, although in ſize and ſhape theſe ſtones are ſeldom found alike. It is moſt commonly roundiſh or ſomewhat inclining to the oblong form, with obtuſe edges, on one ſide as nearly as poſſible flat, and on the other, ſomewhat convex. It is prepared from the aſhes of a certain root, which is burned, and from a particular ſort of earth, ſaid to be found near *Diu.* Theſe two ingredients being mixed together, are burned a ſecond time, and reduced to a dough, which is then moulded into the form of a ſerpent-ſtone, and dried. All have not the ſame colour; thoſe which have been moſt burned, being of a lighter,

lighter, and those which are less burned, of a darker grey: most frequently they are variegated with black and grey spots. The stone is pierced through with fine holes, which however may often be seen with the naked eye, and it is at the same time so brittle, that it will fly in pieces, if it be let fall on a stone-floor. When a man happens to be bit by a serpent, one of these stones is laid upon the wound, over which it is bound tight, and left there, till all its pores are filled with the extracted poison. In this case it is said to drop off of its own accord, like a glutted leech; and if it be then steeped in sweet milk, the poison is supposed to be extracted from it; upon which the stone may be applied afresh to the wound, in case the patient is of opinion that any poison remains behind. They attribute likewise here great virtue to this stone in malignant fevers, even in putrid fevers, if a small quantity of it, being scraped fine, is taken in wine. I was informed that counterfeit serpentine stones are made in imitation of the real ones, but which possess no virtue, and therefore great attention ought to be employed in the examination of those which are genuine, and which may be known by the circumstance of their fastening on the palate and forehead, when one is warm, and likewise that on being put into water, they send up in a short time several small bubbles.

Cocoa-

Cocoa-nuts, from the Maldives, or as they are called, the *Zee-Calappers*, are said to be annually brought hither by certain messengers from thence, and presented, among other things, to the Governor. The kernel of this fruit, which greatly resembles the kernel of the ordinary Cocoa-nut, is looked upon here as a very efficacious antidote. They take of it half or even a whole drachm. It is deemed a sovereign remedy against the Flux, the Epilepsy, and Apoplexy. The inhabitants of the Maldives call it *Tavarcare*, and it seems to belong to the genus of *Borassus*.

From the ordinary Cocoa-nuts, which formed the daily food of the Indians, was pressed, in many places, a great quantity of oil. The Cocoa-nut was broken in pieces intire and in the state in which it came from the tree, between two cylinders. The oil, as long as it is fresh, is very mild, and is used for the table, in lamps, and for various other purposes, both by Europeans and Indians. From the fibrous husk, which invelopes the nut, was generally prepared cordage for sloops, and other uses, and even what to me seemed very singular, strong cables, for the use and service of the Dutch ships, when they lie in the harbour off this island.

The Indians, who have such a number of poisonous animals, juices, and fruits in their country,

country, are likewise richly provided with antidotes; among which they reckon the *Lignum Colubrinum*, *Ophiorhiza*, *Mungos*, to which the Moors add the *Rhinoceros's-horn*.

The Moors conduct themselves in the Churches (or *Mosques*) very devoutly and with great decorum. With the most exemplary devotion they offer up their prayers, during which I never once saw them turn their heads aside, and still less offer to converse with each other. In this respect they might well serve as a pattern to Christians, who but too often behave with very little decorum in the house of God, and frequently offer up their prayers with so little devotion, that a Moor would be apt to imagine, the whole of their divine service to be a mere pastime.

On account of the extensive trade which Columbo carries on with the whole coast of the Continent, as likewise in consequence of the vast numbers of Moors, who reside here on account of this commerce, I had abundant opportunities of procuring a variety of scarce and current Indian Coins.

Among the Cingalese Coins was one very remarkable, on account of its form, and it was even said to be current on the Coasts of Malabar and Coromandel. It was struck, as I was informed, by the Emperor in *Candi*, of various sizes and value, and was commonly called *Laryn*.

It

It confifts of a filver-cylinder, hammered out, which in the middle is bent together, the ends being afterwards turned up like a hook, and the upper end diftinguifhed either with certain letters, or ftars, or elfe with engravings. One of them which I procured by barter, coft twelve Dutch ftivers, and another of a fmaller fize nine; both of them were of fine filver.

In fome parts of Ceylon was dug up out of the earth itfelf a copper coin lefs than a farthing, but rather thicker, with an impreffion upon it, and Malabar characters. It was fuppofed to be a Malabar Coin, which was formerly current here.

Among the poorer fort of people were very current Copper Coins of the Dutch Company, of different fizes, and of that kind which bears upon one fide the Company's arms.

Otherwife the moft current Coin in traffic between the Europeans and Indians, were *Rupees* of gold and filver and *Pagodas*. The Rupees were here of different forts, being ftruck by feveral Princes, and confifted of whole, half, and ftill fmaller pieces. *Pagodas*, which are feldom feen in the Eaften part of India, were here extremely common. They are, with very little exception, the only Coin which bears any impreffion, and the gold in them is mixed with a fmall proportion of copper. They contain, on the nearest average, a Ducat, and pafs for two Rix-dollars, one Stiver, Dutch money. On the one fide they are convex, and on the other fomewhat flatter, refembling in appearance a peppermint-drop. One fide has a figure upon it, and the other fide, in thofe which are moft current in the Dutch Factories, has only fome embofled dots, whilft thofe which pafs in trade in the Englifh Factories, have a ftar. Great caution is neceffary not to be impofed upon with thefe Pagodas, as a great many counterfeit ones are in circulation, and are fo ftrongly gilt, that it is difficult to diftinguifh them from the true ones, except by the found.

A *Pagoda*, with the image of an Elephant upon one fide, was very fcarce to be met with. It was faid to be of great antiquity, and was larger than the common fort, and at the fame time confifted of fine gold.

The Pagodas of *Maffulipatnam*, which are brought hither from Coromandel, where they are current, have three figures upon them, confift of fine gold, and are both in whole pieces, and divided into eighteen parts.

The *Mangalor-Pagodas* are of two forts, the one old, having characters on the reverfe, and the other current, with a moon on the reverfe, and ftamped with two images on the oppofite fide;

side; it is of fine gold, and is met with in whole and half pieces.

The small Coin, for change, which otherwise was made use of here, and was likewise current on the Coasts of Malabar and Coromandel, consisted either in very small gold and silver Coin, called *Fanum*, or in copper Coins of various sizes, which have been struck by the Factories established by the Europeans.

The *Fanums* were all small and thin, of gold mixed with copper, and of silver, struck at several places, and by different Princes on the Continent. They were marked with several lines and dots on both sides. The value of them varied, according to their different contents and size.

Among the copper Coins were several different sorts, struck by Dutch, English, French, and Danes, of various sizes, thickness, impressions, and value. Some of these were likewise struck in silver at Madras, Pondicherry, and Tranquebar. To give a minute description of all these, would be too tedious and prolix; for which reason I shall rather reserve them for a separate Treatise on Indian Coins.

Two leaden Coins, somewhat larger than the Javanese, were likewise brought hither from Malabar; one of them with a round, the other with a square hole in the middle.

As were likewise two copper Coins, called *Dudu*, or *Baifa*, with the figure of an elephant on one fide, the one of a larger, the other of a fomewhat fmaller fize.

The Cingalefe Ape (*Simia Silenus*?) is called *Rollewai*, and is kept by many perfons tame in their houfes. He is eafily tamed. When he fees any of his acquaintance, he directly comes jumping to him, fawns upon him, grins, and with a peculiar kind of cry teftifies his joy. He is of a very friendly and gentle nature, and is very loth to bite any one, unlefs he is immoderately irritated. If any one kiffes and careffes a child, he feeks to do the fame; if you beat a child in his prefence, he rears himfelf up on his hind legs, grins and howls in a wretched manner, and, if let loofe, will attack the party that beats the child. He leaps fafter than he runs, becaufe his hind legs are longer. He eats fruit of every kind, as for inftance, cocoa-nuts, apples, pears, greens, potatoes, bread, &c. He is very delicate and tender, with refpect to his tail, which is longer than his body. In fize he is nearly upon a par with the *Lemur Catta*, or fomewhat larger. His body is entirely grey; although the colour fometimes borders more upon black, and fometimes more upon white, the latter particularly when he is old. His face is blackifh, bald, and very little fhaded with hair. The beard upon his chin and cheeks is white, and turned backwards; on the chin and upper lip it is short, but upon the cheeks it is upwards of an inch in length, and stands erect towards his ears, which are in some measure covered with it in front. His hands and feet are blackish, and naked; his nails long and blunt; the thumb detached and short. The breech has hard tuberosities, which are bare. The tail is round, tapering towards the extremity, hairy, and longer than the whole body, so that the animal can twist it round and hold himself by it among the branches of the trees. The tips of the ears are rounded off, almost bare of hair, and black. When he sits down, he always keeps his hands crossed over each other. I had one on board in my voyage homeward, but could not keep him alive, as he died on our coming into a colder climate, just before the Cape of Good Hope; he is exceedingly tender, not being able to support the least degree of cold.

SECOND JOURNEY TO MATURE.

DECEMBER 7th, I made a second journey from Columbo to Mature, at the instigation of the Governor, to visit Count *Rantzow*'s Lady, who
laboured

laboured under a fevere and tedious illnefs. Count *Rantzow* was Comptroller of this Factory of the Company, and fhewed me great favours during the few weeks of my abode here. I travelled both day and night in a palanquin, borne by twelve ftout Moors, who fupported the whole journey, without refting, fo that I made the journey in the fpace of three days.

I daily made excurfions in the vicinity of this place, and as the precious ftones of the ifland are found and dug up more efpecially in thefe parts, I procured the proper intelligence, as well concerning the different kinds of them, as the manner in which they are fought for and made ufe of. Several of them are exported to Europe, quite in their rough ftate, but the major part are polifhed and fometimes fet here, and afterwards fold in India itfelf. It was generally the occupation of the poorer fort of Moors to cut and polifh them, which was done upon a plate of lead, and for a very moderate charge. I purchafed of the Moors fuch forts as were to be met with, not only in their polifhed, but likewife in their rough ftate; the latter, in order to be preferved among other collections of Foffils. At firft I was obliged to pay very dear for them, efpecially as I then had my choice of them, and felected them, as I pleafed; but in the fequel I found,

found, that I could procure them much cheaper, by taking them one with another in the lump.

The Minerals and precious Stones which I had an opportunity of meeting with and collecting, were the following, viz.

Iron-ore is found interlarded in earth and clay, and that sometimes to a considerable depth under ground. It is melted in crucibles over a fire, which is blown with two bellows. The scoria is separated from it with tongs made expressly for the purpose, and the melted mass is poured into a mould made of clay, after which it is purified farther, and forged for smaller uses.

Mica (or Glimmer) in large laminated masses, is called *Mirinan* by the Cingalese. The shivers of this are used for ornamenting Talpats or Umbrellas, made of large Talpat (*Licuala*) leaves.

Plumbago, called by the Cingalese *Kalu Miniran*, is found along with Mica, at the foot of mountains, in clay and red earth, most frequently at a considerable depth. Plumbago is sometimes likewise met with by itself in a dry soil.

Stahlstein, or crystallized Pyrites, which contains a little copper, is used for making buttons of.

In Ceylon all such Stones as are transparent and sufficiently hard to take a polish by grinding, are called precious Stones. These are known to the Moors from Malabar and Mogol, as likewise to the Cingalese and the Dutch that live in
their

their country, by the following Dutch, Malabar, and Cingalese names:

The *Ruby*, Robyn, Malab. *Elinges Chogeppu*, and Cingal. *Lankaratte*; is a genuine Ruby.

The *Amethyst*, Malab. and Cingal. *Scuandi*; is a purple-coloured Mountain Cryftal.

Robals, Malab. *Rauwa*, Cingal. *Rawa*; are fmall tranfparent Garnets of a dark-red colour.

Hyacinths, which are made to pafs for Rubies.

The *Red Tourmalin*, Malab. *Pani turemali*, Cingal. *Penni turemali*; is a Quartz inclining to a red colour.

The *Blue Saphire*, Malab. *Nilem*, and Cingal. *Nile*; is a genuine blueifh coloured Saphire, frequently with blue fpots.

The *Blue Tourmalin*, Malab. and Cingal. *Nile turemali*; is a Quartz, in colour inclining a little to blue.

The *Green Saphire*, in the Malabar and Cingalefe languages called *Patje Padian*, is a genuine Saphire.

The *Green Tourmalin*, or Maturefe Diamond, Malab. and Cingal. *Patje Turemali*, is a name given both to Chryfolites with tetraedal prifms, and even fometimes to the Chryfopras.

The *Topaz*, Malab. *Pureffjeragen*, and Cingal. *Purperagan*, is a genuine Topaz.

The *Cinnamon-stone*, Cingal. and Malab. *Komedegam*, is a fine flame-coloured or yellowifh-brown Garnet.

The

The *Yellow Tourmalin*, or Maturese Diamond, Malab. and Cingal. *Kaneke Turemali*, is a Topez of a greenish-yellow colour.

The *White Tourmalin*, or Maturese Diamond, Malab. and Cingal. *Sudu Turemali*, is a Topaz of a pale yellow colour.

The *White Cryſtal*, Malab. *Wille Palingu*, Cingal. *Sudu Palingu*, is a tranſparent and colourleſs mountain Cryſtal.

White Saphires, or *Water-Saphires*, Malab. *Wille Padjan*, Cingal. *Sudu Padjan*, are ſmall fragments and ſhivers of the moſt tranſparent white mountain Cryſtals.

The *Taripo*, is a milk-coloured Quartz.

The *Yellow Cryſtal*, Malab. *Manjel Palingu*, Cingal. *Kaha Palingu*, is a lighter coloured ſmoky Topaz.

The *Brown Cryſtal*, Malab. and Cingal. *Tillia Palingu*, is a ſmoky mountain Cryſtal, or a dark coloured ſmoky Topaz.

The *Black Cryſtal*, Malab. *Karte Palingu*, Cingal. *Kallu Palingu*, partly in cryſtals, partly in fragments, is the Electrical Tourmalin of Ceylon.

The *Cat's-eye*, Malab. and Cingal. *Wairodi*, is a Pſeudo-Opal.

The Ruby is more or leſs ripe, which, according to the Indian mode of expreſſion, means, more or leſs high-coloured. The Amethyſt is violet,

violet, but the Ruby is red, and for the most part blood-red. The deeper red the colour, the larger the stone, and the clearer it is without any flaw, so much the greater is its value. However they are seldom found here of any considerable size, for the most part they are small, frequently of the size of particles of gravel, grains of barley, &c. The higher the colour, the clearer and more transparent they are. The unripe are not so clear, and sometimes those that are more saturated, are found with spots or streaks in them; some of these latter approach very near to a violet colour. Most of them are round and flat, from having been agitated and rolled about in the water; some I have found crystallized with eight sides, of which four were broad, and four very small, and terminated by two points, consisting of four sides each. The Moors say that these approach nearest to the Diamond in hardness, and polish them, in order to render them fit for being set in rings.

The Amethyst is, in fact, no other than a violet-coloured mountain-crystal, which differs very much in the degrees in which it is coloured. Among these one finds some that are almost white, with so faint a tinge of violet, that, if they were found by themselves, one would rather take them for mountain-crystals, especially one that was no great connoisseur in these matters. Others are

found

found to be tinged towards one end; others only in the middle, and others again in spots and patches, and that in a greater or less degree. Some are so saturated, that, when they lie on a table, they appear almost black, and exhibit, when held up to the light, a very beautiful violet colour. Frequently as well the spots as the streaks are seen to be in some parts paler and in others of a more saturated colour, in specks and patches. They are of various sizes, seldom so large as a walnut, and for the most part very small. The larger they are, the paler and the less coloured they are, and therefore the less valued and esteemed. The small ones have in general the deepest colour, but yet are of no great value, as they furnish only small stones for cutting. The dearest and most valuable are those which are high-coloured, without flaws, and of some tolerable size. The more saturated the colour is in them, the more ripe they are called, and on the other hand unripe, the paler they are. It is beyond a doubt, that these were originally in a fluid state, and previous to their crystallization, were tinged with a violet colour, which incorporated itself either with a part, or else with the whole of the fluid. Some are found rounded off at the angles, and by the rolling about in the water have contracted a high polish; others are of an irregular figure, broken on every fide, frequently with deep and large impreffions; fome have fix fides, and one hexagonal point. Not one was I able to find quite perfect and undamaged. It is very feldom that one meets with any which have both their ends; though even in that cafe they have always received fome damage from external violence. Some have very long violet ftreaks variegated with ftreaks of white. The largeft are generally cut into buttons for waiftcoats, which, in the Eaft-Indies, it is much the fafhion to wear of white linen; and thofe that are of an inferior fize, are manufactured into jacket and fleeve-buttons.

The *Robal* is a dark-red ftone, darker than the Ruby, and not fo hard. It appears moft opaque in a lying pofition, when it is highly faturated. Thefe are moftly found in fmall pieces, which are rounded off at the angles, and worn fmooth by friction. They are cut for fetting in rings, and are frequently expofed to fale for Rubies.

Hyacinths are fmall yellowifh-brown or reddifh prifms, which, as well as Robals, are frequently offered for fale under the denomination of Rubies.

The *Red Tourmalin*, when laid down upon a table or other fupport, appears dark and opaque, but, being held againft the light, is of a pale red hue. The largeft I could procure are of the fize of a pea, but moft of them are fmaller,

about

about the size of a grain of rice. Here and there I met with one crystallized, but in general they are always damaged and imperfect. They seem to have had four similar sides on their oblong column, and a quadrangular pyramid. Most of them are worn smooth and polished from their agitation in the water. The colour is in general equally distributed in every part, and seldom paler or more saturated in one place than in another.

The *Blue Saphire* is, as well as other Cingalese coloured stones, ripe or unripe in different degrees, that is, more or less of a deep blue cast. Sometimes they are so pale, that they almost exhibit the appearance of water, and it is more seldom that they are dark blue. They are however more uniformly coloured than Amethysts, without spots and streaks; although I saw one which was quite of a light blue colour at one end, and dark blue at the other. All those which I saw had been worn smooth by their agitation in the water, into round and various other shapes. I have met with one as large as a hazle-nut; but most of them are many times smaller. They are all made use of, when cut, for buttons and rings.

The *Blue Tourmalin* is nothing but a Quartz, with a tinge of blue.

The *Green Saphire* occurs of a bright green, a greenish, and a pale whitish colour, and is a

genuine

genuine Saphire, which, as well as the former, is fit for cutting, and applied to that purpose.

The *Green Tourmalin* is of a dark hue, sometimes bordering a little upon yellow, sometimes upon blue, sometimes upon green, and most frequently upon black. It is in not a few instances transparent, in others covered with an opaque surface; sometimes it is totally opaque, like Shirl, of a shining and frequently tortuous fracture, with many flaws longways and across. Sometimes it is found in a crystallized state, with an oblong shaft of four similar sides, and a quadrangular point, but mostly occurs worn down and broken in thick or thin pieces of an irregular form, sometimes as large as a walnut, sometimes as small as groats. The Green, or Chrysoprase is beautiful, of a grass-green colour, clear and transparent, and is used for cutting. This is the mineral properly called Green Tourmalin, although this name is likewise given to several other species.

The *Topaz*, properly so called, occurs mostly in yellowish splinters, and is a more or less dark genuine Topaz.

The *Cinnamon-stone* derives its name from its colour, which in some measure resembles the oil drawn from the best and finest Cinnamon. It is not however always alike, but more or less pale, or of a deep orange-colour. One seldom finds any of these stones of a considerable size,

which

which are undamaged; but they are in general, even the small ones, cracked longways and across, which destroys their clearness, and renders them unfit for cutting. These flaws occasion it to fall into squares and oblique laminæ. Sometimes it resembles, in some measure, Gum Benzoe. When cut, it produces very beautiful stones, especially for rings, stock and other buckles.

The *Yellow Tourmalin* is called likewise Tourmalin Topaz, by the Moors, because it sometimes bears a great resemblance in colour to the Topaz. In appearance it is very much like Amber. Some are more saturated or ripe, almost of an orange colour; some are of a paler and some of a whitish yellow. I never saw it in a crystallized state, but always worn smooth, by being agitated in the water, and from the size of a grain of rice to that of a pea. They are cut for the purpose of setting in rings, and are exceedingly handsome.

The *White Tourmalin* is that which is properly called the Maturese Diamond. It is more or less white, almost always of the colour of milk, so that its transparency is not perfectly clear. For this reason it is frequently calcined in the fire, in consequence of which the colour vanishes, and the stone becomes much clearer, although not perfectly white. It is then enveloped in fine lime, and burned with rice-chaff (oryza).

One often finds pieces which have spots or streaks in them. They are mostly found worn smooth by the water, and sometimes crystallized, with an oblong shaft, which has four similar sides and a tetraedral point. It is cut for setting in rings, especially for a border round other larger stones, and for sleeve and small jacket-buttons. It is among the most common stones in Ceylon, and not extremely dear.

White crystal is found here both crystallized and worn smooth by the water, in uneven, flat, and long pieces, full of pits and hollows. The colour is clear, more or less of a watery hue, or shining white. The smaller pieces I have often seen with their column and pyramids. The larger ones have been generally worn smooth by agitation in the water. It sometimes is of the size of two doubled fists. Of it are cut waistcoat and jacket-buttons, stones for buttons, for drawers, and for setting in shoe-buckles, &c.

Water-Saphire is the name of a stone, which very much resembles white crystal, but, when viewed against the light, is both clearer and whiter; it is especially distinguishable by its hardness, in which it surpasses the Crystals. I could never procure any of those which had their sides and points, but they had always been worn down by the water into shapeless pieces, or else flat and rounded off, with a rugged surface, full of small

small impressions like dots. The largest I saw had been of the size of a walnut. They are much dearer than Crystals, and are cut for waistcoat and jacket-buttons, and for shoe-buckles.

Taripo is the name given in Ceylon to a white stone, which in all probability is nothing more than a Quartz or white Crystal. Its colour is pure white, or somewhat of a watery cast, but not so clear and transparent as the Crystal, but rather like a Quartz. I have never seen it crystallized, but always in shapeless lumps. Of these likewise stones are cut for setting.

The *Yellow Crystal* is probably the same as the white, only with this distinction, that it appears of a disagreeable yellowish colour. I never saw it crystallized, but always worn down smooth by the agitation of the water into round pieces, with a rough knobby surface.

The *Brown Crystal* distinguishes itself from the former merely by its being of a blackish cast, or of the colour of pale ink. When laid down upon any substance, it does not seem to be transparent, but may be seen through, if viewed against the light. The specimens I saw were always rounded off in pieces as large as a large hazle-nut or small walnut, in consequence of the agitation they had undergone in the water. The surface is rough, in consequence of the fine dots impressed on it, and a grey crust, which sometimes

times renders it impervious to the light, when in its intire state, although the inside is transparent, as appears when the stone is broken in pieces. It is cut into buttons for drawers, and other uses.

The *Black Cryſtal* is a quite black, shining, but not transparent Shirl. It is often found broken into shapeless pieces, round or oblong, being worn smooth by agitation in the water. It is of a shining fracture, and falls into slate-like shivers, which are transparent at the edges. Of this I have seen pieces as large as a walnut, and others quite small, like a pea. Some I was able to meet with, which were cryſtalline, although not altogether undamaged, with six diſſimilar sides and an obtuse triangular point. They are cut and polished for buttons, which are worn upon jackets and upon the clothes of those who are in mourning. They bear a great resemblance to canel-coal buttons. This Cryſtal is very common, and not of any great price or value. I could not observe, that the Indians were acquainted with its electrical properties, which they never denote by the name of Tourmalin, but bestow that denomination upon several other species.

Cat's-eye is the name given to a very hard stone, which approaches more or less to white or green, and is semi-diaphanous, with a streak of
the

the breadth of a line in the middle, which streak is much whiter than the stone itself, and throws its light to what side soever this is turned. In this respect therefore it resembles a cat's eye, whence it derives its name. The largest I saw was of the size of a hazle-nut, others are found much smaller. In its rough state it seems to have no angles nor signs of crystallization. Its value is in proportion to its size and purity. One of the size of a nut, without flaws and other imperfections, is sometimes valued at fifty or sixty rix-dollars and upwards. They are cut convex and oblong, without faces, so that the streak, which intersects them, comes in the middle, and they are afterwards set in rings, which are worn by the Malabars and Moors.

From these descriptions it may be seen, that the stone known in Europe, under the name of Tourmalin, and celebrated for its electrical virtues, is not known by the same name to the Indians; but that they denote by the word Tourmalin, several stones, which possess no electrical properties, and which are even of different species, of different colours, and of different degrees of transparency.

Most of these stones I shewed to Professor BERGMAN, who very kindly furnished me with their mineralogical names.

It is chiefly the Moors who fell thefe ftones in Columbo, Gale, and Mature, both in their rough ftate, and after they have been polifhed and fet: but a ftranger ought to be very cautious how he deals with them; as well becaufe they are apt to afk extravagantly more than the ordinary price, as alfo becaufe they often impofe upon the purchafer with glafs-fluors and ftones cut by them, which they manage with fuch art and dexterity, that one that is not ufed to them is eafily duped.

All thefe precious ftones, which are found in Ceylon, more efpecially occur in the region round Mature, in the vallies and at the foot of the mountains, in a compound of earth and fat clay. Several different forts are found in the fame foil and the fame place. Sometimes they are found likewife upon the furface of the earth, when they are wafhed off from the mountains by a violent rain or a ftrong current of water.

In fome places one finds ftones without much trouble, at the depth of one, two, or three feet beneath the furface, whilft, on the other hand, in other places, one muft dig to the depth of twenty feet and more. When one is within the reach of water, the work goes on much eafier, becaufe the wafhing can then take place upon the fpot; the earth dug up being put into a large rattan-bafket, which is kept in water, that the earth may be feparated. For this reafon, thofe

pits

pits, which lie near rivulets, though they are not the richest, are considered as the least troublesome.

The digging of precious stones in the circumjacent district of Mature is farmed out annually in the month of August, to the highest bidder, on account of the Dutch East-India Company. In 1777 and 1778 a Moor is said to have farmed it for 180 rix-dollars. The land farmed out for digging does not always lie in one contiguous stretch or tract, but different spots, scattered up and down in different parts, are sought out, which are found to contain stones. Before they are farmed out, these spots are inspected by Commissioners on the Company's account. To such portions of land appertain frequently the gardens of the Cingalese, which in this case are not free to be dug. One and the same tract of land can be hired out, and consequently dug several times. In general and chiefly such plots of ground are chosen for this purpose, as lie contiguous to mountains, and more especially to rivulets, on account of the washing. Afterwards the Farmer-General frequently sells licences to several others to dig with a certain number of men; for instance, for fifteen rix-dollars, to those who employ ten men, and so in proportion for five or twenty men. These have the privilege of digging the whole year, and whereever they pleafe, but not with more men than they pay for to the Farmer-General. Thofe who purchafe the privilege of digging, have, exclufive of this, to pay their diggers themfelves. What is got every month after digging and wafhing, is put into a bag, which is fealed up, and fent home to the Proprietor, who then has to felect and arrange the ftones, which, with more or lefs profit to himfelf, he has been able to acquire.

The *Ficus Religiofa* is called by the Dutch *Duyvel's-boom*, or Devil's-tree, and by the Cingalefe *Boga*. The latter regard it as a facred tree, becaufe they believe that the God *Budu* repofes under it; for which reafon they never fell one of thefe trees, but, on the contrary, make their moft folemn vows under it. Whenever they have taken an oath, or entered into any covenant under fuch a tree, one may reft affured of their obfervance of it.

Leeches (*birudines*) are found in abundance in the woods, efpecially near the fummit of a mountain. Thefe are of a reddifh-brown colour, of the thicknefs of a knitting-needle, and an inch in length. When one is walking in thefe places, they faften on the feet, and can fuck out the blood through two pair of cotton ftockings. Count RANTZOW informed me, that a European, on whom one of thefe leeches had faftened,

pulled

pulled it forcibly off, and afterwards loft his life in confequence of that, and a neglect in the cure.

The *Hyſtrix* (or Porcupine) is found in plenty in the woods, and the Dutch frequently hunt this animal with dogs. His ſharp quills faſten in the bodies of the dogs, when they ruſh too eagerly upon him, ſo that it is not uncommon for them to loſe their lives in the purſuit. The animal makes its abode and burrow in the ground, the entrance to which is no larger than to admit a moderate-ſized hunting-dog to creep into it, and drive the animal out at another aperture of the ſame burrow. The *Hyſtrix* has frequently Bezoar-ſtones in its ſtomach, which here, ſcraped to a fine powder, are adminiſtered in all kinds of diſorders. Theſe ſtones conſiſt of very fine hair, which has concreted with the juices of the ſtomach, and have one layer over the other, ſo that they conſiſt of ſeveral rings of different colours. I have ſeen them of the ſize of a hen's egg, moſt commonly blunt at the end; but one I had an opportunity of ſeeing, which was as large as a gooſe's egg, perfectly globular, and all over brown.

I was informed, that the *Hyſtrix* has a very curious method of fetching water for its young, viz. the quills in the tail are ſaid to be hollow, and to have a hole at the extremity; and that the animal can bend them in ſuch a manner, as that

that they can be filled with water, which afterwards is discharged in the nest among its young.

Scorpions abound here in great numbers, although it is seldom that any detriment is experienced from them. When it rains, one may often see these animals, as well as the *Scolopendra morsitans*, sally forth from their hiding-places, and creep in shoals into those houses, the doors of which are left open on account of the heat.

The Stink-tree was called by the Dutch *Strunt-hout*, and by the Cingalese *Urenne*, on account of its disgusting odour, which resides especially in the thick stem and the larger branches. The smell of it so perfectly resembles that of human ordure, that one cannot perceive the smallest difference between them. When the tree is rasped, and the raspings are sprinkled with water, the stench is quite intolerable. It is nevertheless taken internally by the Cingalese, as an efficacious remedy. When scraped fine, and mixed with lemon-juice, it is taken internally, as a purifier of the blood in the itch, and other cutaneous eruptions, the body being at the same time anointed with it externally. I was at great pains to procure some blossoms of this tree, in order to ascertain its genus, but was constantly disappointed. Of the Cingalese, whom I sent out for that purpose far up the country into the woods, I could only obtain some branches without any blossom, from which, however, I could perceive, that the tree was neither the *Anagyris fœtida*, nor the *Sterculia fœtida*. I had likewise set some live but small plants of this tree in boxes, and carried them with me alive quite to the English Channel, where they were totally destroyed, together with several other scarce trees and plants, by cold and storms. Of the wood I carried with me some pieces to my native country, which, however, afterwards lost their scent to that degree, that now not the smallest traces of it can be perceived.

Another kind of tree was called the *Serpent-tree*, by the Dutch *Slangen-hout*, and by the Cingalese *Godagandu*, which had a very bitter taste. It was not only used as an efficacious antidote against the bite of Serpents, but likewise in ardent and malignant fevers. The Europeans have cups turned of the wood, into which wine is poured, which, in a short time, extracts the virtue from the wood, has a bitter taste, and is drank as a stomachic, or strengthener of the stomach. Water likewise extracts a green tincture from it. Most probably this tree is the *Ophioxylon Serpentinum*, which grows here, although I had no opportunity of seeing any of the flowers. The wood itself resembles that of the Oak, by its grey colour, and numerous small
pores,

pores, which, in the cups that are turned from it, frequently let the water filter through them.

The Shingles (*Herpes*) are cured here with the Capsules of the *Hibiscus Tiliaceus*, by rubbing the juice of them over the eruption. This beautiful tree is planted at Columbo and other places, in alleys, continues in bloom for several months together, and with the varying hues of its lovely blossoms is a great ornament and embellishment to the spot.

From the root of the *Capuru Curundu*, Camphor is said to be distilled in Candia, which is the capital of the island, and the residence of the Emperor of Ceylon. It is situated upon an eminence, almost in the centre of the country. Not far off stands a very high mountain, which rears up in the air a still higher summit. The mountain bears the name of *Adam's Mountain*, and the summit is commonly called *Adam's Peak*, where Adam, the father of the human race, is supposed to lie buried. The Cingalese make pilgrimages to this place, and pretend that the impression of Adam's foot is still to be perceived in the mountain.

The *Ophiorhiza Mungos*, called *Mendi*, is used by the Indians against the bite of Serpents. The leaves and bark are said to be boiled and taken in the form of a decoction.

The

The *Ophioglossum scandens,* a creeping plant, that twines round the trees, is here made ufe of in feveral places as a fubftitute for Ivy, to cover pales and garden-fences with, and defend them againft the fea-wind. The pales are covered with it on the outward fide, and confift themfelves of nothing more than a number of fmall ftakes driven into the earth, clofe to each other.

I faw *Cocoa-trees* alfo ftuck in the water, like poles, and was told, that they would laft a whole century, without going to decay, although this appeared to me incredible.

The *Sciurus Ceilanicus* was not fcarce, but kept by feveral people in their houfes tame in a cage. It is called by the iflanders *Rockia,* or *Ruckia,* and is black on the back and fides, and yellowifh under the belly. The tail is likewife black, and longer than the body. This Squirrel, which at this time was altogether unknown in Europe, and has fince been defcribed by Mr. PENNANT, is very eafily tamed, and is as large as a cat, but more flender in the body.

On the 28th I travelled from *Mature* to Columbo, in company with the young Count RANTZOW, who was now going on a vifit to his brother, and failed as Gunner on board a Dutch fhip. This youth, who was of a very hafty difpofition, had, at the fame time, the misfortune to be lame in his feet. Notwithftanding this defect,

defect, he had learned to fence with great skill, and, in spite of his crooked legs and thighs, to dance incomparably well. We arrived in safety at Columbo, on the evening of the new year.

Soon after the new year, according to annual custom, three Ambassadors from the Emperor in Candi, arrived in Columbo. These were received on the part of the Company by Deputies at *Situvaka*, and, the usual ceremonies of congratulation having passed, were conducted to the old Town, without the fortifications, where they were quartered, and remained, till the day appointed for public audience.

February 5th was fixed for sending an Embassy to the Emperor, on part of the Company, which Embassy consisted of a Merchant and two Clerks.

About this time was celebrated, with much pomp and rejoicing, the installation of the Governor-General, in Batavia, in his high office, intelligence of his nomination having arrived from Europe. The joy of the day was testified by the discharge of cannon from the ramparts and the ships, and the evening was spent in dancing and diversions, with a public supper in the Governor's palace, to which all the public Functionaries and naval Officers were formally invited, together with the Ladies of distinction in the town.

Among

Among the various kinds of Cottons and Chintzes, which are brought hither from Coromandel, those appear to me to merit the preference, which come from Suratte and Bengal, of which the latter seem to be the most beautiful. From *Tutucorin* I saw likewise some which were not printed, but had flowers painted upon them with a hair-pencil, after the manner of Tapestry. It is incredible to what a degree of fineness Cotton is sometimes spun upon the Indian coast. I had an opportunity of seeing Cotton-stuffs so exceedingly fine, that half a dozen shirts could be squeezed together in one hand. These are however not readily made use of, but are kept as rarities by people of distinction, to shew to what a degree of perfection the art of spinning can be brought.

Some differences had arisen on the coast of Malabar, which obliged the Governor to send some troops from this place to Cochim. And as preparations were now making for this purpose, the Governor was pleased to propose to me to make a journey to the Continent of Africa with this expedition, although the ship in which I had come hither lay ready to sail on her return to Europe. But as I had already in Batavia formed the determination to revisit Europe, I requested, instead of the proffered favour, his Excellency's kind permission to exchange my place

place with another ship's Surgeon, and to remain still a month longer upon this beautiful island, and by this means to have an engagement on board one of the ships, which were to sail from hence in February; which request was graciously accorded me.

January 17th, 1778, I undertook a journey, in company with Messrs. SLUYSKEN and CONRADI, to *Negumbo*, at which place we arrived the following day. This is a small fortified place, with a gate of brick-work, and ramparts of earth, where an Ensign is stationed in quality of Commandant.

On the 19th, a quantity of Cinnamon was packed up, during which time, in company with a Cingalese, I undertook a journey on horseback somewhat further up the country, to see an *Elephant-toil*, or snare, which served for capturing and inclosing a great number of Elephants. The toil was constructed of stout Cocoa-trees, almost in the form of a triangle, the side nearest to the wood being very broad, and augmented with slighter trees and bushes, which gradually expanded themselves into two long and at length imperceptible wings. The narrower end was strongly fortified with stakes, planted close to each other, and held firmly together by ropes, and became at length so narrow, that only one single elephant could squeeze itself into the opening.

opening. When the Governor gives orders for an Elephant-chace on the Company's account, which happens at the expiration of a certain stated number of years, it is performed in the following manner: a great multitude of men, as well Europeans as Cingalese, are sent out into the woods, in the same manner in which people go out on a general hunt for wolves and bears in the North of Europe. These diffuse themselves, and encompass a certain extent of land, which has been discovered to be frequented by Elephants. After this they gradually draw nearer, and with great noise, vociferation, and beat of drum, contract the arch of the circle; in the mean time that the Elephants approach nearer and nearer to the side on which the toil is placed. Finally, torches are lighted up, in order to terrify still more these huge animals, and force them to enter into the toil prepared for them. As soon as they are all come into it, the toil is closed up behind them. The last time that Elephants were caught in this manner, their number amounted to upwards of a hundred, and on former occasions has sometimes risen to one hundred and thirty.

The major part of the Elephants, which are caught in the manner related above, are afterwards sold at Jasnapatnam, to the Princes of Coromandel. So that the first care of the captors

captors is, to bring them out of the toil, and to tame them. For this purpose one or two tame Elephants are placed at the side where the opening is, through which each Elephant is let out singly, when he is immediately bound fast wi.h strong ropes to the tame ones, who discipline him with their probofces, till he likewife becomes tame, and suffers himfelf to be handled and managed at pleafure. This difciplinary correction frequently proceeds very briskly, and is fometimes accomplifhed in a few days, especially as the wild Elephant is at the fame time brought under controll by hunger. After thefe large and powerful animals have been in this manner brought forth and tamed, it remains to view and meafure them; which latter operation is performed in a place paved fmooth and even with corals; on this they are arranged in due order, and meafured with a long rod, by a man who rides between their ranks, fitting upon a tame Elephant. The review and examination of them extends over the whole body, in order to difcover whether they have any natural or acquired blemifh. After this a defcription is drawn up, expreffive as well of the height as of the blemifhes of each, and according to the fize and perfections of the animal is its value eftimated. The meafure is computed by *Covidos*, three of which conftitute four feet. The admeafurement is made from the ground to

the

the shoulder-blade; and in general an Elephant stands ten *Covidos*, or about fourteen feet high. A tame Elephant is commonly sold for 200 rix-dollars; but if it has any blemish, for instance, if its tail has been plucked off, one of its ears slit, if some of the nails be wanting on its feet, or if it has suffered any other kind of damage, they deduct from the purchase-money for every defect, from 50 to 60 or 80 rix-dollars, according to the different nature and importance of the blemish. And as it is very rare to find an Elephant free from every kind of blemish, those that are so, are most commonly sold for from 500 to 1,000 rix-dollars. When the time arrives for holding the auction, it is customary for two, three, or more persons, to purchase conjointly 50, 60, 80, or 100 Elephants, which they afterwards dispose of in separate lots, with great profit. Previous to the sale, the Elephants are marked on the rump with the Company's arms. For this purpose the animal is bound fast to a strong tree, and burned with red-hot iron.

The Elephant is incontestably one of the most sagacious and gentle animals in nature, an animal which, notwithstanding its unparallelled size and strength, very readily suffers itself to be tamed, and trained to various useful services. When he is brought into trouble and distress, he whines almost like a child, and learns, when tamed, in a very short time, to understand what is said to him. When he is first caught, he pines away with grief and anxiety, especially if he was tame before, and has had a good master. It sometimes happens, at such a hunt as I have just described, that tame Elephants, belonging to the Emperor in Candia, and which have been turned loose to graze in the woods, are caught with the rest. In this case it is often impossible to prevail with them, whilst they are in the toil, to eat or take any kind of nourishment, before the arrival of the servants who are accustomed to tend them, whom they not only recognize, but, when let loose, follow. The Elephant is very fond of the fruit of the Pisang-tree, as likewise of Cocoa-nuts, whether these are given him broken or whole, and in the latter case he cracks them himself. The young sucks the dam with the mouth, and not with its trunk, and many experiments made by M. SLUYSKEN have ascertained its daily proportion of drink to be commonly forty-five gallons of water. The females, when tame, are sometimes employed to catch wild Elephants, for which purpose they are turned loose in the woods, and from hence allure the wild males to some toil, where they can be inclosed. Males, caught in this manner, I have more than once seen bound to a large and stout tree, and at the expiration of a few days become

tame.

tame. The male Elephants, which the Dutch make use of to discipline and tame the wild ones they have captured, are commonly called Kidnappers (*Zeelverkooper*). When an Elephant has once been properly tamed, he may be governed even by a child, and does not willingly injure any one, provided he is not ill-treated, and thereby spurred on to revenge. I have frequently seen him bend one of his legs, in order to let his rider climb up by it, as it were by a step, on his back, and likewise take up little boys very carefully with his trunk, and place them upon his back, and take them down again. The Dutch East-India Company make use of Elephants every where to transport beams and other heavy articles, as likewise for carriages and large carts. When he is harnessed to any such vehicle, a strong rope is always bound round his neck, to which another strong rope is fastened on either side, which runs along the sides near the back, and is made fast to the tackling of the carriage. In case two Elephants are harnessed to the same carriage, a pole runs between them. When the Elephant moves, one may clearly perceive, that he bends the knee-joint, notwithstanding that the whole leg otherwise appears to be of an equal thickness, and inflexible. The proboscis is not only a great ornament to this stately animal, but at the same time one of its moſt neceſſary inſtruments, for gathering in its food, drinking, and laying hold of all ſorts of things; for which reaſon he is very careful of it, and will upon no account ſuffer any ant to come upon it.

The Elephant is never, or at leaſt very ſeldom, ſhot in this country, as they prefer catching it alive; neither does one find here any great Elephant-hunters. I was informed that upon a female, which was bound faſt to a tree, thirteen ſhot were fired from a common muſket, before ſhe fell. The reaſon for killing her was, for the ſake of cutting out the fœtus, with which ſhe was pregnant, in order to ſend it, preſerved in arrack, to his Royal Highneſs the Hereditary Stadtholder's Collection of Natural Curioſities at the Hague. That the wild ones in the woods, however, are ſometimes fired upon, ſeems evident from a circumſtance, of which I was informed by M. Frobus, viz. that he had ordered one of the teeth of an Elephant, that had been caught, to be ſawed through, in which he found a common leaden bullet, which had lodged in the tooth, and in proceſs of time was ſo totally incloſed and covered over, that externally no marks of it could be perceived. This tooth he ſent likewiſe in the year 1765, to the above-mentioned Collection at the Hague. As the Ceyloneſe Elephants are ſo eaſily caught and tamed, it ſeems extraordinary,

extraordinary, that many obstacles should lie in the way of those that make similar attempts at the Cape in Africa. And yet, in 1775, shortly before my departure from thence, a young one had been taken alive, after the dam was shot, and the attempt was made, though without success, to rear it. It had need of the milk of three cows daily for its support, but could not be preserved alive.

After I had minutely examined the large and extensive toil, which was constructed for the capture of such a considerable number of these large animals, I returned back to the companions of my journey, and arrived at *Negumbo* towards evening. In the way I had the pleasure, which I now least expected, to find that beautiful plant, the *Burmannia disticha*, which I had for the space of five months both sought for diligently myself, and likewise exhorted many of the Cingalese to look out and procure for me. It grew in the low lands, and places in the woods, that were still covered with water, and had lately began to expand its blue flowers. I gathered as much of it, as was to be found in this place, and laid it up to dry, as well for my worthy patron and benefactor, Professor BURMANNUS, as for others of my much loved and truly respectable friends in Europe. It is called by the Cingalese *Wilende Wenne*.

We travelled in the delightful cool of the same evening to Columbo, where we arrived on the 20th of *January*, about noon.

Here I met with (and purchased for twelve Pagodas) a Bezoar-stone, which was represented as very scarce, and the largest of the kind ever found in the gall-bladder of the *Simia Silenus* above-described. It was commonly called *Ape-stone*, was smooth on the outside, and is now preserved in the Collection of Minerals belonging to the University of Upsal.

I had observed several times, as I went in and out of the gates of the fortifications, that a soldier, who presented his arms to me, as I passed him, as is usually done to Naval Officers, looked at me with particular attention. This induced me to ask him what country he was of. He then informed me, that he was a Swede, that his name was Bolin, and that he had been a Notary in some College in Stockholm, but being obliged by misfortunes to quit his native country, he had sailed out in the capacity of a soldier, and had spent several years in these parts, without having met with any encouragement or farther advancement. As soon as I had informed myself more circumstantially concerning this man, and had learned, that he wrote a good hand, and understood something of book-keeping, and that he was content to sail to Batavia, I solicited

this

this favour for him of the Governor, who very readily gave his consent. Furnished with my recommendation to Counsellor RADERMACHER and Captain WIMMERCRANTZ, he soon after set sail, and arrived in safety at the place of his destination. The former of these gentlemen promoted him immediately to the post of Clerk, and soon after to that of Principal Accomptant; the latter, with his wonted partiality to his countrymen, received him into his house, and as long as he lived, rendered him the most essential services, which gives this gentleman, who is now returned to his native country, a just claim to our thanks and esteem.

The Coffee-plantations in Ceylon resembled those which I had seen in Java, with this difference, however, that here a large tree of the *Bigonia* genus was planted between the Coffee-shrubs, in order to afford them a thin shade, and screen them with its crowns, from the excessive heat of the sun. The Coffee-beans which are cultivated in this place, are said not be equal in quality to those that are produced in Java.

Rice is cultivated in this island, as well as on the coasts of Coromandel and Malabar, but not in such quantity as to afford these places a sufficient supply. On the coasts of India above-mentioned, the crops sometimes, as I was informed, turn out so exceedingly bad, and in consequence of this such a dreadful famine ensues, fues, that, on the coaft of Malabar efpecially, parents are forced to fell their children for flaves, for one fingle folitary bufhel of rice, or elfe to give them up to flavery without any compenfation, that they may not fee them ftarved to death before their eyes.

Cardamomoms were brought me, which were faid to be cultivated in the internal part of the country. They were triangular oblong capfules, nearly an inch in length, and confequently quite unlike thofe which grow in the ifland of Java. A flower of them I could not procure, to enable me to afcertain their genus; but I imagine, that they were the feed-veffels of fome fpecies of the *Alpinia*.

Gum Lac was very plentiful on the fhrubs of the *Croton lacciferum*, which grew in abundance in the fand-pits without Columbo, and other places. It was fometimes ufed here for lacquering, after being diffolved in fpirits of wine.

Both on the coaft of the Continent of Afia, and the ifland of Ceylon, the leaves of the Boraffus Palm-tree (*Boraffus flabelliformis*) and fometimes of the Talpat-tree (*Licuala fpinofa*) are ufed inftead of paper, which the Indians do not prepare from the bark of a tree, as their neighbours more to the eaftward do. The leaves of both thefe Palm-trees lie in folds like a fan, and the flips ftand in need of no farther preparation than

merely

merely to be separated and cut smooth and even with a knife. Their mode of writing upon them consists in carving the letters with a fine pointed steel (*stylus*). And in order that the characters may be the better seen and read, they rub them over with charcoal, or some other black substance, so that the letters have altogether the appearance of being engraved. The iron point made use of on these occasions is either set in a brass handle, which the Moors and others carry about them in a wooden case, and which is sometimes six inches in length; or else it is formed entirely of iron, and, together with the blade of a knife, designed for the purpose of cutting the leaves, and making them even, set in a knife-handle, common to them both, into which handle it shuts up, so that it may be carried by the owner about with him, and be always ready at hand. On such slips are all letters, all Edicts of Governors, &c. written, and sent round open and unsealed. When a single slip is not sufficient, several are bound together by means of a hole made at one end, and a thread, on which they are strung. If a book is to be made, either for the use of the Churches or any other purpose, they look out principally for broad and handsome slips of Talpat-leaves, upon which they engrave the characters very elegantly and accurately, with the addition of various figures,

figures delineated upon them, by way of ornament. All the flips have then two holes made in them, and are ftrung upon an elegantly twifted filken cord, and covered with two thin lacquered wooden boards. By means of the cords the leaves are held even together, and by being drawn out, when they are wanted to be ufed, they may be feparated from each other at pleafure. One of thefe books, faid to contain various prayers, I had an opportunity of purchafing from a Prieft in Ceylon, by the intervention of Count RANTZOW.

The leaves of the Boraffus, which is a very common Palm-tree in this ifland, are befides ufed for Fans, both here and in other parts. The Palm Licuala, which is fcarcer, produces very large leaves, and rivals in this refpect the Cocoa-tree itfelf. Thefe, which lie in folds, are divided towards the point, and are here commonly ufed as Parafols, for a defence againft the fun, and as Farapluyes to defend them from the rain. One of thefe leaves, cut off about five feet in length, and of almoft the fame breadth, decorated with various elegant embellifhments, bears, like the tree itfelf, the name of Talpat, and is carried over the heads of people of diftinction, both Indians and Europeans, by a flave, inftead of the common Parafols and Parapluyes. One fingle leaf is generally large enough to

shelter

shelter six persons from the rain. This beautiful Palm-tree grows in the heart of the forests, but is scarce. It may be classed among the loftiest trees, and becomes still higher, when on the point of bursting forth into blossom from its leafy summit. The sheath, which then invelops the flower, is very large, and, when it bursts, makes an explosion like the report of a cannon; after which it shoots forth branches on every side, to the surprizing height of thirty-six or forty feet. The fruit attains to maturity the following year. I had the good fortune to see this tree in the different stages of its fructification; but as it had already blossomed the preceding year, I missed the pleasure of examining and noting down on the spot the beauties of its efflorescence.

My abode in this place was much too short to allow me to devote any of my precious time to the learning of the Cingalese and Malabar languages: I perceived, however, that they differed much from each other, as did again the language of the Moors from both of them. I nevertheless noted down the expressions, which the Malabars used in reckoning, viz.

1. unnu, undu.
2. rendu, rindu.
3. mundu.
4. nalu.
5. anji, anju.
6. aru.
7. elu.
8. ettu, ittu.
9. ombedu.
10. pattu.
11. patti-

11. pattinendu.	60. aruedu.
12. pattirendu.	70. eluedu.
13. pattimundu.	80. enbedu, aymbedu.
14. pattinalu.	90. tonnuru, imbedu.
15. pattinanju.	100. nuru, nur.
20. iruedu.	101. nutcondu
21. iruedondu.	200. irnur.
30. muppedu.	300. munur.
40. natpedu.	1000. ayrem, ayrim.
50. anbedu.	10,000. patairim.

From Tranquebar, and the Danish Mission established there, a Lutheran Priest had arrived in Ceylon, for the purpose of preaching in Columbo, and more especially of administering the Holy Sacrament to the Lutherans in this place, who had no separate Church here, nor Priest of their own persuasion. A Clergyman of this profession generally travels hither once a year, prompted by zeal and affection to his brethren in the faith, who, according to their circumstances, though for the most part moderately enough, reward his labours. The Danish Mission in Tranquebar was very highly extolled by several people here, who at the same time assured me, that, had the Catholics, in their endeavours to propagate Christianity in India, conducted themselves with equal gentleness, moderation, and Christian charity, devoid of avarice, haughtiness,

ness, and violence, the major part of the numerous inhabitants of Asia would at this present time have been converts to this doctrine.

The Bread-fruit, which in the warmer climates feeds many thousands of hungry mouths, grows in great abundance on this island likewise, where this fruit supplies the place of daily bread for several months in the year. There are two sorts of trees which produce the Bread-fruit, and both are found here, as well in a wild as cultivated state. The one, which yields smaller fruit, without seed, I found at Columbo, Gale, and several other places. The name by which it is properly known here is the *Maldivian Sour Jack*, and its use is here less universal than that of the other sort, which grows more plentifully in Ceylon, bears larger fruit, and is in greater request. The first sort bears fruit about the size of a child's head, and can only be propagated by the roots. The latter sort weighs from thirty to forty pounds, and contains from two to three hundred kernels, each of them four times the size of an almond, and this sort can be propagated by seed. The trees of both sorts are replenished with a resinous milky juice, of such a viscous nature, that birds may be caught with it, in the same manner as with bird-lime. The fruits are all over prickles, with a thick and soft rind: the internal part of the fruit only is used for food by the

the human race, and the rind is left for the hogs. Both fruits have an unpleasant cadaverous smell, and the taste of the internal esculent part is not unlike that of cabbage. The trees will flourish for whole centuries, and bear their fruit (which ripens by degrees) not only upon its thickest branches, but also upon the stem itself, for the space of eight months together, to the inestimable benefit and advantage of the islanders.

The manner of preparing and using the larger sort of Bread-fruit, which is most universally consumed in Ceylon, is as follows. According to the different ages of its growth, at which it is used for food, it receives from the Cingalese three distinct names. It is called *Pollos*, when it has attained to the size of an Ostrich's-egg, and is a month or six weeks old: *Herreli*, when it is half ripe, and of the size of a Cocoa-nut; the pulpy esculent part is then still of a white and milky cast. At both these ages the fruit cannot be eaten without previous preparation. When it is perfectly ripe it is called *Warreka*: the pulpy part is then fit for use, and that which environs the seed has a sweetish taste, is yellow, and, without any preparation, both eatable and relishing. It has the name of Bread-fruit, because the poorer class of Cingalese eat this fruit instead of bread or rice. I frequently have seen them eat Bread-fruit cut into very small

small pieces, and mixed either with the raspings of cocoa-kernels alone, or with the addition of a little rice, and sometimes some salt, Cayenne-pepper, or onions. The seeds may be eaten either alone, like chesnuts, or, together with the pulpy part of the fruit itself, prepared in different ways. They are used for food, both boiled and roasted; the poorer sort generally boil and eat them with the scrapings of cocoa-nut and salt: the rich fatten pigs, as well as geese, and other fowls with them, which are afterwards roasted.

Fifteen different dishes may be prepared from this fruit, and are more or less in use; viz.

1. *Caldu Curry* is prepared from Pollos, cut into thin slices, which are first boiled a little in water with turmeric, till the liquor turns yellow; after which two pinches of dried and pounded fish and about a pint and a half of cocoa-milk are added, and the mixture is then boiled again for the space of half an hour, during which time it must be continually stirred. This soup is the most common in use, and is not seldom made with the flesh of various animals.

2. *Seco Curry* differs from the former, in the addition of several ingredients and spices, such as roasted and pounded cocoa-nut, coriander-seeds, pepper, cinnamon, mace, salt, boiled bacon cut into small square pieces, and cocoa-milk, which are all thoroughly incorporated to-gether,

gether, and boiled in water for the space of half an hour. To this are added onions fried in butter, lemon-juice, fometimes Cayenne-pepper, and falted water, which being well mixed with each other, are boiled, till they attain the confiftence of a hafty-pudding.

3. *Chundido Pollos* is, like the former difh, prepared from flices of Pollos or Herreli, with turmeric, fcraped cocoa-nut, Cayenne-pepper, chopped onions, and falt, which are boiled over a gentle fire to the confiftence of thick porridge.

4. *Chefnut Curry* is prepared from the feeds cut into long narrow flips, and boiled with turmeric in water: to this are added dried fifh, chopped chives, and cocoa-nut-milk, with which the other ingredients are boiled up afrefh, being ftirred about all the time.

5. *Niembela* correfponds with the former difh, with this fingle diftinction, that the Pollos or Herreli here made ufe of, is cut very coarfe.

6. *The Fruit is ftewed with Bacon*; on which occafion they take thick flices of the unripe fruit, chopped chives, boiled bacon cut into fquare pieces, mace, cinnamon, and falted water, which are boiled up together, and ftirred continually.

7. *The boiled Fruit*, ripe, with the kernels and pulpy membranes cut into three or four parts, and boiled up with turmeric, and the addition of a

little

little salt, is a very common dish with the poor. It is eaten nearly after the manner of stewed cabbage, with scraped cocoa-nut; and the more opulent add to this dish pepper and dried fish.

8. *Fried Pollos* is prepared in the following manner. To the unripe fruit cut into thin slices, cocoa-milk and a little flour are added, which being kneaded up together into a dough, are rolled up in the slices of Pollos, and the whole fried in a pan in fresh cocoa-nut oil.

9. *Empade* is the name of a dish, that, in addition to the fried slices above-mentioned, consists of chopped onions, dried fish, roasted and chopped onions, and pounded cinnamon, which are boiled in a broad and shallow vessel over a gentle fire, the mixture being continually diluted with cocoa-nut-milk.

10. *Forced-meat Balls* of Pollos are prepared in this manner. The unripe fruit is boiled and beat up to a kind of hasty-pudding; to which are added chopped onions, cinnamon, pepper, nutmeg, salt, pounded biscuits, and the yolk of an egg. Of these ingredients, well mixed, they make balls, which are rolled in the white of an egg, that they may hang together. These are afterwards fried in butter, or in butter and cocoa-nut-oil, till they turn red; after which a sauce is poured upon them, consisting of butter, powder of cinnamon, pepper, salt, and lemon-juice.

11. A *Confection* likewise is sometimes prepared of the seeds and their pulpy membranes. For this purpose the membranes, which surround the seeds, are cut into two or three parts, and fried in fresh cocoa-nut oil. The oil is then wiped off well with a towel, and the fried membranes laid in a sieve, that the oil may drain the better from them. They are next boiled in syrup of sugar, dried, and put up in glass-bottles, which must be well corked, in which case this Confection may be preserved several months, and used with tea. The kernels of the seeds separated and well purged from the pulpy membranes by which they are surrounded, are frequently fried in oil, and boiled up in the same manner in syrup, and in the same manner likewise preserved, and used with tea; and, in proportion as the syrup evaporates, a fresh supply may be poured into the bottles, in which case they may be preserved for half a year.

12. *Fios* is made by dipping the ripe kernels of the seeds in a batter composed of cocoa-nut milk with the yolk of eggs, and frying them in fresh cocoa-nut oil.

13. *Pancakes* are fried in the usual manner, and composed of the juice of Siri, cocoa-nut milk, the dried meal of the kernels, and yolks of eggs, which have stood over night to ferment.

14. *Pei* or *Jambal*, is rather a sauce than a separate dish. And indeed it is only used by way of a relish to other dishes, such as fish, rice, &c. To make it, boiled unripe fruit are required, mustard-seed and turmeric, each of which ingredients must be first beaten up separately into a paste, and afterwards all together thoroughly incorporated with vinegar. Some add to this Cayenne pepper, ginger, and salt, previously reduced to powder, and well mixed together.

15. *The fruit is dried* sometimes for future use, during those months, when it is not to be had fresh. For this purpose they gather the fruit when it is half ripe, and extract the pulpy part, which they either leave intire, or cut it into slices. It is then boiled a little, and dried in the sun, after which it is hung up in order to preserve it, either in the chimney or some other dry place. When thus prepared, it may be kept a whole year, and the poorer sort eat it with scraped cocoa-nut, either thus in its dried state, or boiled up afresh.

Of this tree, bearing such beneficial fruit, I was at no little pains to carry with me some live plants to Europe. For this purpose I collected of the smaller sort, that produces no seed, about fifty live roots, which I planted in a large wooden box, and had the satisfaction to see them, at the expiration of a few weeks, spring up and thrive greatly. Of the larger sort I collected several hundred seeds, of which I set upwards of a hundred in another large box; these quickly sprang up, and throve extremely well. In order that the remainder of my seeds might not grow dry during my voyage, nor become rancid, nor be damaged in any other way, I devised several methods of preserving them. Some I only wrapped up in paper, laid in a drawer, and, during the voyage, exposed now and then to the open air; another part I put into glass-bottles, which I carefully sealed up; a great part I environed with wax to exclude the air from them; another part I laid in dry sand, and another part again I sowed every month in earth, during my voyage, in order that it might grow up gradually.

The Pearl-Fishery was formerly carried on here with advantage in the channel between the island and Coromandel, which is shallow, and is said to have a sandy bottom. At present this Fishery has been discontinued for several years, on account of certain disputes between the Nabobs on the Coromandel-coast and the Company, which the English are said to encourage, concerning the legal right to this Fishery. I saw several beautiful and large Pearls, which had been fished up here; and pearl Bandeaus, composed of large as well as small Pearls, are frequently worn by
the

the rich Merchants' ladies over their hair. This Pearl-fishery was formerly always farmed out to one or more individuals annually for a certain sum. These Farmer-Generals after farmed out again to others the privilege of fishing for Muscles with a certain stated number of boats and men. After the Muscles are brought up by the Divers, they are thrown carelessly in heaps upon the shore, and sold at random to the Merchants, who at this time assemble there. The Muscles are said to open, as soon as the animal they contain is dead and begins to putrify, when they may easily be examined, and the Pearls extracted. Sometimes not the least profit is made by this traffic; whilst at other times one single Pearl pays for the purchase of several heaps.

On the 28th, after taking an affectionate leave of my friends in Columbo, I travelled by land to Gale, in the company of M. BELLING, Secretary of Police, who carried with him the letters which were to go by the ship, that lay ready to sail, in the harbour of Gale.

Previous to my departure, I purchased a quantity of the dried fruits of betel-pepper, which is sold here at a cheap rate, and at the Cape of Good Hope brought a considerable profit, of at least one hundred per cent. As the slaves and Indians have every where free access to fresh betel-leaves, which they chew daily, it necessarily follows, that the slaves in those places, where the coolness of the climate does not allow of the cultivation of this pepper, must content themselves with using the fruit instead of the leaves.

February 6th, I embarked on board the ship *Loo*, very early in the morning, together with the Captain and Passengers, who were bound for Europe.

The harbour of Gale is well guarded with fortifications; by its winding it forms an elbow, and is not easy to clear. From this harbour sail all the ships bound to Europe or India, and here they take in their last lading.

We set sail with a favourable wind, crossed the Line on the 11th of *February*, and the Tropic of Capricorn, on the 16th of *March* following. The ship was commanded by Captain Kock, a native of Norway, and was loaded with about 1500 bales of cinnamon, of the Company's own gathering, and some cinnamon from Candia, besides a great many bales of manufactured cotton, from *Suratte* and *Tutucorin*, together with pepper from the coast of Malabar.

Above thirty slaves were likewise carried out by the officers, and sold to great advantage at the Cape. They were all males, the major part from the coast of Malabar, and some few Pampuses with curly hair. This rendered it necessary for

for me to be very circumspect and careful, that all the slaves should have had already the small-pox and measles, and that no symptoms of these disorders should be discovered on board during our voyage. For when unfortunately this is the case, the ship is obliged to perform quarantine at the Cape, and to anchor off Robben-Island, without one single man being suffered to come on shore; inasmuch as the inhabitants of this colony stand equally in dread of the small-pox and measles, as of the plague, and yet will not, after the example of the Europeans, adopt judicious and wholesome regulations and institutions for inoculation, as well as other means of opposing these epidemic distempers, which are capable of depopulating almost a whole country.

Most of the diseases that occurred during this voyage, were venereal, with their whole train of formidable symptoms, which both the sailors and the slaves had contracted by their dissolute courses of life in Ceylon.

As we approached the south between 30 and 35 degrees, we had very frequently storms of thunder, with hail, rain, and snow, which latter however dissolved immediately; and on the 28th of *March*, during a thunder storm, the electrical fluid was perceived to glisten from the tops of the fore and main-mast.

April

April 7th and the following nights, several long and lucid worms (*Scolopendra electrica*), were perceived to fall down upon the deck. These came always from the same side as the wind, which beyond a doubt blew them down, and indeed they always fell upon the windward side. So that they never came from the sails, but from the masts and top-gallant masts. When trodden under foot upon deck, or otherwise crushed to pieces, a phosphoric fire constantly issued out from the whole length of the body. No appearance of wings could be discovered in them: but they probably crawled up the masts with their feet, of which they have a great number, and afterwards fell down from them, on the wind blowing up a brisk gale.

April 22d, between the 45th and 46th degrees of latitude, not far to the eastward of the Cape of Good Hope, we saw at noon, or a few minutes after, a rain-bow, which lay upon the surface of the water itself. It blew a fresh gale at the time, and the sun stood at the highest point of the heavens at N. N. W. and the rain-bow was in S. S. E. It began with a lucid segment of a circle at the horizon itself, which gradually got up higher and higher, and spread at the same time at the sides, having at top a narrow dark-red border. From the two extremities of it proceeded two branches, like two horns, which

bending

bending inwards extended to two-thirds of the distance between the brink of the shore and the ship, being variegated with most beautiful colours of red, yellow, green, and blue-purple. In this situation it continued half a quarter of an hour, after which it gradually vanished in an inverted order. On the left side, towards the east, appeared another rain-bow, the colours of which were in an inverted order, when compared with the former, which shews that it was only occasioned by the reflection of the rays of the former. It was not very high at the top, though it stood higher than the segment of the former at the brink of the shore. After a quarter of an hour indeed there arose again a similar segment, but it did not extend itself out so as to form a rain-bow. The sky was during the whole time covered all over with small light clouds, and it was with difficulty we could distinguish that rain fell, even the horizon. Such rain-bows as these, which can only occur on the ocean and large seas, are probably not often observed.

Several times likewise in the course of this voyage we saw water-spouts hovering in the air in various forms. These began always to disappear at the bottom. And indeed at the time of their appearance we had most commonly thunder-storms, which came at stated intervals, together with violent gusts of wind.

Boobies

Boobies (*Pelecanus Sula*) began at length to shew themselves, and confirmed our joyful hopes, that we should speedily descry land. These birds are always a sure sign to mariners, that they are not far from the African coast, and it frequently happens, that, when they make their appearance, land is at the same time descried from the mast-tops. They seldom venture farther out on the ocean, than will allow of their return to the creeks and bays against evening, where they frequently spend the nights. We likewise discovered land immediately afterwards; but as there blew a hard gale from the south-east, we could not loof up into the road; but were obliged to cast anchor towards evening off *Robben Island*, to which place we with difficulty worked the ship up.

By the violent gale of wind, and at the same time the cold which it occasioned, I had the painful mortification to see several of my Breadfruit trees and other plants, either blighted with the cold, or else unearthed and lost by the violent agitation of the ship.

The following day, *April* the 27th, we came safe and well to the customary anchorage in the road, where we found eleven vessels stationed before us, and after the ship had been duly examined by the Commissioners sent for that purpose, we received permission to land.

I took

I took up my abode with my former host, M. FEHRSEN, and in the same apartments, which I had occupied three years before. As these rooms were putting into order for my reception, a circumstance occurred, which greatly surprized and perplexed me. In the anti-chamber stood a large chest belonging to my host, which I had very frequently made use of, during my former three years abode here, instead of a table, to lay the herbs, seeds, and bulbous plants upon, that I had collected. The last year of my residence here, A. 1775, I had arranged the pulpy plants, which the deserts of Africa produce, in such a manner, as to fit them to be sent to the gardens of Europe by the homeward-bound ships. Whilst I was thus occupied, it happened that a plant, which externally had the appearance of being entirely dried up, and was enveloped in a multiplicity of dry *scales* or *shingles*, fell behind this chest. But, on the chest's being removed from the wall, in order to clean out the anti-chamber, the plant was discovered behind it, from which a branch had shot forth nearly six inches in length, although it had not for the space of six or seven weeks since my finding it in the desart, shewn the smallest symptoms of life, neither had it afterwards, during the three last years, been supplied with any earth, nor the least moisture, except that
proceeding

proceeding from the coolness which might be imparted by a stone-floor. This circumstance proves how hardy and tenacious of life the African plants are, which thrive in the most parched deserts, and how long they can subsist without water and nourishment. This identical plant I afterwards took with me to Europe, and found, that those which I had before sent thither of the same species, had put forth both branches and leaves in the Botanical Garden at Amsterdam, without as yet displaying their blossoms, and making known their names.

A Swedish vessel, which lay at anchor in the road, procured me the pleasure to embrace at this place several of my dear friends, who had come from my beloved native country, and among other novelties, had brought me letters, together with the agreeable news, that I had been appointed Demonstrator of Botany in the University of Upsal, under Professor LINNE', who had succeeded his invaluable father.

The town at the *Cape* had been, during the three years of my residence in India, so greatly changed in most places, by additional buildings, and newly built and improved houses, many of them two or three stories high, that I could scarcely recognize it again.

The foregoing Summer the south-east wind had laid waste the whole country. It raged with uncommon

uncommon violence, and was accompanied with such excessive drought, that complaints were made almost universally throughout the whole land of a scarcity of corn. In most places nothing had been able to grow for the drought, and in some places, where the corn stood well, as for instance, on the other side of the Hottentot Hollands mountains, the rain had fallen again in such abundance, that the grain, which was already reaped, rotted in the corn-ricks, whilst that which still continued on the stalk, began to shoot and grow in the ear. These circumstances raised the price of corn in the town in a most unprecedented manner, insomuch that a load of corn, which had formerly sold for ten rix-dollars, now rose to the enormous price of three and thirty rix-dollars.

I met here with a Mr. PATTERSON, an Englishman, who was come to this place, in order to collect from the interior of Africa, and transmit home to his own country, both the seeds and live roots of such plants, as were scarce and peculiar to these parts. He professed to travel at the expence of certain individuals, and possessed some small knowledge of Botany, but was, in fact, a mere Gardener.

The Dutch Company allows each Officer in the ship a large chest, four feet and a half in length, and two and a half in breadth, which
they

they have permission to store with certain commodities, that are afterwards sold by public auction, for the private advantage of the individuals. Those, who had not already furnished themselves with commodities in the East-Indies, and had stored their chests with *Tamarinds* or other articles, bartered now at the Cape coarse Chintzes and other articles which were not prohibited. Fine Chintzes, and Cottons, Spices, and certain other commodities, which the Company alone deals in, are prohibited to individuals, and considered as contraband.

May 15*th*, 1778, I once more left the Cape, in order to sail to Europe. We set sail in company with four Dutch vessels, which were appointed to constitute a fleet for the defence of the country. A Danish ship, which cleared out at the same time with ourselves, shot past us with great celerity, and, being a much better sailer, soon vanished out of our sight.

The sailors had purchased several Baboons, which they designed to carry to Holland. These animals are always of a mischievous disposition, easily provoked, and bite terribly; for which reason they are generally obliged to be kept tied up. If any of them at any time got loose, it was not an easy task to catch them again, as they climbed with incredible swiftness up the ropes

and

and rigging, and were in no dread at all of the higheſt top-maſts.

May 25. Hitherto we had conſtantly had contrary winds, ſo that we could not proſecute our voyage, nor get out of ſight of the African coaſt. We now had at the ſame time thick fogs, inſomuch that we could not ſee at any great diſtance from us. In the mean time we had approached ſo near the ſhore *on the* 26*th* in the morning, when the weather began to clear up, that we might eaſily have made land, eſpecially the Commodore's ſhip, which drove quite near to the rocks. Had a heavy gale of wind in theſe circumſtances blown from the north-weſt, we muſt infallibly have been loſt; but, fortunately for us, the wind blew from the north, which extricated us out of our danger. Our Commodore KOELBIER, on board the *Canaan*, was beyond a doubt in fault in the preſent inſtance; inaſmuch as the preceding evening he kept cloſe to the land, inſtead of endeavouring to bear away to make the weſt; the other ſhips were bound to follow him, and ſail in his track. The following night we entirely loſt ſight of the Commodore's ſhip, in conſequence of which the command devolved upon Captain KOCK, of the *Loo*. On *the* 28th in the morning, we again deſcried the Commodore's ſhip, but loſt ſight of her again on the 30th.

June 3d, we sailed quite close to the Commodore's ship, which, on account of the wind being contrary, having kept too much towards the land, was now not able to come up with the fleet. This however did not in the least prevent our losing sight of her the following day, notwithstanding it became more calm towards night, instead of blowing with any degree of force. Hence it was easy to conclude, that the Commodore did not wish to keep up with his fleet, but rather, on the contrary, did all he could to separate from it, in order to be able, with less control, to continue and make the greater speed in his voyage home. In fact, we had been greatly detained by his numerous turnings and windings; not to mention that during the whole time likewise, we had either contrary winds, or else were becalmed.

On the 6th, we had a south-east trade wind, and *on the* 12th, passed the *Tropic of Cancer.*

On the 17th we saw something floating upon the water, which resembled large white flowers; I fished for, and caught some of them, and found them to be nothing else than that species of *Lepas* (*anserifera* and *anatifera*) which, by means of its lax and pliable tube had clung to bamboo canes, and pieces of wood, in clusters of a dozen and more, and which now floated upon the water. When the animal opened its five shells, they

bore

bore a perfect resemblance to a full-blown flower.

On the 24th in the morning, we discovered the island of *Helena*, which belongs to England, and the harbour of which is fortified with very strong batteries. The land appears very high and mountainous, and may be descried at a very great distance. The English ships which were homeward-bound from the East-Indies, always assembled at this place during the present American war, in order to prosecute their voyage together afterwards in fleets, accordingly as it may happen, more or less numerous. In the afternoon we had sailed on just before the middle of its road, where at that time no ships lay at anchor; and as we had not met with any traces of our lost Commodore, a ship's council was held, in which it was concluded not to wait for him any longer, but to continue our course with the brisk wind, which we now had. The road was said to have a very bold shore, so that ships might ride at anchor quite close to the land.

June 30th in the afternoon we passed Ascension Island, which frequently serves as a place of refreshment for Swedish and other vessels, which take in Tortoises there on their return home. The ships, which provide themselves with refreshments from the Cape of Good Hope, sail by this island. It is mountainous, sterile, and destitute of fresh water. The surface is likewise covered with a kind of ashes, which plainly evinces, that it must formerly have been a Volcano.

July 7th, having the night before crossed the line, we were consequently saluted towards noon by the other two ships with eleven vollies, which we answered in the same manner.

On the 24th we passed the Sun, when we perceived no kind of shadow whatever on either side of any thing, that was set upright upon the deck. Before we had the Sun at noon in the north, now it stood right vertical over us, and after this was seen in the south, and sank continually lower and lower towards the horizon.

On the 29th the Captains of the other two ships came on board of us, in order to open the sealed letters, which were to direct us, whether the ship should sail through the Channel, or take a circuitous route behind Great-Britain, as is usually done in war-time. We sailed now in the sea called the *Cross Sea*, which is pretty thickly covered with *Sargazo* (*Fucus natans*). This sea-weed floats upon the surface of the ocean in incredible quantities. Sometimes it quite hides the face of the water in calm weather, so that one seems to be sailing through a meadow: at other times it forms large floating islands, and sometimes, during stormy weather, it is driven about more loosely. This *Fucus* seemed to hold out a plain

proof,

proof, that it grows as it floats in the water, and shoots forth new shoots at the extremities, which grow larger by degrees. Among this sea-weed I discovered various animals, that harboured and sought their food in it. The most numerous of these were the *Scyllæa pelagica*, the *Cancer minutus*, of various sizes, and the *Lophius histrio*, a fish, which the Dutch call *Crown-fish*, which was very much variegated, and at the same time beautiful, and, when of a certain size, in high estimation. Some of these I preserved in spirits of wine; they were mostly very small, and it is but seldom that they are found of the length of a finger or upwards. The loose rays, which this fish has upon its head and back, and which resemble a crown, have given occasion to its name. It is seldom that it can be brought to Holland alive; but when this fortunately happens to be the case, provided the fish is of any moderate size, it is said frequently to fetch ten ducats.

August 25th, a hog was killed on board, in whose bladder was found a kind of chalk-stone. It was nearly round, somewhat flattened, and rough all over, with small knobs. The colour was at first a chesnut-brown, but grew paler and paler as it dried. It was somewhat larger than a musket-ball; and of a close-grained texture within. This hog had been purchased in Ceylon.

September the 12th, having heaved the lead, we found ground, and faluted the other fhips with eleven vollies, who returned the compliment.

We had on board a man, whofe fate was equally fingular and unfortunate. He had been engaged as Chief Surgeon on board a fhip from Enkhuyfen, called *de Jonge Hugo*, which was commanded by Captain KLEIN, this unhappy man's implacable enemy. His name was BERG-AKKER, and he appeared to me during the whole voyage to be a fteady, ferious, and worthy old man. Whilft the fhip lay ready to fail, the Captain had taken umbrage at him, and loaded him with all manner of infults, even fo far as to let the boys have him in derifion. At laft he wrote word to the Director who had the infpection over the fhip, that this man was infane, and requefted that another Surgeon might be appointed in his place, who was accordingly fent on board. Upon this the Captain immediately fet fail, without putting the accufed on fhore, whom he kept under an arreft during the whole voyage to the Cape, and would not fo much as permit him to come once on deck, to breathe a little frefh air. During the voyage he caufed a writing to be drawn up and figned by fome of the Officers, who were his creatures, purporting that the above-named perfon was pofitively infane.

sane. On our arrival at the Cape, the unhappy man was conducted on shore, and immediately clapped into prison, without having the privilege of walking out, or having any opportunity to prefer a complaint, and without being examined either by the Governor, the Fiscal, or any of the Senators. When our ship was mustered, he was sent thither like a prisoner, to be conveyed in it to Europe, without salary or any kind of emolument whatever. Notwithstanding that this man had been pronounced insane, I was not able, during a voyage of several months, to perceive any symptoms of derangement in him, or to discover the least probability, by his appearance, that he had ever been so. In the course of seven years, which I spent in India, in the service of the Dutch Company, I had an opportunity of seeing several instances of violence and oppression in Captains, as despotic as they were wicked and brutal: but what struck me with the greatest surprize in this instance was, that neither the Governor nor any Members of the Administration at the Cape sufficiently investigated this business, by means of which the innocent sufferer might have been freed from farther oppression, and the malicious misanthrope brought to condign punishment. All, whom I interrogated about the character of Captain KLEIN, spoke of him with the most sovereign contempt, as of an ill-conditioned, fierce, and savage man, who was not even qualified for the post he held.

On the 16th we came within sight of the English coast at the *Lizards*, and cruized about there for a whole night and day, till we discovered the Dutch man of war, which was sent out to meet and convoy home the richly-laden East-Indiamen. One of these afterwards accompanied us, and convoyed us to the Texel. The first signal was given on our side by the discharge of four guns, and by alternately hoisting and lowering our colours. Upon this the man of war answered us in the same manner, by hoisting and lowering her pendants, together with the discharge of five guns. As soon as the ships were come somewhat nearer to each other, a Lieutenant and Clerk were sent from the man of war, in order to search our ship, whether it carried any contraband wares, and this search was made in the Captain's cabbin only among his wine bottles.

On the 18th the Captains of the three homeward-bound ships repaired to the man of war, in order to open a sealed letter from the *Overduyn*, one of the ships that came from China, by which letter we now first received intelligence, that the lading was consigned to Amsterdam.

At the same time we likewise obtained the intelligence, that our Commodore KOELBIER, with the ship *Canaan,* had arrived two days before,

and

and had sailed on, which ship we had missed from our company four months ago, off the African coast.

On the 28th we sailed in the Channel between Dover and Calais, with a good and favourable wind; but in the evening about ten o'clock, a sudden and violent storm arose, which drove us more and more against the land, rent our sails, and tore down our top-masts. The ship tossed about so violently, that it was impossible to stand always upon one's feet. We were so near the Breakers, that all gave the ship up for lost, without any possibility of deliverance; for which reason indeed at last none of the sailors could any longer be persuaded or encouraged to attempt any thing for the preservation of the ship. Besides the darkness, we had this additional misfortune, that the crew was feeble and quite worn out, owing to the excessive covetousness of the Captain and First Mate, so that many of the crew, exhausted with their toils, fell down from the rigging, and several fainted away on the deck itself. Their fare had been wretched during the whole voyage, and consisted of nothing but meagre food, as for instance, rice and fruits, with very little of those more strengthening viands, which are indispensably necessary for a Mariner. The Captain and First Mate, who had expected that the voyage would not prove so tedious, had very unwarrantably confulted their own private intereft and advantage, by difpofing at the Cape of a great part of the meat, pork, and other articles of provifion, which are allowed for the crew, and were by that means reduced to great ftreights, in confequence of the procraftination of the voyage. This had not only reduced the men's ftrength, but had likewife occafioned much difcontent and murmuring among them. For this conduct both the Captain and Firft Mate were in the fequel arraigned, and both declared incapacitated for farther fervice. As foon as the morning began to dawn, we perceived that we had driven in between the fand-banks, almoft directly oppofite Oftend, and that we were entirely feparated from our company. And as we were now, through the particular providence of God, delivered from deftruction, and from the calamities which had threatened us the preceding night, the crew imbibed frefh courage to extricate the fhip from its dangerous fituation; which attempts likewife fucceeded, with the favourable wind that now prevailed. Exclufively of all other damage, which I fuffered on this occafion, I had the misfortune peculiar to myfelf, of feeing my plantation of upwards of a hundred fhrubs of both fpecies of the Bread-fruit tree, and other extremely

tremely scarce plants, entirely thrown topsy-turvy and absolutely destroyed.

After surmounting these misfortunes, we arrived at length just before the opening of the Texel, *on the* 29*th* following.

October the 1*st*, we sailed between the Texel and Helder, saluted the road, and let fall our anchor. All now with joyful hearts invoked the Almighty; and I had, more than any of them, reasons of the most binding and compulsory nature to bring him my thank-offering, having, during a seven years series of toilsome and not unfrequently irksome peregrinations, enjoyed in the highest degree the benefit of his powerful protection and special guardian care.

On the 6*th*, M. BEAUMONT, the Director, came on board, in whose presence all our cloaths-chests, and other things were searched, and the crew discharged, excepting about sixty men, who staid behind to unlade the ship.

I sailed in company with some of the other officers in a hired boat, and arrived in safety at Amsterdam, where my much-respected Patron, Professor BURMANNUS, with the utmost kindness and benevolence made me an offer of his house and table.

I spent my time in viewing with him the most remarkable Collections, which are to be found in Amsterdam, among which that in the
possession

possession of the Merchant van der MEULEN, was the most valuable, especially with regard to Birds and Insects.

After this I made an excursion into the vicinity of Haarlem, in order to pay my respects to my three worthy Patrons, van der POLL, van der DEUTZ, and ten HOVEN, as likewise to see their country seats, and the beautiful plantations of all kinds of Exotics, which, at an incredible expence, they have raised in the most sandy and barren plains near this spot. It was not without the most sensible pleasure, that I observed here several of the vegetable productions both of Africa and the Japanese islands, which testified that the pains (not unattended with danger) which I had been at in collecting them, had not been wholly lost. I had likewise the extreme happiness to receive from my Patrons testimonies of their satisfaction on the score of my diligence, together with the most handsome recompence, on account of which the last-mentioned Gentleman, M. ten HOVEN, paid me, on my return to Amsterdam, an unexpected visit. This Gentleman, who is said to have a yearly income of more than 300,000 guilders, did not deem it beneath his dignity to pay me a visit in the Dutch fashion, on foot, and without any attendants, and at the same to make me a

present

present with his own hand of 128 Dutch Ducats in gold.

I afterwards, in company with Dr. *Klochner*, made an excursion purposely to Haarlem, to see M. VRIEND's fine Collection of Insects, together with the curious animals of every class, which are kept in the house belonging to the Society of Sciences at Haarlem.

The *Phalæna brumata* was at this time very common in the orchards and fruit-gardens. It was prevented from laying its noxious eggs in the buds of the blossoms, by the method invented by Professor BERGMAN, and which was here very much celebrated, viz. by means of the tarred bark of a birch-tree bound round the stem of the tree.

It is very common in Amsterdam, as well as in other parts of Holland, to dispose of Collections of Natural Curiosities, by public auction. Such auctions were now held several times, agreeable to printed Catalogues, after the Cabinet had been previously exposed for a certain time to the inspection of the public.

Among other rarities which I saw in Amsterdam, was likewise a very pretty Collection of Coins in the possession of the Minister of the church called the *Oude Kerk*. I had here the unexpected pleasure to see, for the first time, the Zodiac Rupees, as they are called, in gold, the whole twelve

twelve together complete, which I could in India neither procure a fight of, nor obtain in change, and of which one feldom finds a complete collection in Europe. He had redeemed thefe twelve Coins with 300 Dutch Guilders, and had the goodnefs to part with them to me at my earneft follicitation for 700 Guilders. This Collection, together with the Portrait of Selim Ift. had been made a prefent of by the Governor-General Imhoff, from Batavia, to fome of his relations in Holland, who were afterwards under the neceffity of difpofing of them. This Coin had been ftruck both in Gold and Silver by the Emprefs Nour-mahal, the above-mentioned Selim's Confort, in the fpace of twenty-four hours, during which fhe, with the Emperor's permiffion, reigned with abfolute fway. And as thefe, after the Monarch's demife, were prohibited, called in and melted down, it is now very uncommon to meet with all the twelve, which bear upon one fide the impreffion of one of the twelve figns of the Zodiac, and on the other are marked with Arabic or Perfian characters.

I could not well accept of Profeffor *Burmann*'s very kind invitation to refide in his houfe, as he and his family were themfelves ftraitened for room, for which reafon I hired an apartment of a worthy friend and countryman of mine,
Eric

Eric Floberg, who was Proprietor of a Silk-Stocking Manufactury, and was settled in this city, where all foreigners are at perfect liberty to earn their bread, let them be of what country and of what religion they will. This did not however prevent me from visiting daily in his house, and being quite overwhelmed with his kindnesses, the remembrance of which shall remain deeper impressed in my breast, and be preserved as a more sacred deposit there, than if they had been engraved on th' most costly Parian marble.

In like manner I had the happiness, (and the remembrance of it even at this distant period of fourteen years, in which I prepare the present narrative for the press, awakens the most lively sense of joy and gratitude in my soul) I had the happiness to experience from several of my respectable countrymen every possible civility, mark of friendship, favour, and real service; as for instance, from the Consul-General, M. Hasselgren, Messrs. Faohræus, Swart, and Lunge, &c.

Having finished my engagements with the Dutch East-India Company, and received my salary, together with the customary gratuity, I resolved to travel to England, and spend part of the winter in London.

With

With this view I went in the month of November to the Hague, where I inspected his Royal Highness the Hereditary Stadtholder's valuable Cabinet of the productions of Nature and Art, and paid a visit to M. LYONET, in order to see his choice Collection of Shells; after which I travelled to Rotterdam, and from thence farther on to *Helvoet Sluys*.

Here contrary winds prevented my passage over for several days, and when afterwards I was able at last to set sail, in company with several other passengers, in the English Packet-boat Royal, such a heavy storm arose, and at last contrary winds, that we were driven a great way out of our course, and landed at a place a great distance from London, from whence we were obliged to go by land to the Metropolis, where I arrived on the 14th of *December*.

Mr. DRYANDER, my friend and quondam fellow-student, had very kindly taken upon himself the charge of providing lodgings for me: my first care therefore was to wait upon this Gentleman, at the house of Sir JOSEPH BANKS, agreeably to the address he had given me. As soon as I had sent in my name, I was received in the most polite manner by Dr. SOLANDER, who did me the honour to introduce and present me immediately to Sir JOSEPH BANKS, in his Cabinet of Natural History.

This

This Gentleman was not only pleafed to receive me with the greateft kindnefs in the prefent inftance, but continued, during the whole time of my abode in London, to fhow me all poffible favour, and, what was the chief object of my wifhes, granted me free and uncontrolled accefs to his incomparable Collections, made (that appertaining to the vegetable kingdom in particular) from every part of the globe. I accordingly fpent the forenoon of every day in his houfe, and went with the utmoft attention through his extenfive Herbarium, which was a moft commodious as well as efficacious method of enlarging my ftock of knowledge in this department of my favourite Science. And as at the fame time feveral learned men daily affembled here, as though it were to an Academy of Natural Hiftory, I had frequent opportunities likewife of forming connexions, that proved as ufeful as they were truly creditable and honourable.

I farther faw, during my fhort abode in this country, every thing worthy of notice, efpecially with refpect to Natural Hiftory, as for inftance, the *Britifh* and *Leverian Mufeums*, &c. The former is on a very large and extenfive fcale, and contains Collections in many different articles, fuch as Books, Manufcripts, Antiquities, Coins, and the Apparel of remote nations, Utenfils, &c.

KÆMPFER's Manufcripts and Collection of Herbs, together with the Drawings and Defigns, were the articles, which it gave me the greateft pleafure to fee here. Thefe were now almoft a hundred years old, and had been bought up by Sir HANS SLOANE, after the Author's death. The latter was the property of an individual, was fhewn for a certain fum, and confifted chiefly of minerals and animals.

In like manner I made feveral excurfions in the vicinity of London, to fee the beautiful gardens of Kew, abounding with living plants, and under the direction and care of Mr. AITON: Mr. LEE's garden, which is uncommonly rich in trees and fhrubs: Dr. FOTHERGILL's garden, CHELSEA, &c. At Mr. LEE's I likewife faw his daughter's fine Collection of Infects, which had been increafed with the uncommonly beautiful Infects from the Coaft of Bengal, which Lady MONSON had collected there, and, previous to her death, bequeathed to Mifs LEE.

Profeffor FORSTER, fenior, whom I waited upon one day, received me with much friendfhip, and not only procured me the pleafure to fee the plants and fhells, which he had collected during his voyages in the Pacific Ocean, but was farther pleafed to prefent me with a whole Collection of them, which has entitled him to my fincereft gratitude and eternal acknowledgements.

The

The English spend the day in a much better manner than any other nation I have hitherto seen. Nine o'clock in the morning is the common hour of breakfast, which generally consists of tea and some light diet. After breakfast they follow their occupations, till three in the afternoon. At four o'clock, when the merchants return from Change, dinner is generally served up, though people of fashion dine an hour or two later; after which the evening is either spent in company or some other pastime. This mode of living appears to me much more rational than what is customary in other places, viz. during one's occupations to fast till one o'clock, and afterwards to consume the best, lightest, and finest part of the day at dinner, after which one is little qualified for attending to any business in the afternoon.

For this reason Assemblies are always held at six in the evening. The members of the Royal Society of Arts and Sciences assemble likewise at that hour on a stated day in the week, and I had the pleasure to be present at their meetings several times. The Meeting-room is furnished on one side with benches for the accommodation of the members, like a church, and the President with his Secretary sit before a table. Each member has the privilege to take with him one of his friends, but he muſt in this caſe deliver in his name to the Preſident.

With the new-year a ſevere froſt ſet in, accompanied with a very violent ſtorm, which blew down ſeveral ſtacks of chimnies upon the houſes, and ſome even broke through the roof, and at times even penetrated to the ſecond ſtory, ſo as to occaſion much damage and calamity.

Among other favours, with which Sir JOSEPH BANKS overwhelmed me, I conſider this a ſingular proof of his friendſhip that I was permitted, previous to my departure, to view the Collection of Plants made from the iſlands in the Pacific Ocean, which were not as yet placed among the other plants, and are not ſhewn indiſcriminately to every ſtranger. Dr. SOLANDER, who, as well as Mr. DRYANDER, ſtrove to render my abode in London both agreeable and advantageous to me, had the goodneſs, on this occaſion, to order the whole of this Collection to be brought down from the upper ſtory, and to go through with me every ſingle and diſtinct ſpecies of it.

The Library, which Sir JOSEPH BANKS has collected, is in fact the completeſt in the world, with reſpect to Natural Hiſtory, both in old and new works. It is erected in a large ſeparate room, before you enter into the Cabinet, by

means

means of which one has a most incomparably fine opportunity, when one is examining any particular plant, of referring to, and consulting whatever author one chuses, without loss of time, and without being under the necessity of fetching books from a general Library, which frequently stands at a great distance off, and is most commonly incomplete, and not always accessible.

January the 30th, I set off, in company with Captain, now Colonel Cronstedt, who was lately returned from North America. We took our route through Holland and Germany to Ystad and Lund. From Harwich we went across the Channel to Helvoet Sluys, and from thence travelled on to Amsterdam, where we staid a few days only.

February the 16th we proceeded farther on our journey to Groningen: on the 22d to Bremen; from thence to Hamburg, on the 24th; then to Lubeck, Wismar, Rostock, Damgard, and Stralsund, where we arrived on the 2d of March.

Whilst we waited for the sailing of the Packet-boat to Ystad, we made an excursion to Gripswald, in order to see this celebrated Seat of the Muses, its Library, &c. and on our return, sailed from Stralsund in the Packet-boat to Ystad, and on the 14th following, arrived in our dear and long-desired native country.

THE END.

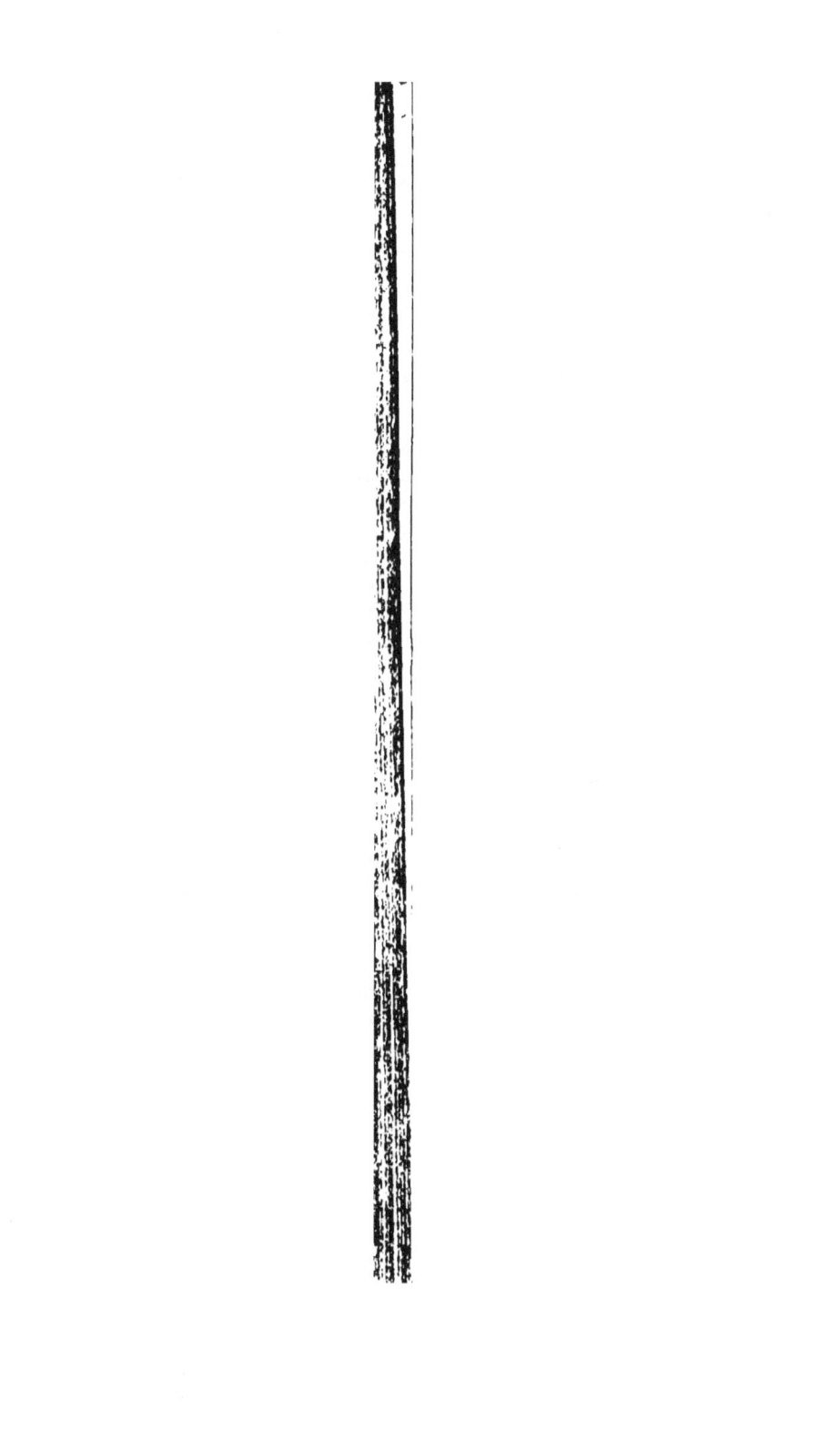

INDEX.

A.

Abrafin, 38.
Abu, 124.
Acheta, 100.
Acorus, 149.
Acu punctura, 73, 75.
Adamsberg, 236.
Adianthum, 147.
Agaricus, 89.
Agate, 105.
Agriculture, 54.
Agrimony, 146.
Agrion, 101.
AITON, 290.
ALBEDYL, 174.
Almanacks, 6.
ALNOOR, 171.
Alpinia, 250.
Amakusa, 103.
Ambassador, 27, 238.
Amber, 105.
Ambergrise, 98.
Amethyst, 218, 220, 221.
Amida, 24.
Amomum, 89, 147.
Amphibia, 99.
Anas, 99.

Anatomy, 55.
Andewalu, 161.
Anger, 171.
Anobium, 100.
Anomia, 102.
Ant-eater, 178.
Ape, Cingalese, 214.
Ape-stone, 248.
Apis, 101.
Aqua Mercurialis, 79.
Ara, 39.
Arca, 102.
Ardea, 99, 160.
Areca, 150.
Areek-Tree, 183.
Argonauta, 102.
Aristolochia, 185.
Arkidomas, 158.
Artemisia, 74, 145.
Arum, 121, 149.
Arundo, 91.
Ascension, Isle of, 275.
Assesors, 69.
Aster, 90.
Asterias, 101.
Astromony, 55.
Atsingo, 104.

Atsuki,

INDEX.

Atſuki, 88.
Auctions, 285.
Aukuba, 90.
Awa, 88.
Azalea, 90.
Azedarach, 38.

B.

Baboons, 272.
Baſia, 214.
Bamboos, 85, 91, 142, 160.
Bangle, 147.
BANKS, Sir Joſeph, 288, 292.
Barbary, 193.
Barley, 84, 86.
Barringtonia, 177.
Batavia, 129.
Batatas, 38, 84, 89.
Bath, warm bath, 158, 159.
Bathing, 175.
Beans, 84, 88.
—— French, 87.
BEAUMONT, 283.
BEEK, van der, 153.
Belemnites, 102.
BELLING, 263.
Belot, 145.
BERGAKKER, 278.
BERGMAN, 229, 285.
Betel, 263.
Bezoar-ſtone, 233, 248.
Bidara Laut, 150.
Bignonia, 38, 249.
Bingo, 104.

Binnuge, 186.
Birds, 98.
Biſen, 105.
Bitſju, 105.
BLADH, 171.
Blatta, 100.
Blind, 150.
—— order of, 28.
Boa kirai, 161.
BOENNEKEN, Dr. 139.
Boerhavia, 205.
Boga, 232.
Bogor, 162.
Bolange, 179.
BOLIN, 248.
Bombylius, 124.
Bombyx, 100.
Bong, 46.
Boobies, 268.
Boomjes, Iſlands of, 156.
Books, 177.
Boraſſus, 183, 205, 252.
Bor taurus, 97.
Botany, 55.
Bows, 113.
Braſſica, 87, 88, 93.
Bread-fruit, 255—262.
Bridges, 12.
Brimſtone, 105.
Britiſh Muſeum, 289.
Buccinum, 102.
Buck-wheat, 84, 85.
Budha, Budſo, 19, 23, 187, 232.
Buffaloes, 97.

Buffles-

INDEX.

Buffles-blad, 141.
Bugios, 8.
Building, mode of, 142.
Bulla, 102.
Bungo, 30.
Bupreſtis, 100.
Burgomaſter, 69.
Burmannia, 247.
BURMANNUS, 134, 247, 283, 286.
Burning with Moxa, 74.
Buytenzorg, 158, 162.

C.

Caballe, 178.
Coleworts, 84.
Cole-ſeed, 84, 87.
Cactus, 90.
Calaminder-tree, 205.
Calebaſhes, 89.
Calendula, 90.
Callionymus, 100.
Caltere, 193.
Camellia, 38.
Camphor-tree, 92.
Canaan, 280.
Cancer, 101, 277.
Candles, 93.
Canes, 172.
Canis, 97.
Cannabis, 140.
Canons, 14.
Cape, 269, 270.
Capſicum, 89, 145.
Capuru Curundu, 236.

Cardamoms, 147, 259.
Cardium, 101.
Carrots, 88.
Caryota, 149.
Caſhier, 69.
Caſſia, 149.
Caſſida, 100.
Caſtles, 10.
Cats, 95, 97.
Cat's-eyes, 219, 228.
Cayenne-pepper, 89.
Cedar, 91.
Celoſia, 90.
Cerambyx, 100.
Chabe, 147.
Chai, 147.
Chama, 102.
Champaca, 152.
Chelſea, 290.
Chalk-ſtone, 277.
Chemiſtry, 55.
Chenopodium, 145.
Cheribon, 136.
Cherries, 89.
Cherimelle, 178.
Cherroton, 163.
Cheſnut, 38, 90.
Cheſnut Curry, 258.
Chiluar, 158.
Chimangis, 158.
Chimbine, 146.
CHINAJOS, 9.
Chineſe, 164, 170.
———— Trade, 108.
Chipannas,

INDEX.

Chipannas, 158.
Chipinong, 158.
Chiferoa, 158.
Chriſtian doctrine, 30.
Chryſanthemum, 90.
Chryſalite, 218.
Chryſomela, 100.
Chryſopras, 218, 224.
Chundido, 258.
Churches, 21, 24.
Cicada, 124.
Cicindela, 100.
Cicuta, 149.
Cimex, 100.
Cinnamon, 194—204.
——— Stone, 218, 224.
Cities, 100.
Citrus, 118, 120.
Clematis, 146.
Climate, 160, 175.
Cloathing, 5.
Clupea, 29, 100.
Coals, foſſile, or pit, 105.
Coccinella, 100.
Cock, 99.
Cocoa, 191, 209.
Cochim, 239.
Coffee, 152.
——— plantations of, 249.
Coins, 117, 123, 124, 169, 210—214, 285.
Collections, 283, 285, 288, 289, 290, 292.
Columba, 99, 161.
Columbo, City of, 175.
Columbo Root, 185.
Commerce, 105.
——— articles of, 168.
Conflagration, 70.
Confections, 260.
CONFUCIUS, 34.
Conomon, 89.
CONRADI, 248.
Convolvulus, 84—89.
Conus, 102.
Copper, 59, 104, 125.
Corals, 101.
Coriander, 150.
Corn, falts of, 84.
Corvus, 99.
Coſtus, 146.
Cotton, 59, 91.
Cottons, 239.
Court, 5.
Cows, 95, 97.
CRAAN, 157.
Crabs, 39.
Crinum, 150.
CRONSTEDT, 293.
Crotalaria, 185.
Croton, 250.
Crow, 99.
Crown-fiſh, 277.
Crown-lands, 8.
Cryſtall, 219, 226—228.
Cucumbers, 89.
Cucumis, 89.
Cucurbita, 89.
Cudweed, 150.
Culex, 101.

Cupreſſus,

INDEX.

Cupreſſus, 122.
Curcuma, 147.
Curry Caldu, 257.
—— Cheſnut, 258.
—— Seco, 257.
Cynogloſſum, 148.
Cynoſurus, 88.
Cyprus, 148.
Cyprœa, 102.
Cypreſs, 122.
Cyprinus, 100.

D.

Dadap, 153.
Daidſu, 88.
DAIJOSIN, 113.
Daimio, 1.
Dairi, 3, 6, 17.
Dances, 143.
Dancing Girls, 51.
Dandang, 147.
Daucus, 88.
Dead, 53.
Death, penalty of, 64.
Dermeſtes, 100.
Deſima, 33.
DEUTZ, 284.
Devil's Rock, 156.
Diarrhæa, 77.
Dimboring, 145.
Dioſcorea, 123, 143.
Dioſpyros, 90.
Diſeaſes, 76.
Dogs, 95, 97.
Dolichos Soja, 38, 88, 121, 177.

Domolo, 145.
Donax, 101.
Dranguli, 149.
Drawing, art of, 57.
Dreſs, 5.
Drink, 39.
Drought, 271.
DRYANDER, 288, 292.
Dryandra, 38, 93.
Ducks, 95.
Dudu, 214.
Dukut parang, 146.
DUURKOOP, 124, 164.
Duyvel's-boom, 232.
Dying Materials, 90.
Dyſentery, 77.

E.

Ear-rings, 189.
Eels, 99.
Eggs, 87.
Electrical Fluid, 265.
Elephant, 242—247.
———— Hunt, 241.
———— Toil, 240, 247.
Elinges chageppu, 219.
Embaſſy, 31.
Empade, 259.
Emperors, 12, 89.
England, 288.
Equus, 98.
Erythrina, 153.
Eyes, diſeaſe of, 76.

FAHRÆUS,

INDEX.

F.

FAHRÆUS, 287.
Fagara, 89.
FALCK, 174, 182.
Farma Mufi, 100.
Fans, 252.
Fanum, 213.
FEHRSEN, 269.
FEITH, 132.
Felis, 97.
Fences, 237.
Feftivals, 46.
Ficus, 140, 232.
FIDE JORI, 32.
FIDE TADA, 112.
FIGASI gamma no yn, 9.
Figs, 90, 140.
Fines, 6.
Fios, 260.
Fir, 122.
Firando, 112.
Fires, apparatus againft, 10.
Fifh, 100.
Fifhermen, 126.
Fiftularia, 100.
FLOBERG, 287.
Fokke fokkes, 89.
Food, preparation of, 35.
Forced-meat-balls, 259.
Fornication, 52.
FORSTER, 290.
FOTHERGILL, 290.
Fox, 97.
Fragaria, 146.
FROBUS, M. 190.
Fucus, 276.
Fumaria, 145.
Funerals, 51, 53.
Furniture, 64.

G.

Gale, 194, 263, 264.
Games, 46.
Gardens, 89.
Gardenia, 90.
Garnets, 218.
Geefe, 98.
Ginger, 147.
Ginko, 38.
Ginje, 148.
Genfima, 104.
Glands, indurated, 76.
Glafs, 59.
——— grinding of, 60.
Glimmer, 217.
Gnats, 144.
Gnaphalium, 150.
Goa, 31.
Goats, 95.
Gobius, 99.
Godagandu, 235.
Gold, 102.
Gold-chains, 190.
Goffypium, 91.
Gotho, 92.
Government, 1, 9.
Governors, 126, 138.
Grapes, 90.
Grafs, 88.

Green

INDEX.

Green Tea, 41.
GREGORY XIII. 31.
Gryllus, 100.
Guard, 10, 70.
——— house, 10.
Guns, 13.

H.

Haarlem, 284, 285.
Hague, The, 288.
Haliotis, 82, 102.
Hamagai, 102.
Hare, 27.
HASSELGREN, 287.
Helena, Isle of, 275.
Helvoetsluys, 288.
Hemerobius, 101.
Hens, 95, 99.
Herpes, 236.
Herelli, 258.
Hibiscus, 120, 146, 246.
Hirudo, 232.
Hirundo, 163.
Hister, 100.
History, 54.
HOFFMAN, Dr. 129, 167.
Holcus, 88.
Holidays, 24—26.
HOPNER, 174.
Hops, 90.
Hordeum, 86.
Horses, 9.
Hospital, 165.
HOVEN ten, 284.
Hovenia, 90.

Humulus, 90.
Hyacinth, 218, 222.
Hydrocele, 76.
Hydrocephalus, 77.
Hystrix, 233.

I.

Jacberi, 185.
Jacatra, 168.
Jambal, 261.
Jamanabos, 28.
Jan Lopes root, 205.
Japara, 153.
Jarrak, 149, 192.
Jassminum, 150.
Jatropha, 149, 192.
Idols, 18, 21.
Jedo, 7.
Jemma, 24.
Jessamin, 150.
IMHOFF, 158.
Impatiens, 90.
Imposts, 67.
INABA MINO, 113.
Ink, Indian, 58.
Inns, 11, 113, 192.
Intermaga, 156.
Ipecacuanha, 186.
Iron, 59, 127.
——— Ore, 217.
Isie, 16, 26.
Isis, 102.
Itch, 234.
Juana, 138, 155.
Julus, 101.

Juncus,

INDEX.

Juncus, 119.
Iwa Kik, 102.

K.

Kadondon, 161.
Kæmpfer, 8, 16, 133, 290.
Kæmpferia, 147.
Kaha palinga, 219.
Kaki ular, 150.
Kaki Figs, 38.
Kallu palingu, 219.
Kalu miniran, 217.
Kamadu, 140.
Kambang Pokul Ampat, 148.
Kami, 21.
Kanoke turemaizi, 219.
Karte-paliugu, 219.
Kattami, 104.
Katumjar. 150.
Kellingo, 179.
Keulen; Van; 174.
Kibi, 88.
Kjellin, 174.
Kinsohivo Tei, 88.
Kinsima, 144.
Klein, 278, 279.
Klengengang, 196.
Klockner, Dr. 285.
Ko Kibi, 88.
Koelbier, 280.
Komedegam, 218.
Komukus, 148.
Kopping, 140.
Koosi, 34.
Korang garing, 161.

Kosak, 123.
Koto, 58.
Kubo, 1, 6—9, 22.
Kunjet, 147.
Kunir, 147.
Kyno Xusi, 104.

L.

Lac, Gum, 256.
Lacerta, 99.
Lacker'd Ware, 61.
Lactuca, 89, 145.
Lagundo, 146.
Lamps, festival of, 124.
Lampujang, 147.
Lampyris, 100.
Lan Karate, 218.
Language, 55.
Lanthorn, festivals of, 46; 124.
Laryn, 210.
Laurus, 91, 93.
Law, Study of, 55.
Laws, 62, 71.
Learning, 5.
Lee, Mr. and Mifs, 290.
Leeches, 232.
Lemons, 38, 89.
Leonurus, 38, 146.
Lepifma, 101.
Lepus, 101.
Lettuces, 89.
Lever's Museum, 289.
Library, 292.

Lichens,

INDEX.

Lichens, 161.
Licuala, 25, 253.
Lignum colubrinum, 150, 210.
Lilium, 119.
Lizards, the, 280.
Lombo, 145.
London, 289.
Loo, the Ship, 173, 264.
Lophius, 277.
Loxia, 99, 169.
LUNGE, 287.
Lute, 58.
Lycoperdon, 121.
LYONET, 288.

M.

Mactra, 102.
Madrepora, 102.
Magnoliæ, 90.
Malabar numeration, 253.
Mammalia, 98.
Man of War, 280.
Manjel palingu, 219.
Manikan, 146.
Manis, 178.
Mantis, 97.
Manure, 82.
Manufactures, 59.
Marendan, 183.
Maritjo, 148.
Marmelle, 179.
Marriages, 51.
Mars, the Ship, 170.
Mats, 119.

Matsuri, 46.
Mature, 190.
Maturese Diamond, 218.
Meadows, 81.
Measles, 77.
Medicine, 55.
Medlars, 89.
Mehemedon, 161.
Melia, 93.
Melilothus, 148.
Meloe, 100.
Melons, 89.
Mendi, 236.
Menispermum, 185.
Merchants, 106.
Mespilus 89.
Metals, 102.
MEULEN, vander, 284.
Mia, 21.
Miaco, 4.
Mica, 217.
Miliary Eruption, 77.
Mimasaka, 105.
Mines, farming out, 231.
Miniran, 217.
Mirabilis, 90, 148.
Mirror, 26.
Miso Soup, 38, 88.
Mojei, 147.
MOMO *Zon no Yn*, 9.
MONSON, Lady, 290.
Monoculus, 101.
Mooku, 56.
Moors, 158, 230.
Mortality, 56.

Mordella,

INDEX.

Mordella, 100.
Moringa, 205.
MORO, 33.
Morus, 61.
Monks, 28.
Mountains, 138, 158, 163.
Mountain Cryſtal, 218, 219.
Mugwort, 74, 145.
Mulberry-tree, 60.
Muræna, 99.
Mus, 38.
Muſa, 172.
Muſca, 101.
Muſci, 161.
Muſhrooms, 38, 89.
Muſic, 58.
Muſical Inſtruments, 58.
Mya, 101.
Myrica, 122.
Mytilus, 102.

N.

Na tanne, 87.
Navigation, 63.
Negumbo, Devil of, 78.
NAGATO *no Kami*, 126.
NAKA *no Mikado no Y'n*, 8.
Namba, 105.
Naban, 88.
Nandina, 90.
Natural philoſophy, 85.
Nerita, 102.
New-year, 132, 153.
Nettles, 140.
Niembela, 258.

Nile Nilim, 218.
Nile turcmali, 218.
Ninban, 69.
Nin O, 2.
NOTO *no Kami*, 126.
NOUR-MAHAL, 286.
Nunneries, 30.
Nyctanthes, 151.

O.

Oath, 77.
Ocymum, 149.
Oils, 38, 84, 87, 93, 203, 204, 209.
Oniſcus, 101.
Oo, 3.
Ophicthus, 99.
Ophiogloſſum, 237.
Ophiorhiza, 150, 200, 236.
Ophioxylon, 235.
Oranges, China, 39, 89, 120.
——— Seville, 39, 89.
Orang outang, 160.
Order, 68.
Orders, 28, 30.
Oſtrea, Oyſters, 39.
Oſtracion, 100.
Ottona, 10, 69.
Owari, Prince of, 124.
Oxalis, 145.
Oxen, 95, 192.

P.

Paditulis, 162.
Pæonia, 90.

Pagoda,

INDEX.

Pagoda, 211, 212.
Palanquin; 191.
Pancakes, 260.
Panicum, 88.
Panningai, 179.
Panorpa, 101.
Paper, 62, 150.
Papilio, 100.
PARRA, van der, 130,
Pafs, 182.
Patella, 120.
PATERSON, 271.
Patti, 153.
Patje Pad jan, 218.
Patje turemali, 218.
Payam China, 145.
Peas, 84, 88.
Peaches, 89.
Pearl-fifhery, 262.
Pears, 38, 89.
Pediculus, 101.
Pei, 261.
Pelicanus, 268.
PENNANT, 237.
Penne turemali, 218.
Pepper-fhrub, 89.
Perca, 39, 100.
Perficaria, 146.
PETTERSEN, 171.
Phalæna, 285.
Phafeolus, 87, 88.
Phyficians, 77.
Pigeon, 99.
Pilgrims, 27, 28.
Pinna, 122.

Pine, 91.
Pinus, 91, 122
Piper, 147, 148, 150.
Pifang, 172.
Pifum, 88.
Plantago, 149.
Plays, 49.
Plumbago, 212.
Poetry, 58.
Police, 64.
POLL, van der, 234.
Pollos, 256, 258, 259.
Polygonum, 85, 90, 123.
Pomgranates, 80.
Pondogede, 158, 162.
Porcellain China, 108.
Porcupine, 233.
Portuguefe, 31, 109, 186.
Poft-houfe, 11.
Potatoes, 89.
Poterium, 150.
Priefts, 18, 22, 23, 254.
Princes, 1, 9.
Printing, art of, 57.
——— Prefs, 177.
Prifon, 67.
Prunus, 90.
Pfeudo-opal, 219.
Ptinus, 100.
Pulex, 101.
Pumpkins, 89.
Punica, 90.
Puresjerajen, 218.
Pufperagan, 218.
Pyralis, 101.

Quadrupeds,

INDEX.

Q.
Quadrupeds, 94.
Quails, 99.

R.
RADERMACHER, 130, 132, 133, 167, 249.
Radishes, 88.
Radix Columbo, 185.
Raja, 100.
Rain, 131.
Rainbow, 266.
RANTZOW, 215, 216, 232, 237.
Ranunculus, 146.
Raphanus, 88.
Rat, 97.
Rawa, 218.
Red dog, 77.
Religion, 17, 168.
Rheumatisms, 76.
Rhinoceros's-horn, 210.
Rhus, 38, 62, 91, 93.
Rice, 37, 84, 249.
Ricinus, 118, 149.
RIEMSDYK van, 136.
Roads, 11, 12.
Robal, 218, 222.
Rockia, 237.
Rollewai, 214.
Rosary, 29.
Rotecubung, 147.
Rubus, 145.
Ruby, 218, 219, 220.
Rumpung, 145.
Rupees, 211, 285.
Rye, 84.

S.
Saccharum, 148.
Sacsander, 185.
Sado, 130.
Sagittaria, 123.
Sago, 149.
——— Tree, 149.
Sakki, 37, 39, 40.
SAKKURA *Matje no Yn*, 8.
Salicornia, 146.
Salatiga, 138.
Salmo, 100.
Salmon, 39.
Salplicat, 62.
Samangi Kunong, 145.
Samarang, 137, 138, 144.
Sambucus, 150.
Sanicula, 145.
Saphire, 218, 219, 223, 226.
Sargazo, 276.
Satsuma, 92, 103, 105.
Scarabæus, 100.
Schœnanthus, 146.
Schools, 59.
Sciæna, 100.
Sciences, 57.
Sciurus, 237.
Scolopendra, 234, 266.
Scolopendrium, 145.
Scorpions, 234.

Scuandi,

INDEX.

Scuandi, 218.
Scyllæa, 277.
Scymitar, 14.
Sea-Cocoa, 183, 209.
Secretary, 69.
Sects, 17.
Selim, 286.
Semi, 124.
Sempu, 147.
Senki, 76.
Sepia, 101.
Seroni, 145, 147.
Serpents, 206.
——— bite, 235, 236.
——— Stone, 207, 208.
——— Tree, 235.
Serpula, 102.
Sesamum, 38, 95.
Shaddocks, 39, 89.
Sheep, 95.
Shell-fish, 39, 101.
Shingles, 236.
Shrimps, 39.
Sida, 150.
Sigak, 102.
Silk, 59.
——— culture of, 91.
Silpha, 100.
Silver, 101, 102.
Silurus, 100.
Simia, 214, 248.
Simina, 146.
Sin, 21.
Sinto, 19.
Siomio, 1.

Sire, 146.
Sitawaka, 238.
Sium, 88.
Sjuto, 34.
Skirrets, 88.
Slangenhout, 235.
Slaves, 250, 264.
SLOANE, 290.
SLUYSKEN, 240.
Slymapels, 179.
Smylax, 146.
Smugglers, 66.
Society, Royal, 291.
SOLANDER, Dr. 288, 292.
Solanum, 38, 89, 147, 178.
Solen, 101.
Sombong Madur, 150.
Sonchus, 145.
Soobo, 156.
Sour-fack, 259.
Sowas, 59.
Soy, 107, 121.
Spanish Figs, 109.
Sphinx, 100.
Spireæ, 90.
Spondylus, 102.
Spran, 145.
Sports, 143.
Squirrels, 237.
Stahlstein, 217.
Stavenisse, 124.
Steel, working of, 60.
Steenbrasem, 39.
Stink-tree, 234.
Stockholm's Slot, 173.

Stomoxys,

INDEX.

Stomoxys, 101.
Stones, precious, 216, 230, 231.
Storm, 281, 292.
Strombus, 122.
Strunthout, 234.
STUTZER, 134.
Sudu padjan, 219.
Sudu palingu, 219.
Sudu turemali, 219.
Sugar, 93.
——— Canes, 148.
——— Maple, 93.
Surveying, 57.
Surunga, 103, 104.
Sus, 98.
Suwa, 47.
Swallows, 163.
SWART, 287.
Swine, 95, 98.
Syngnathus, 100.

T.

Tagal, Mount, 136.
Tagetes, 90.
Tai, 3.
Taiko Lamma, 7.
Tamarindus, 149.
Tampal utan, 161.
Tango no Kami, 126.
Tanjong, 157.
Taripo, 219, 227.
Tavarcare, 209.

Taxes, 8, 67, 68.
Taxus, 38, 122.
Tay, 39.
Tea-Tree, 42, 91.
Tea Trade, 107.
———, Preparation of, 41.
Tebu, 148.
Tellina, 101.
Temples, 21, 22, 26—28.
TENSIN, 3.
TENSJO DAI SIN, 226.
Testudo, 99.
Tetrao, 99.
Tetraodon, 100.
Texel, 283.
Threshing, 85, 87.
Tigers, 162.
Tillia Palingu, 219.
Tingling mintik, 161.
Tipula, 101.
Titles, 5.
Tobacco, 43, 44.
Tommegom, 152.
Topaz, 218, 219, 224.
Tortrix, 101.
Tourmalin, 218, 219, 222, 223, 224, 225.
Towns, 10, 11, 60.
Town Officers, 69.
Travelling, mode of, 11.
Treba, 148.
Trees, fort of, 118.
Triticum, 86.
Trochus, 102.
Truffles, 121.

Tsikumgo,

INDEX.

Tsikumgo, 103.
Tsubaki, 38.
Tubipora, 122.
Tundang, 141.
Turbo, 102.
Turmeric, 147.
Turneps, 84.
Turtle doves, 161.

U.

Umbilicus veneris, 102.
Unarang, 139.
Unicorn's Teeth, 126.
Unicornu, 126.
Upan upan Karpo, 146.
Upan upan Sarpi, 148.
Urenne, 234.
Urtica, 118, 140, 146.
Uteratje, 189.
Uvaria, 120.

V.

Varnish, 62, 265.
———— Tree, 92.
Venereal disease, 78.
Venus, 101.
Verbesina, 101.
Vespa, 101.
Vicia, 88.
Vier uhrs bloem, 148.

Villages, 11.
Vitex, 146.
Vitis, 90.
Voluta, 102.
Vows, 29.
Vreedlust, 135.
Vriend, 285.

W.

Wairodi, 219.
Walnuts, 9.
War, art of, 56.
Warreku, 256.
Watch, 10.
———— house, 10, 70.
Water, diminution of, 155.
———— Nuts, 38.
———— Spouts, 267.
———— Saphire, 219.
Weapons, 13.
Whale-bones, 98.
Whales, 98.
Wheat, 84, 86.
WILLIAM V. 173.
Wille padjan, 219.
Wille palingu, 219.
Wilunde Wenne, 247.
WIMMERCRANTZ, 157, 249.
Winds, 136.
Worms, 101.
Writing, mode of, 58.
WURMB, van, 157.

INDEX.

Y.

YE FAI KOO, 9.
YE NOB KOO, 9.
YE SIEGE *Koo*, 9.
YE TSU KU *Koo*, 9.
Ye *Varu*, 7.

YORITOMO, 6, 7.
YOSI MUNE *Koo*, 9.

Z.

ZENTOOGOZIO, 9.
Zeeduyn, 124.

This Day are published,

In One Volume Octavo, Price 5s. 6d.

The PSALMS of DAVID,

A NEW AND IMPROVED VERSION.

Printed for M. PRIESTLEY, Pater-noster-row; and J. MATTHEWS, in the Strand, near Charing-Cross.

N. B. This Version is taken from a TRANSLATION lately made of the PSALMS into the SWEDISH LANGUAGE, by the learned DR. TINGSTADIUS, PROFESSOR of ORIENTAL LANGUAGES in UPSAL.

www.ingramcontent.com/pod-product-compliance
Lightning Source LLC
Chambersburg PA
CBHW031855220426
43663CB00006B/636